THE MULTILATERAL DEVELOPMENT BANKS

VOLUME 1

THE AFRICAN DEVELOPMENT BANK

THE MULTILATERAL DEVELOPMENT BANKS

VOLUME 1
THE AFRICAN DEVELOPMENT BANK

E. PHILIP ENGLISH
HARRIS M. MULE

LYNNE RIENNER PUBLISHERS

THE NORTH-SOUTH INSTITUTE
L'INSTITUT NORD-SUD

Published in the United States of America in 1996 by
Lynne Rienner Publishers, Inc.
1800 30th Street, Boulder, Colorado 80301

and in the United Kingdom by
Lynne Rienner Publishers, Inc.
3 Henrietta Street, Covent Garden, London WC2E 8LU

Paperback edition published in Canada by
The North-South Institute
55 Murray Street
Ottawa, Ontario K1N 5M3 Canada

Library of Congress Cataloging-in-Publication Data
Multilateral development banks.
  p.   cm.
  Includes bibliographical references and index.
  Contents: — 1. The African Development Bank / by E. Philip English
  and Harris M. Mule.
  ISBN 1-55587-467-3 (alk. paper : v. 1)—
  ISBN 1-55587-493-2 (pbk. : alk. paper : v. 1)
  1. Development banks. 2. African Development Bank.
HG1975.M848 1995
332.2—dc20   94-45003
                                                                      CIP

Canadian Cataloguing in Publication Data
Main entry under title:
Multilateral Development Banks
  Includes bibliographical references.
  Contents: v.1. The African Development Bank / by E. Philip English and
  Harris M. Mule.
  ISBN 0-921942-84-2 (v.1) (pbk)
  1. Development banks. I. North-South Institute (Ottawa, Ont.)
HG1975.M85 1995 332.1'52 C95-900188-3

British Cataloguing in Publication Data
A Cataloguing in Publication record for this book
is available from the British Library.

Printed and bound in the United States of America

The paper used in this publication meets the requirements
of the American National Standard for Permanence of
Paper for Printed Library Materials Z39.48-1984.

5 4 3 2 1

CONTENTS

TABLES

FOREWORD

In the course of the past decade, the majority of countries in Africa have undergone rigorous structural adjustment and monetary liberalization. The hope is that the resulting free market forces, together with the focus on the private sector as the engine of growth and the state playing a positive and facilitating role, will purge underdevelopment and place the continent on a new and stable long-term growth path. Success in this process still eludes the majority of countries.

Some thirty years ago when the African Development Bank was created, and for the greater part of the Bank's history, the present tolerant political regimes and the liberal macroeconomic and development environments did not exist. The Bank has had to operate as best it could in a politically unstable setting and among stagnant and declining economic regimes. Nonregional members of the Bank in particular complain of the problems that the Bank must overcome if it is to play the developmental role expected of it in the future.

It is because such problems face the Bank that this book is of extreme value to both African and non-African investors in the Bank, as well as all Africans. The Bank's operational and policy shortcomings are clearly described and analyzed. Every major point in the book has been dispassionately made on the basis of thorough research or from the wealth of experience of the authors. Where credit is due, such as the Bank's success in capacity building, it has not been denied. However, the authors also point out deficiencies, such as in project management, levels of debt arrears, the lack of credit rating, and excessive politicization, and make suggestions for their correction. Even the delicate issues of equity balance between regional and nonregional members, and the method of appointment and dismissal of the Bank's chief executive are addressed.

Currently there is an urgent need for a premier African development institution that can be a catalyst for development and resource mobilization, as well as a credible source of leadership for Africa in an increasingly competitive world. The recommendations in the concluding chapter are especially valuable and should be seriously considered by the new management of the African Development Bank, its share-holders, and by any person or institution concerned with public policy or public opinion in Africa.

Jonathan H. Frimpong-Ansah
African Policy Research Company
Accra, Ghana

PREFACE

In 1991 the North-South Institute launched its research project on the multilateral development banks ("the MDB Project"). The principal focus of the project was the group of regional development banks (comprising the African, Asian, and Inter-American Development Banks) plus the subregional Caribbean Development Bank. All these banks, created more or less in the image of the World Bank, had been around for two to three decades. Yet, in contrast to the World Bank, they had been subjected to little critical scrutiny.

The project was designed to provide a consistent framework for examining each of the banks. Besides providing a brief history of the origins and evolution of its subject, each study reviews the experience of a selected group of borrowing countries, as well as the bank's performance as a lender and as a mobilizer of resources. In all the studies, the operations and policies of the regional bank are compared with those of the World Bank; also addressed are relations between the two agencies and the division of labor between them. Finally, each study looks ahead at the challenges facing the banks in the future.

In a word, the studies seek to determine the *development effectiveness* of the regional banks by examining their impact on growth, poverty, the environment, and social indicators of development. It is hoped that the project will contribute to ongoing discussions on the future of the multilateral system of development financing, now in its fiftieth year after the Bretton Woods Conference. In addition to this volume on the African Development Bank, the project will yield four other major publications—one each on the Inter-American, Caribbean, and Asian Banks, as well as a "synthesis" volume. There are also two studies on Canada's role in the MDBs, one on Sweden and the MDBs, and one on Jamaica's relations with the MDBs.

The project has been generously supported through grants from the Canadian International Development Agency, the Inter-American Development Bank, the Asian Development Bank, the African Development Bank, the Ford Foundation, the Swedish Ministry for Foreign Affairs, the Caribbean Development Bank, the Norwegian

Ministry of Foreign Affairs, and the Netherlands Ministry for Development Cooperation. The views contained in this volume and in others issuing from the project, however, are those of the authors alone and do not necessarily reflect the views of the project's sponsors, the funders of the multilateral development banks project, the North-South Institute, its supporters, or its board of directors.

Roy Culpeper
MDB Project Director
The North-South Institute

ACKNOWLEDGMENTS

In a book of this type, the best ideas and information come from those on the inside—in this case, the staff and management of the African Development Bank (ADB) Group. We had the pleasure of working with many competent and committed employees and were impressed by their willingness to assist us and to discuss in a very candid and honest way both the strengths and the shortcomings of their institution. This open-minded attitude continued when our draft report was reviewed by Bank management, making our work both easier and more satisfying. We were particularly gratified by the positive reception accorded to many of our final recommendations. Such openness can only bode well for the future of the organization.

Our first round of thanks goes, therefore, to the management and staff of the ADB Group. Several in particular warrant special mention. Delphin Rwegasira and Anselm London, the contact points for the North-South Institute throughout this exercise, were most supportive. Lual Deng provided invaluable assistance in arranging a full slate of interviews for our most important research visit to the Bank. The executive director from Canada, Sandelle Scrimshaw, and her office were also very helpful, especially when it came to providing detailed comments on our draft report. To our many other friends at the Bank, we simply say thank you.

We benefited from exceptional cooperation from the Canadian International Development Agency (CIDA) in the persons of Rick Stapenhurst and, especially, the officer responsible for the ADB Group, Nicole Gesnot. Our appetite for documentation must have appeared insatiable to her, but she never complained. She also provided lengthy comments and clarifications on our draft, and the book is much better as a consequence.

The chapter of country case studies would not have been possible without the three consultants who provided us with background reports on their respective countries. We are most grateful to Andrew Katili, senior economist at the Kenyan Ministry of Finance, and to consultants Moustapha Deme and Wafik Arif for Mali and Egypt, respectively. At the same time, we alone remain responsible for the way in which their material was finally interpreted and presented.

Philip English would like to thank the International Development Research Centre of Canada, where he was working at the start of this project, for the flexibility offered to him to take some time off for the initial research and writing. In particular, he would like to thank his former secretary, Marleny Tanaka, for the support she provided to this extracurricular activity. Similarly, Harris Mule wishes to thank his secretary, Margaret Amoke, for the long hours she devoted to typing parts of the draft report.

Outside the Bank and CIDA, several other reviewers provided helpful feedback. However, none of them could compete with Gerry Helleiner, who lived up to his well-known reputation for providing both rapid and rich reactions.

Finally, we owe a special and heartfelt note of thanks to the staff of the North-South Institute. Various members of that family helped in more ways than we know to shepherd this project through to completion. Four stand out in particular: the ever ebullient editor, Clyde Sanger; Rowena Beamish, for a sharp-eyed proofing; Roy Culpeper, the man who was crazy enough to initiate the whole MDB project and tenacious enough to see it through; and Sarah Matthews, who handled everything on the many occasions when Roy was not available (and often when he was). It was indeed a pleasure to work with Roy on both professional and personal levels—a major fringe benefit of taking on this assignment.

We hope that all those associated with this book feel that their efforts on our behalf were worthwhile, and that in some modest way we have been able to contribute to the stronger African Development Bank that so many would like to see.

E. Philip English
Harris M. Mule

ACRONYMS

ABR	African Business Roundtable
ACBF	African Capacity Building Foundation
ADB	African Development Bank
ADF	African Development Fund
AFREXIMBANK	African Export-Import Bank
APDF	African Project Development Facility
AsDB	Asian Development Bank
BCEAO	Central Bank for the West African Franc
BMCE	Moroccan Bank for External Trade
BUA	Bank Unit of Account
CEAO	West African Economic Community
CFA	Communauté Financière Africaine
CIDA	Canadian International Development Agency
DANIDA	Department of International Economic Cooperation, Danish Ministry of Foreign Affairs
DMU	debt management unit
ECOWAS	Economic Community of West African States
ED	executive director
EIA	Environmental Impact Assessment
EPCP	Economic Prospects and Country Programming
ESAF	Enhanced Structural Adjustment Facility (of the IMF)
ESAIDARM	Eastern and Southern African Initiative in Debt and Reserves Management
GCI	general capital increase
GDP	gross domestic product
GIS	geographical information system
GNP	gross national product
IBRD	International Bank for Reconstruction and Development
IDA	International Development Association
IDB	Inter-American Development Bank

IDRC	International Development Research Centre
IFC	International Finance Corporation
ILO	International Labour Organisation
IMF	International Monetary Fund
MDB	Mali Development Bank
MDB	multilateral development bank
NESDA	Network for Environmental and Sustainable Development in Africa
NGOs	nongovernmental organizations
NTF	Nigeria Trust Fund
OAU	Organization of African Unity
ODA	official development assistance
OECD	Organisation for Economic Co-operation and Development
OPEC	Organization of Petroleum Exporting Countries
PSDU	Private Sector Development Unit
PTA	Preferential Trade Area (Bank)
SAF	Structural Adjustment Facility (of the IMF)
SAPs	structural adjustment programs
SDA	Social Dimensions of Adjustment
SDR	special drawing right
SEAF	Special Emergency Assistance Fund
SILICs	severely indebted low-income countries
SIMICs	severely indebted middle-income countries
SPA	special program of assistance
TA	technical assistant
UNCTAD	United Nations Conference on Trade and Development
UNDP	United Nations Development Programme
UNECA	United Nations Economic Commission for Africa
UNSO	United Nations Sudano-Sahelian Office
USAID	United States Agency for International Development
WID	women in development

1

INTRODUCTION

The African Development Bank Group has had a turbulent history, and the Bank has come a long way since it was created in 1963. Widely regarded as Africa's premier multilateral organization, the group has recently been the subject of increasing scrutiny and criticism, which reached the boiling point in 1994.

As an all-African initiative without nonregional shareholders for the first ten years, it was unique among the major regional development banks, but it paid a price in terms of a very slow start and relatively low lending levels. Change came only gradually and somewhat ambivalently, with conditions attached to preserve its African character. The ADB Group soon reaped the benefits, with rapidly expanding lending levels through both the concessional and nonconcessional windows. However, tension developed between the African (or regional) and nonregional members of the board, which has continued to affect decisionmaking over the years.

The Bank is caught in the turbulence throughout the African continent, where civil wars have wracked a dozen states in recent years and where already low incomes have fallen back to independence levels. What then is the ADB Group's role in this difficult environment? In the view of some, the ADB Group must expand its role in order to meet the limitless needs of African development. For others, it is time for modesty, a refocusing on a few core activities. While most of this report concentrates on evaluating the past record of the ADB Group, it concludes with some recommendations for the future direction of the institution.

Governance and the Governed

The ADB Group is characterized by a large and dispersed ownership with no single member or group playing a pivotal role. The nonre-

1

gional shareholders have not had an obvious leader, and their influence has been counterbalanced by the two-thirds majority of Bank votes held by regional members, whose board representatives have vigorously protected their vision of an "African bank." In addition to their controlling share of ownership, this has included an African president, an overwhelmingly African staff, sensitivity to African government priorities, and a reluctance to copy foreign models, most notably the World Bank.

For a variety of reasons, neither "side" has given the ADB Group a high priority. This has been a mixed blessing. It has meant a relative freedom from attempts to influence lending policy, but also a low level of support from ministries back home and little involvement by governors. As a result, there has been a shortage of initiative to solve problems when they do arise and a certain vulnerability to the personalities of the executive directors in place.

The notably democratic process of selecting the president has generated the usual benefits and costs. It has encouraged the president to be responsive to the priorities of borrowing members, raising the possibility of both better service and more political interference. This has helped generate a more sympathetic, less arrogant culture than that of the World Bank—and hence more cordial relations with African governments—but also a reputation for more "political projects."

The governance structure has also produced a particularly active role for the Board of Directors. With no one country claiming the right to nominate the president, his or her reelection depends to a large extent on satisfying as many of the executive directors (EDs) as possible. Furthermore, this board has the authority to suspend the president. Because there are usually some regional EDs who have served on the board longer than the president, they are particularly comfortable in asserting their power.

Unfortunately, the board has not historically focused on the developmental impact of the ADB Group's lending operations. Regional members have concentrated on defending the projects proposed for their constituent countries, as well as countering the more sensitive propositions of their nonregional colleagues. The latter have devoted the most attention to financial and administrative policies and procedures, to the point of micromanagement. Each group has often defined its position in opposition to the other, leading to considerable acrimony.

Political considerations reach down to the level of vice-president, as these positions are appointed by the Board of Directors and must be renewed every three years. This is also the most obvious source for future presidents. Thus, presidents have not had complete authority over them, while having cause for concern as to the ultimate ambitions of some incumbents. This is probably one explanation for the occasional flare-ups between presidents and vice-presidents that have affected the history of the institution, as well as the limited delegation of authority to the latter.

The professional staff has been constrained to rather low numbers compared to other major multilateral development banks. This was due partly to budget limitations and partly to continued demands by the board for prior reforms in personnel policy before authorizing further increases. The board has been rightly concerned about the large shares of staff in middle management, support positions, and service departments and the significant numbers who are probably no longer sufficiently qualified for such an international organization. The concentration of experienced African professionals at the Bank does represent one of its strongest attributes, for they are uniquely placed to understand and relate to their counterparts in recipient institutions. However, there is too much variation in the quality of staff. This is a particularly serious problem in management, because weak managers provide a poor model, undermine morale, and are more likely to hire weak subordinates.

Lending a Hand

The ADB Group saw impressive growth from 1985 to 1992, in both absolute terms and relative to other funding agencies. Its share of net official flows to Africa tripled to 8.1 percent by 1992, while its net transfers actually exceeded those of the World Bank for a time. The recent downturn in Bank lending, the temporary cessation of new African Development Fund (ADF) commitments of concessional loans, and the pessimistic outlook for the near future suggest that the institution can no longer look to an increasing volume of resources as one of its main contributions.

The geographical distribution of lending has been relatively egalitarian as compared to bilateral agencies, with less attention to political factors in determining lending levels and increasing attention to economic performance as a criterion. North Africa may have received a large and growing share of Bank resources, but this is explained by that region's relative economic strength and creditworthiness and would seem well founded.

Country programming has not been particularly influential, due in part to some inherent difficulties. Given its governance structure, but also its institutional philosophy, the ADB Group has probably been more flexible in its programming than most other donors and has certainly been understood as such by recipient governments. For many countries the ADB Group is still considered the "lender of last resort," the one who will help out when others say no.

Agriculture has continued to receive the highest priority for support, although in practice its share of resources equaled that of the public utilities sector in 1989–1992. Compared with the World Bank, the ADB Group sectoral lending pattern could be characterized as less diverse and more traditional. On the other hand, there has been no hesitation to launch into policy-based lending. Its initial foray was probably too hasty, given the macroeconomic expertise at its disposal, but the Bank Group subsequently restrained such lending within agreed limits and concentrated on cofinancing programs with the World Bank to benefit from the latter's expertise.

One can hardly fault the decision to participate in such lending, given the urgent need for balance-of-payments support and the limited absorptive capacity for traditional projects. Unfortunately, there is very little evidence that the ADB Group was able to provide a needed second opinion or countervailing perspective to that of the World Bank in this contentious area. Lack of staff expertise was combined with reluctance to confront either the World Bank or recipient governments. The recruitment of additional economists in the programming departments has resulted in improved capacity over time, suggesting some impact—and greater potential.

The performance in classic project lending is more extensive and more difficult to assess. The stock of postevaluations is suboptimal in coverage and consistency, but it does provide some idea of the Bank's record. A majority of projects have been judged as basically successful, albeit usually with "minor shortcomings." A tenacious, and perhaps tenuous, comparison with similar World Bank data indicates that the ADB Group's overall performance across the continent is comparable to that of the World Bank in sub-Saharan Africa, but lower when disaggregated by sector, and decidedly lower once the latter's North African portfolio is included. There is no evidence of a deterioration in project quality over time and even some that suggests an improvement. Recent improvements in the postevaluation system will make such comparisons somewhat easier in the future.

However, good work has been the exception rather than the rule, while even "successful" projects could have been done better. Inadequate project preparation was the most fundamental shortcoming, while the absence of staff involvement at this stage or in subsequent supervision was particularly striking. Neglect of the institutional and administrative capacity of the borrower proved especially egregious. Projects have been conceived first and foremost as engineering challenges or simply financial transactions, not as attempts to support human initiative and introduce new ideas.

It is not easy to work in Africa, and no donor has a shining record, but the ADB Group has not done enough to reduce the risks and to shift the odds in its favor. There is little evidence that its special African character is being put to good advantage to do things differently, and better, than other donors. Particularly disturbing is that in the project cycle for traditional investment loans, it appeared that not much changed in the six years before ADF resources dried up in 1994.

Country Case Studies

The strengths and weaknesses of the Bank's lending operations were confirmed in country case studies of Kenya, Mali, and Egypt. The ADB Group is clearly sensitive to government priorities and tends to build on past experience. There is evidence of some concentration even if it is not the result of explicit strategies but simply because past experience was positive. In general, where the executing agency was competent, the results were encouraging. The Kenya case study identified a fundamental difference in the style of the ADB Group when compared with the World Bank, a difference that was found elsewhere as well. From ideas, through country programming to project appraisal and implementation, the World Bank is proactive while the ADB Group is decidedly more passive. The World Bank pioneers new approaches to development and aggressively sells them; the ADB Group follows, often with a time lag of several years. The World Bank is less receptive to government priorities, more thorough in its appraisals, and much more involved in monitoring execution.

Fortunately, the difference in final results was not as marked, and there were even encouraging, if limited, signs that sometimes the ADB approach paid off. In Kenya, both institutions had serious problems in agriculture and both were broadly successful in road construction. Indeed, the executing agency felt that the ADB Group road projects were if anything better. In Mali, the ADB Group demonstrated a patient commitment to local capacity building in two struggling institutions, which eventually proved justified. The ADB Group's relationship with the government was judged to be less conflictual than that of the World Bank. The hands-off approach of the ADB probably contributes to a stronger sense of borrower ownership, with positive repercussions when the owner is competent, especially for the long-term sustainability of investments. This does not appear to have been a well-articulated policy, however, and the costs of this approach where executing agencies were weak may have more than offset any gains to date.

The ADB Group strikes one as being at the mercy of its environment, and the environment is typically harsh. In most cases, it has gone beyond responsiveness to become a captive of its borrowers. It must rely on governments to identify priorities without providing an informed second opinion; in difficult circumstances, it tends to lean on other donors. Its personnel are not present to help troubleshoot, or when they are—in the form of a regional office—they lack the mandate and staff to do a proper job. Executing agencies are left to sink or swim. Even the more developed borrowers would benefit from a more active development partner, especially one from the same environment and culture. The borrowers themselves are asking for it.

The Knox Report dramatically highlighted these same issues in 1994 and pointed to three causal factors: the lack of resources, a lending culture, and problems of governance. The convergence of this report's release, a tightening of donor purse strings, and the general crisis of governance have brought the situation to a head and gives reason to believe that these problems may finally be addressed. Fewer funds for new loans are freeing up staff time for current projects, while a major reorganization promises significant increases in the professional staff assigned to the operations departments. Meanwhile, serious challenges remain in the more intractable area of the institution's governance.

Mobilizing and Managing Money

The ADB Group's capacity to mobilize new resources in the mid- and late 1980s was remarkable. It made innovations in the use of subordinated debt, while obtaining and then protecting AAA rating on its senior debt. Eventually, the professionalism of its borrowing and investment activities earned it respect and prestige. Its own trading room mastered the intricacies of foreign exchange markets. The plaudits of the international financial press indicated that the Bank had reached world-class status, making it the pride of Africa.

Then the tide shifted. Questions were raised about the pace of growth in lending, the absorptive capacity of borrowing members, and the risk implications. Arrears began to rise alarmingly, the demand for nonconcessional lending narrowed, and net income plummeted. The ADF dried up as shareholders argued over different approaches to the financial dilemma.

While the underlying problem is the persistent debt crisis facing

African countries, the Bank has made significant efforts to strengthen its financial policies, often with the constructive prompting of nonregional members. It has tightened its sanctions and nonaccrual policies by reducing the grace periods involved; increased loan-loss provisions; enforced the share transfer rules to reduce arrears on capital subscriptions; reduced liquidity levels to control borrowing requirements and hence financial charges; strengthened asset/liability management in its trading room; changed to a variable lending interest rate to protect its income from interest rate fluctuations; and reduced its administrative budget. It has cut its total nonconcessional lending and stopped it completely for low-income, category A member states, other than Nigeria. The loan portfolio is not particularly concentrated when compared to other MDBs, and country exposure among those still borrowing from the Bank does not yet appear to be excessive.

Still more could be done, notably in the areas of country-risk assessment and Bank credit policy. The Bank is now paying the price of what, at least in retrospect, was imprudent lending to a few risky clients, but it has generally adjusted its policies appropriately, if sometimes reluctantly, walking that fine line between regional hopes and nonregional fears.

Nonetheless, the Bank cannot escape its operating environment. Only the nonregional members live outside that environment, and finally they must provide most of the funds to refinance the debt. Ideally, the nonregionals should also help the ADB Group shift the bulk of its lending from the Bank to the ADF windows, through a higher ADF replenishment, but this seems unlikely. And so the ADB Group must do its best in a second-best world.

Crosscutting Issues

A development bank is rightly viewed as a powerful instrument that can support other public concerns beyond sound public investment, directly through those investments and indirectly through the authority it commands as a leading development actor. The list of issues has grown considerably in recent times, especially in Africa where the development debate has been particularly fertile due to the failure of the traditional models to make much headway.

The most important issue is also the one with the least impact on the content of the lending program: the external debt crisis. More than half the continent's countries remain classified as "severely-indebted." Various attempts have been made to control and eventually eliminate the problem, but they have been piecemeal and half-hearted. The ADB Group has tried a few things, notably a debt securitization proposal and a more modest debt management capacity-building unit. Neither received much support from the nonregional members, and little was achieved.

The ADB Group has been promoting regional integration longer than any other special concern—from the institution's very beginning, in fact. Like the debt problem, but unlike most other, newer themes, the impetus for its promotion emanates largely from within the Bank, and it also enjoys significant support inside Africa. Yet multinational projects have claimed a small and falling share of total lending. More recent regional initiatives of a different type may be more promising: the 1993 study of economic integration in southern Africa and the establishment of the African Export-Import Bank, AFREXIMBANK.

The theme of private sector promotion has been adopted by the ADB Group with some effectiveness, through the creation of the Private Sector Development Unit and the African Business Roundtable. The Bank also stands out in its efforts to promote local procurement in the course of its traditional public sector projects. The private sector, both in agriculture and in industry, will inevitably be the engine of growth in coming years. Given the continued ambivalence of many African governments and the weak state of the commercial banking sector in most countries, there is undoubtedly a role for the ADB Group in private sector promotion. The Bank's unequivocal move into this field has helped raise the sector's legitimacy in the eyes of African officials; but with the extra risks involved, the Bank and ADF will have to make a careful assessment of their comparative advantage.

Three emerging priorities—the environment, gender, and poverty—are closely related and have risen to the top of the agenda in similar ways. All three have been primarily driven by the donor community, and all three have found their strongest proponents among Western nongovernmental organizations (NGOs). In many cases, they have taken root within the continent among the burgeoning local NGO community and civil society more generally, as well as at the United Nations Economic Commission for Africa (UNECA). However, these themes have rarely found strong advocates among African governments.

The latest and possibly largest movement within the ADB Group is that toward good governance, including democratization and human rights. Like so many previous forces, this one has been strongly influenced by the West, but it also draws on many local strengths. It is a force that the ADB Group cannot ignore, but one that it must address selectively.

As a general rule, the ADB Group has proved open-minded and innovative in recent years, embracing issues of interest to the donor community even though most of its borrowers attach a low priority to them. It has undoubtedly helped promote an awareness of these issues, and indeed their very legitimacy, within Africa. In principle, the ADB Group is well placed to translate these sometimes delicate issues into a language that African counterparts better understand.

Yet one wonders how much of an impact is actually being made. New staff have tended to come from outside the Bank and to be concentrated in central policy units, while project officers have complained that each new set of guidelines increases their workload. Management has been encouraged to lay out ambitious programs and then look elsewhere to raise additional resources. This process is time consuming and leaves the institution dependent on the priorities of individual bilateral agencies. Although lower lending levels will relieve some of the pressure on staff resources, they will also mean fewer of the concessional resources needed for specialized projects. Borrowing members may be reluctant to use their allocations for environmental or women's projects if it means squeezing out public utility or agricultural funds. If an increasing share of declining resources is devoted to a donor-driven agenda, the legitimacy of the Bank may be at stake.

The ADB Group is caught in the turbulence created by the confluence of waves from many different directions. Although all these new concerns are worthy in their own right, one wonders if the Bank, especially in its weakened condition of 1995, may be overloaded and in danger of capsizing. Bank management and the shareholders must ultimately decide what they think can be accomplished given the resources available. Nevertheless, we offer here a few ideas based on our assessment of the Bank's performance to date.

The Way Ahead

If there is one defining feature of African underdevelopment, it is the lack of indigenous capacity to master the crises that continually beset it. The ADB Group represents one key effort to build capacity within the continent, and on this score it has been successful. The nonregional shareholders must continue to support the institution if they are serious about helping Africans help themselves. Regional shareholders must rise to the present challenge if they are serious about taking charge of their own destiny. However, capacity building is only a means to an end. The ADB Group must be able to point to the impact it is having on the development of the African continent and on the lives of ordinary people. While there is some evidence, it is still difficult to pinpoint the unique contribution of the ADB Group.

The Basic Building Blocks: Projects and Personnel

Projects are the foundation on which the ADB Group is built, because of their role in absorbing and replenishing the resources of the Bank and because it is through projects that one gains an understanding of how development succeeds. Yet project work has been neglected over the last ten years. The reorganization approved in early 1995 attempts to respond to some of the deficiencies identified here and in the Knox Report, but it can only be judged by its implementation. There are other issues that cannot be addressed through such an exercise. We would make the following additional recommendations:

1. The project operations component of the new subregional departments must be given special priority in personnel policy. A special effort should be made to increase the number of women and to supplement scarce skills through greater recruitment of non-Africans. The difficult process of removing weak employees must be pursued vigorously, and subsequent rewards of salary, promotions, and training should be more closely tied to merit.

2. More attention must be paid to supervision missions. This must not mean hands-on interference that effectively undermines local ownership of projects and programs.

3. A permanent local presence is essential in as many countries as possible, probably through country offices rather than regional ones, and probably starting with some of the smallest countries where the Bank is a major player. New country offices must be given high-quality staff with both responsibility and accountability. Such postings might be made prerequisites for entry into management.

4. More attention should be paid to analytical sector work, particularly in sectors where the Bank has project experience, to improve understanding of policy and institutional constraints faced by projects, facilitate project selection, and feed into sectoral adjustment lending.

5. It is probably at the expense of macroeconomic work that greater sectoral work must come. It should accept the comparative advantage of the International Monetary Fund (IMF) and the World Bank in this area and focus on a few cases where it can offer ideas and knowledge, not just money. Its best economists should be assigned to the smaller countries that are serious about reform but lack national expertise comparable to that at the Bank.

6.   The results of postevaluations must be incorporated more effectively into new project lending. Economic Prospects and Country Programming (EPCP) papers are now supposed to include such data, but this policy is not yet honored systematically. A similar policy should be adopted, and enforced, for project appraisal reports.

7.   Until 1994, the quantity of lending was a crucial factor hindering improvements in quality. Finally, the pressure has been removed, at least temporarily. Management should view this not as a crisis but as an opportunity. If and when resources become available again, the temptation to make up for lost ground through future expansion of the lending program should be avoided until it is clear that the reforms are taking hold.

The Engineers and Architects: Management and the Board

To achieve these changes a revitalized management will be required, together with a new understanding between management and the Board of Directors, and among the directors. In addition to the measures contained in the recent reorganization, the following should be considered:

1.   The vice-presidencies should be made career positions appointed by the president. Vice-presidents who wish to compete for the presidency should be required to resign one year beforehand to avoid internal conflict.

2.   A clearer division of labor is needed between the president and the Board of Directors. The president should be allowed to manage, but ways must be found to judge the results more effectively. The board needs to focus on Bank policies, define a more coherent strategy, and then assume that management will respect its decisions (with regular progress reports).

3.   The Board of Directors must learn to achieve greater consensus, particularly between regional and nonregional directors. Term limits of six to eight years are probably part of the answer. At the same time, an increase in the normal term to, say, four years may be helpful for both nonregional directors and those regional representatives who regularly rotate.

4.   It would also be preferable to have a smaller board. It may be impossible to develop consensus on a regular basis among eighteen members plus the president, and the cost of the current arrangement is too onerous as a share of total administrative expenses.

5.   The regional member states must be encouraged to take a greater interest in the Bank, through more frequent meetings of a sub-

committee of the Board of Governors and more extensive contact among senior management and government officials and ADB country offices.

6.   The president should be appointed and, when necessary, dismissed only by the Board of Governors.

7.   The imbalance between the voting shares of regional and nonregional members is no longer tenable. A fifty-fifty split in the voting shares of regionals and nonregionals would better reflect reality, especially if the boards of the Bank and the ADF were combined, as in all other multilateral banks.

8.   The EDs should do more by way of public reporting in their constituencies, and the Bank should expand its own outreach program if it is to be accountable to the taxpayers who sustain it and the citizens it ultimately serves.

Paying the Bills: Mobilizing and Managing Money

The ADB Group has recently made important improvements in its financial policies. To maintain the crucial support of nonregional members, as well as that of the international capital markets, it will have to go further still. When it does, the nonregional members should be prepared to hold up their share of the bargain.

1.   Management and the regional members of the Bank will have to take a greater interest in the Bank's financial health. In general, they have shown a remarkable complacency about the problems facing the Bank, with the pressure for reforms coming almost exclusively from nonregional executive directors—the representatives of the minority shareholders.

2.   The Bank must take whatever measures are necessary to reverse the decline in its net income, including various incentives and penalties to encourage timely loan repayment. An effective measure would be an agreement from the World Bank and the IMF that they would not approve new balance-of-payments loans or at least not begin disbursements where there were arrears with the ADB.

3.   The Bank will have to set its own example by holding the line on administrative expenses, one of the few areas under its direct control. Given the many operational functions requiring greater resources, cuts will have to be achieved in other parts of the Bank. Staff should not be targeted until significant savings are achieved at the level of the board.

4.   Among the various measures that would reassure the capital markets and rating agencies, none would go further than the increase in the nonregional share of authorized capital and votes, as already recommended.

5.   The Bank should limit its total nonconcessional lending to levels well below those of the early 1990s in order to control borrowing requirements, maintain prudent degrees of country exposure, and avoid exacerbating the external indebtedness of regional members.

6.   The Bank must adopt a more explicit country-risk policy. Internationally acceptable criteria for creditworthiness must be adopted, which will inevitably exclude most if not all low-income, category A members from Bank lending.

7.   A trust fund facility is needed to clear up arrears that may otherwise be intractable. If donors agreed some time ago to provide similar assistance to the much stronger World Bank, there is no obvious rationale for depriving the ADB Group of such help.

8.   If Bank lending is to be cut back, and borrowers encouraged to accept this measure, more concessional lending will be needed to meet the foreign exchange and other development requirements of regional members.

The Blueprint: Bank Strategy

The time has come for some tough decisions about where the Bank is going to make a difference. The standard response is that its unique contribution comes from its African character. But what does that mean? The major role of African shareholders, the process of electing the president, and the dominance of African professionals on staff have made for a distinctly different culture from that of other lending and donor agencies, most notably the World Bank. These have resulted in a Bank that is generally more responsive to the demands of African borrowing members, more sympathetic to their problems, and more "diplomatic" in conducting its business.

It is difficult to document how the African character of the Bank has improved the lives of Africans to date. We believe it has. It is more difficult to contend that this impact matches the resources so far committed to the enterprise. The management and staff cannot apply to good advantage their special understanding of Africa, and their unique rapport with African counterparts, without a greater emphasis on portfolio and staff quality and the expertise that comes from concentration on a manageable set of problems. To this end, we recommend the following:

1.   The Bank must get back to basics: its core lending operations and, especially, its projects. A bank without a record of quality projects is ill placed to launch new initiatives.

2.   The Bank cannot neglect policy-based program lending. It should identify a few issues and countries where it wants to take the

initiative, such as adjustment lending in sectors where it has gained project experience, as well as broader macroeconomic reform in selected smaller countries.

3.   It might do well to specialize in areas of adjustment lending that draw on any superior qualitative understanding of the African condition that its staff should possess. It may be better placed to support capacity building and to help build a sense of local ownership. Pursuing institutional support is probably the best way for the Bank to contribute to good governance in the short run. Highlighting the social dimensions would provide a needed focus for its poverty alleviation strategy.

4.   Among the traditional sectors, agriculture deserves to retain the highest priority. It will continue to be the economic backbone of most African countries for the foreseeable future, while themes like the environment, gender, and poverty alleviation also recommend such an emphasis.

5.   Themes like governance, poverty alleviation, the environment, and gender should influence the choice of priority sectors and then be addressed with a view to improving traditional lending operations. Apart from agriculture, they suggest a focus on education and small business and microenterprise. Efforts to collaborate with NGOs should continue across all these sectors, emphasizing alliances with public agencies.

6. Mechanisms must be put in place to ensure that projects really do benefit the poor. Staff should be assisted in identifying where environmental concerns or the role of women are critical to project success and in planning how to alter project design and implementation accordingly. In the interest of focus, the Bank should probably resist the temptation to launch specialized environmental protection or women's projects. In policy-based lending, efforts to incorporate poverty concerns into program design deserve more attention than separate social funds.

7.   The private sector should become a high priority for the ADB Group. An independent structure along the lines of the International Finance Corporation may be the answer, though the case for a separate African equivalent will have to be examined carefully. The Bank may have a special role to play in attracting foreign investment by providing the necessary advice and reassurances that both investors and national governments often require.

8.   Although the debt problem continues to be the overriding constraint to long-term growth in most of sub-Saharan Africa, it is not getting much attention. The ADB Group, as the only regional creditor, is the obvious champion for continued efforts to resolve the problem. Appropriate action could include lobbying in international

forums, elaborating new debt-relief plans, and assisting member governments in debt management.

9.   As Africa's most successful regional institution, the ADB Group is a logical standard-bearer for regional integration. It must continue its efforts, but with its eyes wide open and past experience squarely in view. It could follow up on its southern Africa study in various ways, as well as finance similar ones in other regions. Now that the AFREXIMBANK has been successfully launched, the Bank will have to invest time and effort to see that it succeeds.

10.   There remains the vision of the Bank as a center of excellence in development thinking. Too many of the ideas "in power" in Africa originate outside. It is time for the Bank to draw lessons from its extensive history of lending, going beyond project postevaluations to conduct sectoral and thematic work. To broach the larger issues of development strategy, it must strengthen its cooperation with the UN Economic Commission for Africa and reach out to the African research community. A small but significant additional investment in a genuine research capacity could make a big difference. Outside researchers should be used more extensively, but an in-house capacity is needed to coordinate their contributions, absorb them, supplement them, and provide the institutional endorsement that makes ideas so much more effective.

PART 1

HISTORICAL SETTING AND RECORD OF PERFORMANCE

2

HISTORY IN THE MAKING

The history of any institution is an important, but often neglected, element in understanding and evaluating it. The African Development Bank Group has had a turbulent history but has come a long way since the Bank's creation in 1963. It has been widely regarded as Africa's premier multilateral organization, "adapting Wall Street's standards to the poorest of nations."[1] But recently, the Bank has been the subject of increasing scrutiny and criticism, once again reaching the boiling point in 1994. Whether its history has been forgotten in recent debates is a moot question; it is, in any event, an essential point of departure for this study.

African states began discussing the establishment of a regional development bank in 1960. For some, it was the day they achieved political independence and even before many of their neighbors were in a position to join them. It was a bold statement of their determination to take economic as well as political control of their own affairs— bold because other regions in the South with much more political and developmental experience were hardly any further ahead on this front. The Inter-American Development Bank (IDB) had opened its doors only the year before; the Asian Development Bank (AsDB) would not begin operations for another six years.[2]

The vision behind the establishment of the African Development Bank was clearly one of self-reliance through cooperation among African states, as proclaimed in the preamble to its 1964 Agreement:

> *The Governments* on whose behalf this Agreement is signed;
> *Determined* to strengthen African solidarity by means of economic co-operation between African States; . . .
> *Realizing* the importance of co-ordinating national plans of econom-ic and social development for the promotion of the harmonious growth of African economies as a whole and the expansion of African foreign trade, and in particular, inter-African trade; . . .
> *Have agreed* to establish hereby the African Development Bank.

None of this boldness had dissipated when it came to working out the details of the project. Thus, it was decided that the ADB would be a strictly African affair, with no nonregional members—no matter how much money they might bring, no matter what the IDB might have done.[3] It followed then that the Board of Governors, the Board of Directors, the president, and the top management of the Bank would be wholly African. The memory of colonial domination was too recent, and for many too bitter, to countenance new ties to the North.

While entirely understandable, this decision came with its costs. It meant that the members were confronted with relatively high subscription costs to enable the ADB to function and a very small operating budget. Total paid-in capital was set at $125 million,[4] though several of the original thirty-five signatories were unable to meet their obligations for many years.

Perhaps more significant, the restriction on non-African participation meant that there was limited outside help in organizing the institution or staffing it. In the words of a future president, "The member states themselves were desperately undersupplied with the technical manpower required to make this kind of organization work effectively" and could seldom afford to release staff for the benefit of the new institution.[5] At the same time, it was decided that the Bank could not offer internationally competitive salaries, thereby hampering its ability to attract overseas Africans. This human resource constraint seems to be the main reason why, by the end of 1969, the ADB had disbursed less than $1 million.[6]

By 1970–1972, total annual loan approvals were averaging only $21 million, whereas the corresponding figures for the IDB and the AsDB were $685 million and $272 million, respectively. Thus, the Bank got off to a very slow start. Such is the nature of self-reliant capacity building.

A Cautious Change of Heart

The ADB was set up to run on a nonconcessional basis—that is, lending at interest rates similar to commercial levels (5–6 percent in the early years), with repayment periods of twelve to twenty years. As the World Bank and the IDB operated concessional windows, which were particularly appropriate for the poorest countries, this option was explored at an early stage by the ADB. Because such lending involves very low interest rates and a long repayment period, its funding would require regular replenishment. This was beyond the capacity of the African member states, so talks began with industrialized countries.

The African Development Fund (henceforth "the Fund," or ADF) began operations in 1973 with grants of $82.6 million from thirteen nonregional states plus the ADB itself.[7] Its loans, like those of the World Bank's International Development Association (IDA), would have very "soft" terms—generally fifty years to repay, including a ten-year grace period, and a "service charge" of only 0.75 percent per annum.[8] It would use the same staff as the African Development Bank (henceforth "the Bank," or ADB). But, to minimize the influence of non-Africans, it was given its own governance structure—one that allotted African members far greater voting power than justified by their financial contribution. A separate Board of Directors was defined that would have equal representation and voting power for the regional and nonregional contingents, even though the former's contribution, via the Bank, was a token 3 percent of the initial target amount. The nonregionals were participating in a special fund that would not give them any broader privileges related to the institution in which it was housed. In this way, the "Bank proper" was still preserved as an African institution.

Nonetheless, the Bank began to reach the limits of its lending capacity. A committee was struck to examine the possibility of opening up the capital stock to nonregional states, and a proposal to this effect was tabled at the 1973 annual meeting. It was rejected, as was a similar motion put forward three years later. Instead, the African states dug deeper into their own resources, pledging to triple the authorized capital from its original $250 million over the period 1972–1978.

Various efforts were made to attract other resources from countries that were not members of the Organisation for Economic Co-operation and Development (OECD), particularly the Arab and African countries that belonged to the Organization of Petroleum Exporting Countries (OPEC). The response proved disappointing, though Nigeria did agree to set up the Nigeria Trust Fund (NTF) in 1976. With its oil wealth rapidly growing as a result of the recent OPEC price increases, Nigeria was not borrowing from the Bank and felt some obligation to help its poorer neighbors. Protecting the Bank from outside influence was also a prominent factor in its calculations. The naira equivalent of $89 million was provided as the initial subscription. Its terms were fixed between those of the ADF and the ADB: 4 percent rate of interest and up to twenty-five years amortization period. The ADB, ADF, and NTF together constitute the ADB Group.

However, the very next year, 1977, it became clear that the Bank's lending capacity was barely keeping up with inflation. The 1974–1975 oil crisis had dealt a major blow to most African economies, and members were finding it very difficult to match their promises with actual cash even though, as in any such institution, only part of capital subscriptions was to be paid-in. Furthermore, the remaining callable capital was of little use. Theoretically available to back bonds that could be floated by the Bank to raise additional resources on international capital markets, in practice this mechanism had very limited potential given the weak financial basis of most of the guarantor member states.

With paid-in capital only 17 percent higher (after inflation) by 1977 than it had been in 1971, the governors finally changed their minds and approved the entry of non-African members—in principle.[9] The president was requested to prepare a report explaining how this could be done "on conditions compatible with the maintenance of the African character of the institution."[10] It took another five years—until 1982—before agreement was reached, the statutes were modified and ratified, and nonregional members were officially admitted to Bank membership. This was not an easy decision.

The conditions involved limiting the presence and the voting power of the nonregionals to one-third on the Board of Directors, and guaranteeing that the president would always be African and that the headquarters would remain on the continent. In addition, a president could win election only if he or she received both a majority of the votes from African member states and an overall majority. De facto, it also meant a continued preference for African staffing, particularly in management. Thus began a new era at the ADB Group.

Internal Politics

This early period contained its share of internal disagreements and the occasional crisis. A split between francophone states and the rest appeared during the formation of the ADB. The former were rather more ambivalent about asserting their independence and concerned about the practical implications of the ADB on their close relationship with France. As relatively small countries, they also worried about domination within the institution by larger members like Nigeria, Algeria, and Egypt. Consequently, a special voting system was developed to give smaller members a proportionately greater voice. Abidjan, Côte d'Ivoire, was selected as the headquarters of the ADB to help win over the francophone community.[11]

Problems with the process of selecting the president also arose at this stage. It was an issue that was to become a recurring headache for the institution, sometimes approaching migraine proportions. Lengthy negotiations were required to settle the appropriate nationality of the president. There was also confusion over the authority of the Board of Governors relative to that of the Board of Directors. This was temporarily resolved, only to flare up again in 1970. Then, a mere two months after his reelection, President Mamoun Beheiry was confronted with a motion of censure by his Board of Directors and he resigned. Just as the ADB was getting up to speed, it found itself without a president for five months.

Eventually, the acting president, Abdelwahab Labidi, was confirmed in the position. This meant that two arabophones, from Sudan and then Tunisia, had occupied the presidency for the first ten years of the Bank. When it came time for the next elections, in 1975, the sub-Saharan majority was determined to have its turn. But the North African members voted in a block for a Libyan candidate. With their large share of the votes and Nigeria abstaining, a stalemate ensued. The incumbent's mandate had to be extended for another year while heated debate and political maneuvering continued.

A Ghanaian, Kwame Donkoh Fordwor, finally emerged victorious, but the calm was short-lived. Only three years later, he was accused by the Board of Directors of making unilateral decisions without due consultation. Soon these allegations grew to include mismanagement and favoritism in recruitment. He was dismissed from his duties and a vice-president was once again installed as acting president. The ADB had come to the brink of its own demise.[12]

The subsequent presidential election of 1980 was predictably contentious, but Wila D. Mung'Omba of Zambia eventually won (see Table 2.1). It was only in 1985 that the process lost some of its overt controversy. While the introduction of a secret ballot was a key factor, the arrival of the nonregionals also appeared to moderate the intra-African rivalries. There was now another group that sometimes provided anglophones and francophones, Arabs and non-Arabs with a common adversary. Babacar N'Diaye of Senegal, a career employee of the ADB Group, was elected. His uncontested reelection in 1990 was in sharp contrast with earlier episodes. However, as the end of his second term approached in 1994, the institution once again found itself surrounded by controversy, with the presidency inevitably in the middle (see Chapter 3).

By the time the governors met to elect a new president in May 1995, the process was looking very reminiscent of earlier days. Nigeria had finally decided to contest the position but its own

Table 2.1   A History of Presidents

Name	Nationality	Tenure
Mamoun Beheiry	Sudanese	1964–1970
Abdelwahab Labidi	Tunisian	1970–1976
K. D. Fordwor	Ghanaian	1976–1979
Goodall Gondwe	Malawian	1979–1980
Wila D. Mung'Omba	Zambian	1980–1985
Babacar N'Diaye	Senegalese	1985–1995
Omar Kabbaj	Moroccan	1995–

Source: Mingst, Politics and the African Development Bank.

internal politics did not endear it to many member states. After numerous rounds of voting, a stalemate was reached between a Nigerian, a candidate from Lesotho, and a Moroccan. The governors had to reconvene in August and go through another nine rounds of voting before the Moroccan, Omar Kabbaj, finally emerged victorious. Clearly he was going to have to work hard to develop a consensus behind his presidency.

Moving Money

The fundamental role of a development bank is to mobilize financial resources to be lent out for various developmental objectives while covering administrative and other expenses. After its slow start, the ADB Group has been quite successful in increasing the resources at its disposal. The initial three-year target for ADF subscriptions was only $180 million. This has been replenished every three years at consistently higher amounts, to the point where the sixth replenishment, for 1991–1993, attained a level of $3.42 billion. This evolution is summarized in Table 2.2 below.

Theoretically, the original, nonconcessional Bank window had even more potential for growth. The Bank should have been able to borrow on international capital markets, through the sale of ADB bonds backed by its members' capital. However, it was constrained for some time by its pro-African policy. Limited borrowing did begin in the mid-1970s, but foreign creditors were cautious.

This situation changed with the advent of nonregional membership. The major increase in Bank capital permitted greater leveraging through borrowing. Still more significant was the type of capital involved. With the sovereign states of some of the world's strongest economies putting their money on the line, ADB bonds quickly

Table 2.2   Growth in Resources

Year[a]	ADF Replenishments		ADB General Capital Increases	
	Number	Billions of Dollars[b]	Number	Billions of Dollars[b]
1975 base		0.15		0.48
1976	I	0.33	I	0.96
1979	II	0.85	II	1.61
1982	III	1.22	III	5.79
1985	IV	1.52		
1988	V	2.79	IV[c]	22.98
1991	VI	3.42[d]		
1995	VII	(2.80)[e]		

Sources: Gardiner and Pickett, *The African Development Bank 1964–1984,* pp. 29, 58–62; various ADB Group annual reports.

Notes: a. The year in which the replenishment or increase took effect.

b. Converted from Fund or Bank Units of Account (BUAs) at the average exchange rate for the year indicated in the first column.

c. Approved in 1987.

d. Actual subscriptions totaled only $2.96 billion.

e. Negotiations were still continuing at the time of writing. At the end of 1994, the best guess as to the level of the replenishment was BUA 1.9 billion, but as time wore on this seemed increasingly optimistic.

became a very solid investment. Several international credit rating agencies accorded the Bank their highest AAA rating on its "senior debt."[13] Both the quantity and the quality of its financial base had improved dramatically. Its outstanding debt, which had stagnated around $400 million between 1979 and 1983, was doubled by 1984.

The Bank was particularly successful in obtaining a subsequent general capital increase (GCI) in 1987, by reducing the permissible reserve ratio of paid-in capital to Bank borrowing, along with a 52 percent increase in paid-in shares. It was basically a statement of increased confidence on the part of the members. The resulting GCI of some 200 percent was the largest such relative increase ever enjoyed by a multilateral bank. Consequently, the Bank was able to expand dramatically its outstanding debt to $8.2 billion by 1993.

Loan approvals have mirrored this exponential growth. From a cumulative total of $451 million for the first nine years up to 1976, the one-year figure for 1991 alone was $3,447 million. Until then, there was barely a hesitation in this expansion, as the three-year totals in Table 2.3 indicate. (The NTF has been an exception to this trend, due to Nigeria's inability to expand its contributions, but it was never a major resource.)

Table 2.3   Loan Approvals by the ADB Group (in millions of dollars)

	Fund	Bank	NTF	Total
1966–1975	139	312	—	451
1976–1978	408	457	64	929
1979–1981	811	894	21	1,726
1982–1984	1,071	1,467	37	2,575
1985–1987	1,795	3,087	53	4,935
1988–1990	2,825	5,428	47	8,300
1991–1993	3,151	5,735	72	8,958

Source: Various ADB Group annual reports.

This growth is also remarkable when compared to that of the other regional development banks. For the period 1976–1978, ADB Group lending represented a mere 19 percent of the IDB's level and 33 percent of the corresponding figure for the AsDB. By 1988–1990, it had surpassed the IDB and was up to 77 percent of the AsDB's total lending. There can be no doubt that during the 1980s the ADB Group succeeded in its most basic function of mobilizing and allocating funds.

This success has not been without its controversy. Can the Bank properly manage such an acceleration in its activities? Can the recipients absorb such additional resources effectively? What is the impact on the indebtedness of the borrowing member countries? How secure are the Bank's loans and hence its financial viability? What is the impact on the exposure of the nonregional members, through their callable capital—could it indeed ever be "called in"?

We return to these and other questions later in this book. But some of the nonregional members had already made up their minds by 1992. In discussions of the proposed Third Five-Year Operational Program for 1992–1996, the Board of Directors was unable to accept the higher Bank lending program (or "target") put forward by management. Though the regional members could in principle have pushed it through with a simple majority vote, a consensus was sought and the matter was referred to the annual meeting of governors. Finally, a five-year figure of around Bank Unit of Account (BUA) 7 billion was established, which necessitated an 11 percent cutback in the 1992 Bank lending program as compared to the previous year. The debate continued over the lending program for 1993, eventually leading to a further 14 percent cut in planned Bank lending. With Fund lending stagnating, then declining as well, overall loan commitments dropped by 25 percent in two years.[14]

Another, less auspicious, chapter in the ADB Group's history had begun.

The African Development Bank Group Today

The ADB Group marked its thirtieth birthday in 1994, though there was not much cause for celebration. It began the year with fifty-one regional, or African, member countries and twenty-five nonregional members.[15] The only independent African country excluded was South Africa. All such regional members were borrowers except Libya, which has chosen to refrain in light of its relatively ample domestic resources. The nonregionals include three Middle East oil exporters and five Third World countries—India, China, South Korea, Brazil and Argentina. Eritrea and South Africa offered perhaps the only notes of encouragement that year. The former joined the Bank Group at its annual meeting in May, while the latter's application for membership was anticipated with some excitement after the election of a new, democratic government in April. As of the end of 1995 South Africa had applied but had not yet been accepted for procedural reasons.

The policy of the Bank has always been that African members should control two-thirds of its shares. In practice, their proportion has been slightly less, as there have been some members who have had difficulty making their payments. In 1993, African members held approximately 64 percent of votes in the Bank, led by Nigeria, Egypt, and Libya (see Table 2.4). In the Fund, nonregionals have contributed over 98 percent of the resources but are limited by statute to 50 percent of the votes. In both the Bank and the Fund, Japan and the United States are the leading nonregional contributors.

This structure stands in some contrast to that of the other two major regional development banks. In neither the AsDB nor the IDB is there a separate governance structure for the management of concessional funds. Developed country members of the AsDB contribute more than half the capital and claim a comparable share of the votes. The IDB lies between the Asian and African models, with donors holding 49.9 percent of the votes (recently increased from 46 percent).

Some 1,250 full-time staff work at the ADB Group, concentrated at the headquarters in Abidjan.[16] Until recently, there were four small regional offices—in Kenya, Zimbabwe, Cameroon, and Morocco—and three smaller country offices—in Ethiopia, Guinea, and Nigeria. The ADB Group also maintained representational offices in London and Washington. However, continued controversy over the mandate

Table 2.4 Distribution of Votes and Cumulative Subscriptions Among Members (percent, December 31, 1994)

	Bank[a]	Fund Shares	Fund Votes
Regional members	64.2	1.5[b]	50.0[c]
Nigeria	10.2		
Egypt	6.1		
Libya	4.2		
Morocco	3.9		
Algeria	3.6		
Côte d'Ivoire[d]	3.0		
Zimbabwe	2.8		
Zaire	2.5		
Others	27.9		
Nonregional members	35.8	98.5	50.0
Japan	4.9	14.5	7.4
United States	5.9	13.3	6.8
Canada	3.3	9.7	4.9
Germany	3.7	9.4	4.8
France	3.3	8.5	4.3
Others	14.7	43.1	21.8

Source: ADB Group, 1994 Annual Report.
Notes: a. Distribution of votes (distribution of subscriptions is almost identical).
b. Contributed by the ADB on behalf of the regional members.
c. Shared equally among six regional executive directors who sit on the board.
d. The Côte d'Ivoire increased its share significantly in 1995 by purchasing unsubscribed shares.

and cost-effectiveness of these external offices came to a head when internal audits identified some financial irregularities, and falling net income created pressure to reduce administrative expenditures. All these offices were provisionally closed in 1994.

Total loan and grant approvals peaked at $3.45 billion in 1991 before falling off to $2.52 billion in 1993. In this, the last "normal," year, the Bank accounted for 64 percent of the total through twenty-eight loans, giving an average loan size of $58 million. The ADF approved forty-one project and policy-based loans averaging $19 million each for a total of $796 million. Another $98 million was provided for sixty-two studies, through technical assistance grants. The NTF completed the picture with two loans totaling $10 million.

The resources of the ADB Group amounted to $21.1 billion at the end of 1993. The Bank's resources were $11.5 billion, consisting of debt ($8.2 billion), paid-in capital ($2.6 billion), reserves ($1.2 billion), and net income ($0.07 billion), adjusted for losses on currency translation. The Fund had resources of $9.2 billion, essentially all from member subscriptions. The resources of the NTF were $0.4 billion.

The Bank capital was last raised in 1987 through the fourth GCI. Discussions on the next round were scheduled to begin in late 1994 but were delayed because the Fund negotiations had not been completed. Informally, the debate had already started over whether the Bank had adequate capital to see it through to the end of 1996. The seventh replenishment of the Fund was still not finalized in April 1995, sixteen months behind schedule.

The ADB Group was facing a midlife crisis on its thirtieth birthday. For the first time in its history, annual loan commitments had fallen for two consecutive years, in 1992 and 1993. The Fund had run dry and the eventual size of the replenishment was clearly going to represent a significant reduction from the previous level (see Table 2.2). At the same time, the nonregional members were insisting on major reductions in the lending of the Bank, including the exclusion of many borrowing members deemed uncreditworthy. To complete the gloomy picture, a task force on project quality raised serious questions about the status of the loan portfolio and the institution's capacity to improve it. As a result, the annual meetings in Nairobi in May 1994 ended in frustration. By the end of that year, the unheard-of had happened—there had been no Fund lending whatsoever. Bank Group lending was a mere $1.44 billion, half the level of 1992.

The pressure for fiscal restraint in OECD countries combined with uncertainty over the institution's developmental impact to impede the Fund negotiations. However, the dominant preoccupation of the nonregional members was the financial stability of the Bank. Under a tighter definition of nonperforming loans, arrears had doubled since 1992 to reach $700 million by early 1994. Net income had dropped by 39 percent in the previous year as more and more African member countries were simply unable to meet their obligations. Having bucked the negative trends of its continent for so long, the ADB Group finally seemed to be falling hostage to its hostile environment.

A Continent in Crisis

The growth of the ADB Group has indeed been remarkable when one considers its "working conditions." Of the fifty-two countries classified as low-income, thirty-five are in Africa. These represent over 80 percent of the total population of the ADB Group's borrowing clientele. In the disastrous decade of the 1980s, per capita income in sub-Saharan Africa fell at an average rate of 1.0 percent per annum.[17] By this measure, the region had barely made any progress since 1965.

Significant advances have been achieved in health and education. However, by the late 1980s, there was alarming if localized evidence of declining primary school enrollment, deteriorating nutritional levels, and even falling levels of life expectancy.

Civil wars have wracked many countries: Angola, Mozambique, Uganda, Rwanda, Burundi, Somalia, Ethiopia, Sudan, Chad, Sierra Leone, Nigeria, and Liberia. In a very different way, the recent blossoming of political reforms and democratization, unquestionably a promising trend, has nonetheless created new complications in many countries in the short term. Governments have been virtually paralyzed for various periods in Zaire, Togo, and Niger while they grapple with, or resist, the pressures for popular participation. Others, notably Nigeria, Cameroon, and Kenya, have been distracted from economic reforms without resolving their political dilemmas, losing credibility in the process. On the other hand, for a few the political winds have breathed new life into their economic recovery as well—Mali, Zambia, and especially South Africa. A few small countries, notably Botswana and Mauritius, have combined democratic systems with consistent economic growth, providing a welcome example that might inspire others.

Fortunately, the economic picture in North Africa has not been as bleak as in sub-Saharan Africa, with gross domestic product (GDP) per capita continuing to rise over the 1980s by 1.3 percent per annum.[18] However, this was a far cry from the average of 4.1 percent enjoyed over the previous fifteen years. For the two largest economies in the region, Egypt and Algeria, economic growth continued to decelerate in the late 1980s. More worrisome yet was the rise of Islamic fundamentalism, confronting Algeria with a socioeconomic crisis by 1990. Its neighbors have struggled to prevent its spread into their territories.

The continent's problems had already begun in the 1970s, when stagnation or decline in most oil importers was barely offset by the good fortunes of oil exporters. Even these lucky ones were not preparing for the end of the boom. The rest were suffering to varying degrees from high oil prices, rising interest rates, drought, stagnant agriculture, and continued dependence on a few export commodities. A temporary boom in commodity prices in the late 1970s served only to hide the underlying weaknesses.

The most distressing development was in the agricultural sector, the traditional backbone of most African economies. Food production grew at only one-half the rate of population in the 1970s, turning many countries into significant food importers. Nor was this compensated by expanded output of export crops. Indeed, the continent's share of world trade in coffee, cocoa, cotton, and palm oil fell substantially. With growing trade deficits and little foreign investment, many countries turned to foreign borrowing. In retrospect, it was probably unfortunate that the abundance of petrodollars made it relatively easy for African governments to seek short-term respite in this way.

The roof collapsed in 1980 when a second round of oil price increases was followed by a world recession, soaring interest rates, and plummeting prices for commodity exports. The relative price of Africa's exports (its terms of trade), which had slowly deteriorated during the 1970s, went into a free fall. For sub-Saharan Africa, it dropped by 42 percent between 1979–1981 and 1992.[19] Meanwhile, new commercial credit dried up and old debts came due.

By 1986, two out of every three African countries were classified by the World Bank as having a debt-servicing problem. Middle-income borrowers were particularly encumbered with commercial debt, while low-income countries accumulated significant levels of multilateral obligations. As stabilization and structural adjustment programs (SAPs) dragged on, repayments on the associated loans often came due before the benefits were apparent (especially in the case of expensive IMF credits), and with no option to reschedule. Long-term external debt owed by sub-Saharan Africa more than doubled over the course of the decade, equaling its gross national product (GNP), and making it the most heavily indebted region in the world by this measure.[20] Inability to remain current on debt repayments has led to repeated rescheduling of bilateral and commercial debt and a mounting arrears problem. Similar trends were observed in much of North Africa. Thus, by 1994, the situation had actually deteriorated from that of 1986, with four out of every five African states now classified as severely or moderately indebted.[21]

As a result, a vicious cycle has been set in motion. Imports have been drastically reduced, depriving agriculture, industry, transport, and other productive sectors of basic inputs. Falling exports and imports have meant lower taxes and duties, which are generally the major component of government revenues. At the same time, governments must devote more of their resources to debt payments. Thus, public services such as health, education, and agricultural extension have been curtailed. Investment, both public and private, has been particularly hard hit.

The debate over the causes of this crisis, and hence the solutions, has been intense and polarized. One side, comprising many African leaders, has emphasized the role of external factors, such as interest rates and commodity prices.[22] The IMF and the World Bank, on the other hand, have led much of the donor community in focusing on the weaknesses in national government policies. This schism has further delayed the recovery process.

Finally, it appears that the two sides are willing to acknowledge that the truth lies somewhere in between. The saddest thing about this debate is that its resolution does little to change the prescription, while many years have been lost in the process. Most external factors are beyond the control of the actors involved, and the donor community does not seem prepared to make the major capital infusions necessary to compensate for them. Indeed, after slow but steady growth over the 1980s, total aid flows are now declining as aid budgets in one donor country after another come under attack. Thus, African governments are left with little option but to make major adjustments in their policies. The debate is now largely confined to the extent and speed of that adjustment, together with the need to minimize the social costs and protect the most vulnerable groups.

The IMF and the World Bank have emphasized the need for more realistic exchange rates; export promotion; reduced government spending; more support to the agricultural sector; greater reliance on price incentives, markets, and the private sector; and less government intervention. A large and growing number of African states have adopted such measures, commonly referred to as structural adjustment programs. While necessity is undoubtedly the driving force behind this compliance, there appears to be a gradual recognition among African leaders that some important changes in their approach to economic management are essential for sustainable development.

The political reforms sweeping the continent, with the aid of a vibrant civil society, should eventually mean more open and accountable government. In the short run, pressures for reform have sometimes been disruptive and have always made the policymaking environment more complex. At least here the trend is in the right direction. That said, the combination of widespread poverty, negligible growth, high indebtedness, and major economic and political change hardly corresponds to the banker's preferred scenario. But for a development banker, the task becomes only more urgent.

Literature Review

Until 1989, the ADB Group had essentially escaped in-depth review by outside analysts. Two books did appear in the mid-1970s, but because the institution was still at a very early stage in its development, there was fairly little to evaluate.[23] In 1981, a unique book appeared from the ADB Group's recently ousted president, K. D. Fordwor.[24] It is a detailed history of his term in office with, not surprisingly, considerable attention to his version of the events leading up to his resignation. It provides an intriguing insight into some of the internal politics that dogged the Bank in its early days.

These books were followed by official publications to celebrate the twentieth and twenty-fifth anniversaries of the organization in 1984 and 1989. The first of these made a subtle recommendation for more rigorous project selection, better project management, and more attention to economic policies and trends, pointing out that better impact in the field would raise the standing of the Bank and facilitate the attraction of further funds. Apart from mobilizing additional resources for Africa, the authors conclude that "the task of the Bank is to bring Governments of all political persuasions to accept the importance of economic efficiency, and to educate them to an understanding of the objective conditions required to achieve this."[25]

The 1989 anniversary report focused more on the development problems of Africa, with only modest attention given to the role of the Bank itself. This section was essentially divided between a historical introduction to the Bank and a statement of its current program policies and priorities. In one of its few self-critical passages, it admits that not enough has been achieved in the area of economic integration and multinational project funding. Otherwise, it promises to broaden its contribution by promoting new work in the areas of the environment, women in development, the private sector, intra-African trade promotion, and population. In a telling conclusion, the book argues that the Bank's success obliges it to take on such new challenges even if "some of these tasks may be beyond the capacity of the African Development Bank to tackle."[26]

Around the same time, a committee of nine (eventually ten) eminent persons was commissioned to evaluate the Group's performance to date and recommend the sort of future role it should play. Their short report was also published in 1989. It identified a few areas in need of improvement over the next two years: the disbursement process, project selection, project supervision, postevaluation, country programming, and the number of country economists. This "period of consolidation" was, nonetheless, to be accompanied by expanding financial resources and staff. It went on to recommend expansion into an ambitious range of key development issues, starting in 1992, through the creation of a center of excellence that would "reflect the central role of the Bank as an organism of analysis and advice in the field of economic and social policy."[27]

In 1990, Karen Mingst, a U.S. academic, published the first independent book on the ADB Group since it had come of age: *Politics and the African Development Bank.* Mingst's main objective was to demonstrate, and then explore, the political nature of the institution. Having done that, however, she concludes that political conflict has been less significant than at the other main multilateral development banks (World Bank, IDB, and AsDB). This conclusion undoubtedly reflects her focus on the role of the United States, and it is debatable whether the same could be said about the level of political discord among regional members. In the course of her analysis, Mingst also discusses many of the more mundane technical aspects of the Bank's performance, signaling a variety of problem areas. Here she avoids drawing any overall conclusions, but the impression she leaves is that the Bank is making important progress on most fronts. Perhaps her most telling comment is one short, anonymous description: "good staff—weak system."[28]

The debate only heated up when a Swedish publication appeared in the same year: *Banking on Africa.* It was written by Bo Jerlstrom, who drew on his recent experience as alternate executive director at the IDB to identify key issues and provide some comparative analysis. His is an often hard-hitting critique of the organization, which comes down firmly in favor of a long, five- to ten-year period of consolidation, during which it should stop trying "to be all things to all men" and focus instead on a few priorities.[29] His conclusion is "Less African politics and a more professional banking approach would achieve greater development impact."[30] On the other hand, he does not consider that the Bank's financial stability is in jeopardy, nor does he rule out further modest growth in its level of lending.

The Danish aid agency DANIDA commissioned a much larger study of the field effectiveness of eleven multilateral agencies in four countries, including Kenya and Sudan, where the role of the ADB Group was assessed.[31] The study team concluded that it had tried to do too many things too quickly as both a bank and a development agency, with the result that all stages of its field operations (projects and policy-based programs) received inadequate attention. When situated within the broader donor community, it did not seem to have developed a comparative advantage or niche. The consultants hint that the ADB Group might do well to resist further growth for the time being while it defines its role more clearly.

Finally, we must add the 1994 report of the ADB Task Force on Project Quality entitled "The Quest for Quality," often referred to as the Knox Report after the task force chairman, David Knox.[32] Though not published, it has been widely circulated, to the point where it has been cited on the front page of the *Financial Times* of London.[33] Only thirty-five pages long, it is probably the most complete critique of the ADB Group to date, and certainly the most credible. Four of the task force members were former executive directors or staff of the ADB Group, and two others (including the chairman) were former World Bank managers.

The report has sent shock waves through the ADB Group and its shareholders. Its litany of criticisms culminates in the dire warning: "If not strengthened, it may end up destroying itself. That is the stark choice before the entire Bank community."[34] The extensive experience and inside knowledge of the authors is reflected in a cogent analysis that seldom misses the mark, and we will draw on it frequently in this book. Unfortunately, the authors opted for alarmist terminology and a rather one-sided focus on the weaknesses of the Bank Group. This was undoubtedly a decision consciously made in order to hasten reform, one that seems to have succeeded. However, it may have contributed to delays in the replenishment of the Fund and certainly did nothing to protect the level of that replenishment.[35] It also damaged the image of the Bank Group among those not closely associated with it. Headlines about a "chaotic" bank appearing just before the annual meetings did not do it justice.

Thus, we are beginning to accumulate a body of analysis, issues, and opinions. Two competing visions are also emerging. One, as typified by the two 1989 reports, focuses on the big picture—the continuing crisis of development in Africa and the need for the ADB Group to do more as the most influential African institution on the scene. The other, as reflected by the two Nordic studies, argues for modesty, a refocusing on the core activities of the Bank—doing a few things well. The Knox Report stresses that "the Bank is pulled in all directions by conflicting goals and attitudes of its shareholders."[36] There is no consensus over the institution's mandate. The report does not offer an explicit recommendation, which was in any case beyond its terms of reference, other than to urge that the issue be addressed. The biggest single question that we must try to answer in the course of this study is What is the appropriate role of the African Development Bank Group?

Notes

1. "Third World Hope," p. 1.
2. The Caribbean Development Bank was established nine years later, in 1969.
3. The United States was a founding member of the IDB, as it would be with Japan in the AsDB a few years later.
4. As another, more subtle manifestation of the concern for an African character to denominate its financial transactions, the ADB chose a special unit of account, the BUA, rather than the U.S. dollar. This was quietly set to

equal the value of the U.S. dollar. When the link between gold and the dollar was altered and then broken, the BUA was aligned with the IMF's basket of currencies, the SDR (special drawing right), which has differed from the U.S. dollar by as much as 30 percent. The BUA value increased from 1 BUA = U.S. $1.09 in 1985 to 1 BUA = U.S. $1.45 in 1994. The ADB provides U.S. dollar equivalents for all major financial measures, and we will use this currency throughout most of the book for the sake of convenience.

5. Fordwor, *The African Development Bank*, p. 4.

6. ADB Group, *1992 Annual Report*, p. 207.

7. Once again, a special unit of account was adopted, this time the Fund Unit of Account (FUA), as distinct from the Bank's BUA. It was valued at SDR 0.921052. This was finally dispensed with in 1992.

8. IDA has since reduced its normal repayment period to forty years. The ADF terms remain the same, except for lines of credit that are repayable in twenty years, including a five-year grace period.

9. Current price estimates of paid-in capital are given in Gardiner and Pickett, *The African Development Bank 1964–1984*, p. 44.

10. Ibid., p. 56.

11. Fordwor, *The African Development Bank*, p. 7.

12. Mingst, *Politics and the African Development Bank*, p. 22.

13. Senior debt is backed by the callable capital of AA and AAA member countries. As accepted by credit rating agencies since 1982, this means nonregional shareholders plus Libya. Holders of this debt are given priority in the event of financial difficulties at the ADB. The Bank also offers "subordinated" debt, which is guaranteed by all shareholders.

14. Fund lending fell significantly in 1993 because the Italian government failed to approve its planned contribution, and the rest of the sixth replenishment had been exhausted.

15. Yugoslavia ceased to be a member in 1993.

16. At the end of 1993, there were 1,268 full-time employees, including elected officials. One year later this number had fallen to 1,224, although the number of approved positions was 1,309.

17. Calculated from data on GDP and population growth on pages 221 and 269 of the World Bank, *World Development Report 1992*.

18. Ibid. This is an unweighted average for the ADB Group's four borrowing members: Algeria, Egypt, Morocco, and Tunisia.

19. Calculated from data in Global Coalition for Africa, *1993 Annual Report*, p. 67.

20. In terms of debt to exports, arguably a more relevant indicator, it is comparable to Latin America. The latter is still higher in terms of debt service (actual or due) as a proportion of total export earnings, because of the higher share of nonconcessional lending.

21. There were twenty-nine severely indebted and eleven moderately indebted countries. World Bank, *World Debt Tables 1994/95*, p. 187.

22. UN Economic Commission for Africa, *An African Alternative to Structural Adjustment*.

23. Ebong, *Development Financing Under Constraints*; Amegavie, *La Banque Africaine de Développement*.

24. Fordwor, *The African Development Bank*.

25. Gardiner and Pickett, *The African Development Bank, 1964–1984*, p. 163.

26. ADB Group, *Africa and the African Development Bank: 25th Anniversary 1964–89*, p. 188.

27. ADB Group, *Africa and the African Development Bank: Current and Future Challenges,* p. 3.

28. Mingst, *Politics and the African Development Bank,* p. 26.

29. Jerlstrom, *Banking on Africa,* p. 36.

30. Ibid., p. 7.

31. The analysis of the ADB Group is published separately in DANIDA, *Effectiveness of Multilateral Agencies at Country Level: AfDB in Kenya and Sudan.*

32. ADB Group, "The Quest for Quality."

33. "'Chaotic' Bank Threatens Africa Soft Loans," p. 1.

34. ADB Group, "The Quest for Quality," p. 2.

35. One of the two outstanding issues holding up the replenishment in late 1994 was the submission by management of an action plan to deal with the recommendations of the Knox Report.

36. Ibid., p. 1.

3

GOVERNANCE AND THE GOVERNED

Decisionmaking in an international organization is largely deter mined by the organization's governance structure, its policies, and its key personnel. The influence of these different components varies from one institution to another. The sorts of policies that are adopted and the degree to which they are applied depend greatly on the initial structure of governance and the people involved. On the other hand, once the latter are in place, policies may be the main instrument of improvement.

In the history of the ADB Group, strong lending policy positions have generally been avoided, due largely to the dispersed nature of the Bank Group's governance and hence the need to satisfy a wide range of interests.[1] More recently, prompted in good part by the nonregional members, considerable attention has been paid to policy changes within the institution. In other parts of this book, we deal with such policies. To understand much of the past record and the recent policy debate, we devote this chapter to the context in which policies are defined and implemented.

Board of Governors

Ultimate authority resides in the Board of Governors. Every member country nominates a governor, often the minister of finance in the case of the African members. This group is responsible for such matters as the election of a new president, changes in the Bank's capital stock, the establishment of special funds (e.g., the Nigeria Trust Fund), and the approval of the annual financial statements. The full Board of Governors sits only once a year, at the annual meeting of the ADB Group, and subcommittees are rare. Governors seldom have the time to keep up with recent developments and so are heavily dependent on their executive directors, to the point where some are regularly represented by these directors.

This is unfortunate, since the governors should normally play a critical role distinct from that of the executive directors. They should be bringing a different, and broader, perspective on Bank Group policies and priorities. They need not feel bound by the Charter of the Bank, since they have the power to amend it if they see fit.[2] Being closer to the reality of their countries, and farther from the internal dynamics and personality conflicts on the Board of Directors, they are in principle a source of "sober second thought." Indeed, when governors have met in smaller, less formal settings than the annual meetings, it has generally been conducive to dialogue and increased understanding. However, most of their power has been delegated to the Board of Directors.

Board of Directors

Executive directors are the resident representatives in Abidjan of the member countries. They are chosen by those countries' governments and are formally elected by the Board of Governors, but, as in other such organizations, they are paid by the ADB Group. They serve for three-year renewable terms. All officially represent more than one country, except the U.S. representative.[3] There are eighteen executive directors on the Board of Directors of the Bank, six of whom represent nonregional members. Thus, African members outnumber non-African members two to one, reflecting their shares of the authorized capital, as outlined in Chapter 2. Six of the regional EDs sit on the board of the Fund along with the six nonregional representatives, achieving the 1:1 ratio agreed to at the time of the Fund's establishment.

The ADB Group is the only major development bank with separate governance structures for its concessional and nonconcessional windows. The 1:1 ratio for its Fund is similar to that between borrowers and nonborrowers on the board of the AsDB.[4] The 2:1 ratio at the Bank corresponded to that of the IDB until recent changes in the latter.[5]

Some constituencies rotate the choice of ED among the countries in the group because the members' shares are comparable. In other cases, where one country holds a much larger share than the rest, they always provide the representative. In addition to the unique case of the United States, Canada and Japan fall into this category. On the regional side, Nigeria, Egypt, Libya, Algeria, and Morocco all have permanent access to the Board of Directors. Chad has also had de facto permanent representation, even though Zaire has been easily the largest member of its constituency.[6] A complete list of constituencies for the Bank is provided in Table 3.1.

Table 3.1   Constituencies on the Bank Board of Directors in 1994

Director's Nationality	Also Representing
Regional members	
Nigeria[a]	São Tomé and Principe
Libya[a]	Somalia, Sudan, Mauritania
Algeria[a]	Guinea-Bissau, Madagascar
Egypt[a]	Djibouti
Morocco[a]	Tunisia, Togo
Ethiopia	Kenya, Tanzania, Uganda, Rwanda, Seychelles
Chad[b]	Zaire, Guinea, Cape Verde
Sierra Leone	Liberia, Ghana, The Gambia
Mauritius	Zambia, Malawi, Lesotho, Swaziland
Côte d'Ivoire	Benin, Congo, Niger, Cameroon, Burkina Faso, Equatorial Guinea
Angola	Mozambique, Namibia, Zimbabwe, Botswana
Senegal	Gabon, Comoro Islands, Mali, Burundi, Central African Republic
Nonregional members	
United States[a]	—
Canada[a]	Korea, Kuwait, Spain, China
Japan[a]	Argentina, Austria, Brazil, Saudi Arabia
France	Italy, Belgium
Germany	UK, Portugal, Netherlands
Switzerland	Norway, Sweden, Denmark, India, Finland

Source: ADB Group, 1993 Annual Report, pp. 128–129.
Notes: a. Does not rotate due to dominant share of leading member.
b. Has not rotated even though Zaire holds a much larger share than Chad.

The nationality of the director can be important, because the country whose official sits on the Board of Directors has more actual or potential influence. Thus, the United States is a major player here as in so many other international forums, but so is Canada. Not surprisingly, Nigeria is in the same league. But note the strong presence of North Africans, which in fact reflects their relative economic strength in the continent. At the very least, any active board that holds both U.S. and Libyan members is bound to be lively.

Where the board position does not rotate between different countries, there is the possibility of leaving the same representative in place for much longer than the normal three-year term. This has not been the tendency among the nonregional members, but it has on the regional side. Thus, the EDs for Egypt, Libya, and Morocco have not changed for twelve or thirteen years, and those for Chad have served considerably longer.[7] This facilitates familiarity with the institution and increased confidence in challenging the president or other members of the board. As a result, several of these players have proven to be particularly uncompromising on occasion, earning a reputation as hard-liners.[8]

In the past, the large presence of North Africans on the board probably contributed to the cleavage that sometimes developed between North Africa and sub-Saharan Africa. This seems to have declined as a factor over the years, especially since the arrival of the nonregionals. Henceforth, the biggest problems have arisen between the nonregional contingent and the regional EDs, notably the long-serving hard-liners. The influence of the many small sub-Saharan countries has in fact been weakened by both their small share of votes and the frequent turnover of their representatives.[9]

Because the regional EDs all represent actual or potential borrowers, there is a certain reluctance to question the appropriateness of another country's project when it is presented for approval; this is to avoid "reprisals" when the tables are turned. Applying as it does to two-thirds of the EDs, this factor considerably weakens the project quality control function of the board. Such restraint is a fairly common phenomenon across the multilateral development banks, but it is less critical where the share of nonborrowers is equal (AsDB, and now the IDB) or dominant (World Bank).

When the board discusses policies, a more general problem arises. There has always been a strong, if not overwhelming, emphasis placed on the need to preserve the African character of the Bank. Over the years, little has changed to moderate this preoccupation in terms of African influence in other international agencies. Certainly this is true in the World Bank, where the African voting share is less than 10 percent and managers from sub-Saharan Africa are almost nonexistent. The ADB Group is the bank of Africa, essentially the only international organization with significant financial resources Africans control, and they are determined not to lose it. This explains the limitation of the voting power of nonregionals (33–36 percent for the ADB and 50 percent for the ADF) and the restriction of their presence to one-third on the board of the Bank, where most nonproject discussions take place. Indeed, this ratio is usually carried through to the various board subcommittees.

There are other factors at play as well. On both "sides," the ADB Group is not generally considered a high priority. African governments are understandably preoccupied with their own economic and political scene. Their scarce human resources in the field of economic and financial management are inevitably called to focus on the domestic front, while the ADB Group must appear well heeled by comparison. What human resources are available are more likely to be directed at the World Bank and the IMF, where the big money and bigger decisions reside. The ADB Group has been seen as a sympathetic and successful ally that can be relied upon—and hence neglected.

The situation is similar among the nonregionals, if for different reasons. Africa has never been as important to the largest funding sources (the United States and Japan) as Latin America or Asia, and the end of the Cold War has clearly reinforced this tendency. It has been more prominent in the foreign policy of Britain and, especially, France, but neither of them is even guaranteed a seat on the board, and both have other ways to protect their interests.

The institution's low profile and diffuse ownership have been a mixed blessing. They have meant a relative freedom from attempts to influence lending policy as compared with all the other major multilateral development banks. Indeed, Shaw has argued that the United States for one has been marginalized by failing to appreciate the democratic system of policy formulation.[10] Its EDs have typically been instructed to oppose categorically projects that run counter to U.S. interests, without the opportunity to negotiate a compromise solution. Whereas this approach has worked in other contexts in which the United States had some hegemonic power, at the ADB Group the U.S. objections have been easily overruled. Projects that might have been altered if the United States had been willing to bargain have instead been approved unchanged.

Diffuse ownership is a significant asset when things are going well. However, it has also meant that no one country has chosen to take the lead in resolving problems when they do arise. Disagreements have often occurred within the nonregional and regional camps, and the problem persists. Furthermore, the low priority attached to the ADB Group is sometimes reflected in the quality of the representatives assigned to the board—by both types of member countries. The lack of interest from capitals can mean that individual EDs go largely unassisted and unsupervised, leaving the Bank vulnerable to the weaknesses and biases of the individuals chosen. When strong EDs are nominated, they are generally reluctant to spend more than one three-year term (in those cases where extensions are not automatically excluded by the process of rotation).

With the recent crisis, nonregional capitals appear to have increased considerably their interest and involvement in the institution. The same cannot be said of the regional EDs, who continue to be particularly deprived of guidance from their constituencies, partly for reasons already described. The centralized nature of the institution also means that African governments have relatively little contact with it, providing less opportunity to understand the Bank. It can also be much more difficult to communicate between Abidjan and even a neighboring African country than with Europe or North America. Finally, with the rapid pace of change in recent times, it can be difficult for some EDs to keep up with the situation back home, especially as the years in office add up.

This context explains much of the dynamics in the board's everyday work, which sometimes degenerates badly. Regional EDs have tended to downplay policy issues, focusing instead on projects being proposed for their constituent countries. When policy questions do arise, they often see their role as defending the institution from "undue" foreign influence, maintaining its African character. In addition to the regional EDs controlling share of ownership and the selection of an African president, this has included an overwhelmingly African staff, sensitivity to African government priorities, and a reluctance to copy foreign models, most notably the World Bank.

Nonregional EDs, on the other hand, have a tendency to see their role as one of counteracting the supposedly lax managerial and administrative standards encouraged by the regional directors' attitudes. Developmental impact has been of decidedly secondary importance. Often without much support from their capitals, sometimes without much African experience, and rarely spending more than one term in office, nonregional EDs have probably found management procedures to be more familiar terrain than the complex issues of development strategy.

Consequently, the Knox Report on project quality emphasized that all governors and EDs were collectively responsible, along with management and staff, for the problems the report identified.[11] It pointed out that both nonregional and regional members had endorsed the rapid growth of lending without apparent concern for the impact on projects and implied that neither group had really encouraged policies to improve quality. Instead, they had tended to micromanage the institution, scrutinizing, for example, every line of the annual budget.

The debate at the board seems to ebb and flow with the changes in personalities who sit there, depending on the degree of commitment and previous experience they bring to the job. Sometimes a subgroup hits it off and things happen, if they cut across the not-so-invisible line between regionals and nonregionals. At other times, things fall apart.

What might have been considered acceptable under normal circumstances was no longer tenable in 1993 with the deterioration of the Bank's financial situation. A consultative committee was formed from among the governors with the explicit objective of trying to mend fences on the board through a greater involvement by some senior governors. Although once again some EDs filled in for their governors, some success was achieved in developing a consensus on the severity of the Bank's financial problems and the need for urgent corrective measures. Unfortunately, its mandate was limited and short-lived. By the annual meeting of May 1994, open dissension had returned.

The most recent case, involving a new credit policy to define eligibility for ADB loans, has pushed the confrontation to new depths. Faced with an impasse that was blocking the finalization of ADF VII negotiations, the regional EDs drafted a proposal and recalled the full board to consider it, but with no time for consultations. All the nonregional EDs rejected the proposal, at least partly for reasons of process rather than substance, but were outvoted by the regional representatives who also voted as a block. Not surprisingly, this failed to bring the nonregional members back to the ADF negotiating table, and the impasse persisted.

Presidency

With such a fractious board, and no member country taking a dominant role, the presidency is a key component of the governance structure, though not necessarily the most powerful. That the president votes at the board only in the event of a tie is hardly important.[12] The president is the chairperson and can do much to determine the degree to which differences between the regionals and nonregionals are exacerbated or attenuated. Because formal votes are rarely taken, it is the president who must interpret the degree of consensus and draw conclusions. As head of the staff, the president is also the link between board decisions and Bank responses. The president also has the opportunity, indeed the responsibility, to take initiatives and choose new directions for the institution.

In a continent not traditionally associated with Western democratic principles, the election of the ADB Group president is nonetheless more democratic than in any other multilateral development bank. The United States selects the president of the World Bank and plays a pivotal role in the IDB as well; the Japanese choose the head of the AsDB. Yet in the election of the ADB Group president, all member countries are involved in what amounts to a global election campaign. The only restriction on nominations is that they must be African. There has developed a certain understanding that the various linguistic and geographic groups should take turns in the presidency. After two Arabic-speakers served for the first twelve years, two anglophones from West and Southern Africa followed for the next nine. They were succeeded by Babacar N'Diaye, from francophone West Africa. In 1995, Nigeria, which had apparently decided that it was its turn, put forward a candidate for the first time, although he was not elected.

The selection of the president has generated the usual benefits and costs of a democratic process. It has strengthened accountability to the full body of borrowers, encouraging the president to be particularly responsive to the priorities of borrowing members and raising the possibility of both better service and more political interference. This has helped generate a more sympathetic, less arrogant culture than that of the World Bank and hence more cordial relations with African governments; but it has also brought a reputation for more "political projects." It can prove politically impossible to say no to a major loan proposal for a significant shareholder, while even minor matters take on new significance in the year before an election. The risk of political pressure has become an increasingly relevant concern with the upsurge in fast-disbursing, policy-based lending where the criteria for approval and disbursement are less precise than in a standard project.[13]

This situation is further exacerbated by the fact that the Board of Directors has considerable influence over the appointment and de facto control over the firing of the president. It is the directors who recommend the selection of the president to the governors, and it is they who can suspend the president pending a final decision by the governors. The board that is in continuous contact with the president has the ultimate sanction over him or her. Furthermore, with no one country claiming the right to nominate the president, the reelection of that person depends to a large extent on satisfying as many of the EDs as possible. The EDs are thus more empowered in the ADB Group than in the other multilateral development banks. Those regional EDs who have served on the board longer than the president are particularly comfortable in asserting their power. In general, this governance structure has encouraged the board to take a particularly active role in some elements of management.

Not surprisingly, most presidents have had problems in dealing with their Board of Directors, and two have been forced to resign. The ADB has not enjoyed the stability of the IDB, where two presidents oversaw the first twenty-eight years, nor that of the AsDB, where the president is routinely drawn from the Japanese Ministry of Finance. In 1994, President N'Diaye, in his tenth year in office, was making history as the longest-serving president at the ADB Group; but he was also experiencing serious problems of his own.

Vice-Presidencies

Political considerations reach down to the level of vice-president, because it is not a career position. Instead, vice-presidencies are filled by the Board of Directors on the recommendation of the president. In this case, there has been an explicit, if unwritten, agreement that vice-presidencies would be shared among the broad subregions of the continent: North Africa, Nigeria, the rest of anglophone Africa, and francophone Africa.[14] Thus were the four vice-presidencies allocated until 1986. At that time, a fifth position was created, which went to a non-African. In 1992, the gender element was finally recognized, which also complicated the previous formula. A Sudanese woman was appointed to this level, even though one of the other vice-presidents was from Algeria.[15]

While vice-presidents often rise through the ranks, to reach this position professional qualifications are unlikely to be enough, and they have not always been the most important criterion. Once a vice-president, a person shifts from the very secure status of permanent employee to a more tenuous one based on three-year, renewable contracts. This is bound to influence the behavior of all but the boldest. It is not the practice of most other multilateral development banks, where vice-presidencies are career positions.

The position of vice-president is further complicated by the fact that it is perhaps the most obvious breeding ground for future presidents (which is not to say that it is the most successful). Two of the five regular presidents, as well as the one acting president, have come from this pool. A president desirous of reelection is likely to have an uneasy relationship with any ambitious vice-president. This element is also absent in the other multilateral development banks.[16]

It was probably one of the factors that contributed to the crisis of August 1993. In that month, N'Diaye attempted to fire one of his vice-presidents. An emergency session of the Board of Directors was called, and N'Diaye was almost impeached himself. His decision was reversed and a special committee of EDs was set up to investigate. In the end, the vice-president chose to resign. However, the special committee decided to curtail the powers of the presidency by removing his authority over the Operations Evaluation Unit and the Office of the Internal Auditor so that they would henceforth report directly to the board.

This incident reignited the old debate about the respective powers of the president and the Board of Directors. Among other things, the Articles of Agreement establishing the Bank specify that the Board of Directors appoints vice-presidents on the recommendation of the president, yet the president is "responsible for the organization of the officers and staff of the Bank whom he shall appoint and release in accordance with regulations adopted by the Bank."[17] Thus, it is not at all clear where a vice-president's first loyalty should reside.[18]

Grappling with Governance

The unfortunate series of events that unfolded in 1993–1994 were a major blow to staff morale and the institution's reputation at a critical juncture in its history. That the institution should be deprived for one whole year of the concessional resources so important to its poorest members was the clearest sign that relations with the nonregional members had reached a crisis point. Relations were no better with some of the African members. By the annual meeting in May of that year, Bank governors were reported as saying that "there is open war between Mr. N'Diaye and some North African members of the 18-member executive board."[19]

Reform can be postponed no longer. The Consultative Committee of Governors, at the end of their meeting in December 1993, noted the importance of enhanced cooperation between regional and nonregional partners in order to safeguard the views of all shareholders, respect rules of procedure, and improve the division of labor among the various organs of the Bank Group. The Special Committee of Executive Directors concluded in March 1994 that there was an urgent need for transparent and objective processes in most areas of Bank management, including systems through which the board could confirm that its decisions had been implemented. And the Task Force on Project Quality recognized that these matters had a direct impact at the project level. "Fundamental questions of the bank's governance must also be tackled—the role and attitudes of the governors and the executive directors, the relations between the latter and president, and those between the president and staff."[20]

The task force provided a series of recommendations that bear repeating:[21]

1. Only the Board of Governors should have the right to dismiss or suspend the president.
2. The Board of Directors should be responsible for setting policy and oversight of the amount and quality of lending.
3. The president should be responsible for day-to-day management, establishing a program of policy issues to be discussed each year with the board, and ensuring that the board receives all the necessary information to discharge its functions.

4. A limit should be set to the terms of elected officials.
5. Once criteria have been set, the president should have sole authority for the appointment of vice-presidents, with the exception of a newly proposed vice-president for evaluation.
6. The president and the board should refer to the governors fundamental issues of policy and objectives on which they need guidance.
7. The governors should set up a small representative group of governors to consider these matters.
8. Vice-presidents, in consultation with the president, should be responsible for appointing their department heads, and so on down the line.
9. A new vice-presidency for operations evaluation should be established and report directly to the board.

All of these seem appropriate, though it is not obvious that the head of evaluation need necessarily be elevated to create yet another vice-presidency. The first proposal would seem both long overdue and still very relevant. The power to choose and release the president has been the source of major conflict throughout the history of the Bank, and it must be unequivocally assigned once and for all. It must also be separated from the daily business of the institution as much as possible.

The second, third, and sixth suggestions represent an attempt to establish a more balanced division of labor. The fourth is important for the case of some regional EDs, but it ignores the problem associated with nonregional and rotating regional directors, who tend to leave too quickly. It would seem advisable to extend the normal term to at least four years from the current three to encourage greater familiarity with the institution and the issues, as well as to promote stronger working relationships among EDs.

The fifth recommendation would address some of the concerns regarding vice-presidents. Having them nominated by the president but appointed by the board can lead to confusion over where their loyalties should lie. It is also likely to stimulate distrust on the part of the president. It may be necessary to take this reform a step further. Given the extra degree of politicization of the presidency, and its probable inevitability, it would seem advisable to minimize it at lower levels. As discussed below, there is also a continuing need to provide strong leadership to the staff through the example of senior management. To accomplish this, only the most exceptional managers should reach the level of vice-president; once there, they should have every incentive to devote themselves to the needs of the Bank.

Serious consideration should be given to transforming the post of vice-president to a career position.

On the other hand, if vice-presidents do wish to compete for the presidency, they should probably be required to resign a year before the election, except perhaps if the president has already decided to step down. Otherwise, it is difficult to believe that the institution would not be adversely affected by the competition between two (or more) of its most senior managers.

The seventh proposal is basically a call for the continuation and extension of the work of the Consultative Committee of late 1993. In fact, an ad hoc committee on the next GCI was established in 1994 with, as part of its mandate, governance questions related to the general institutional structure, management, and policy issues. Unfortunately, it had not yet convened by the end of 1994.

As the task force rightly underlines, attitudes are a major part of the problem, which many of the above recommendations would hopefully address. Ultimately, both regional and nonregional members must develop a greater sense of ownership. The regional members, who effectively have ownership, tend to focus on protecting their status without assuming full responsibility for the continued health of their property. The nonregional members have sometimes appeared to treat the ADB Group as the Africans' bank, something they could abandon if they did not get their way. Such an environment is hardly conducive to cooperative problem solving.

It may be necessary to consider an increase in the voting share of the nonregional members in order to instill that sense of joint ownership. Nonregional members are basically the sole source of financing for the Fund, and they provide the callable capital that underwrites the majority of the Bank's debt financing. Even in terms of the paid-in capital subscriptions to the Bank, the African members have consistently found it difficult to honor their two-thirds share, and at one point their effective share dropped close to 50 percent. Yet regionals maintain a clear majority of the votes on the Board of Directors at the Bank and two-thirds of the seats. Under such circumstances, nonregionals are prone to feel that they are "paying the piper without being able to call the tune."

Perhaps a more equitable fifty-fifty split in the votes and the seats on the Board of Directors of the Bank would reinforce the commitment of the nonregionals and promote an unambiguously constructive approach to solving the problems of "their" bank in Africa. Simultaneously, because no one group would hold the simple majority necessary to carry most votes, this could encourage cooperation between regionals and nonregionals. With the recent changes at the IDB, the ADB is now the only multilateral development bank that reserves a majority of the votes for its borrowing members, and it seems to be paying a high price for this distinction.

The proposals for a limit to the tenure of EDs and for a more active role for governors should help enrich the participation of regional members. It may be necessary to supplement these with other measures. More African representatives should participate in the replenishment negotiations for the Fund, which for all practical purposes are now dominated by management and donor countries. The creation of more country offices would also improve the two-way flow of information, perhaps stimulating more interest in the Bank Group's policies—and its needs. Senior management should make greater efforts to touch base with recipient governments. While the president spends a great deal of time traveling, those trips are inevitably tied to "political" concerns. Vice-presidents and directors need to follow up these contacts with more technical meetings to cover everything from arrears to procurement procedures.

Finally, it would seem reasonable to consider reducing the size of the Board of Directors, which is larger than that of either the AsDB or the IDB. This could help improve the atmosphere in the board by facilitating familiarity among the members and increasing the sense of teamwork. The simple reduction in the number of potential opinions would enhance the prospects for establishing a consensus. In addition, this would make a modest yet significant contribution to keeping costs under control and would demonstrate to staff that all levels are being examined. At 9 percent of total administrative expenses, the board's share of costs seems to exceed usual norms.[22]

Staff

The best-laid plans of executive directors and presidents will amount to little without a competent and motivated staff to see them through. The many small decisions staff make every day ultimately determine the effectiveness of the institution. Bodies set up to deal with governance issues, such as the Special Committee of the Board or the Consultative Committee of Governors, invariably turn to personnel questions at some point. These were also a focus of the Knox Report.

The personnel of the ADB Group has been the subject of widely varying judgments, usually on the basis of anecdotal evidence. Some would have it that these are the best and the brightest of Africa, overworked because of understaffing. Others counter that it is a bloated bureaucracy full of deadwood. Here we assess the appropriateness of the staff in terms of its size, composition, quality, and middle management.

Size

One of the many recurring points of disagreement between management and the Board of Directors (in particular the nonregionals) has been staff size. Management has regularly requested increases, which the board has just as regularly rejected. Thus, the actual staff in post numbered around 1,100 from 1987 through 1991. Over the same period, total loan approvals grew by some 60 percent, while various new policies, procedures, and initiatives placed further demands on staff. With much of this additional work generated by decisions of the board, management's frustration was palpable.

A comparison with the World Bank is instructive, if somewhat complicated. In 1995, the World Bank had approximately 1,720 employees working on North Africa and sub-Saharan Africa combined.[23] This included over 100 long-term consultants and some 400 local staff in regional offices but excluded all the central departments that provide various services to all regions of the World Bank. Thus, it cannot be compared to the total staff size of the ADB Group—which was still only 1,224 at the beginning of 1995. Rather, it would be more accurate to compare it to the staff working only in the project and country program departments, where the authorized number of person-years (before the 1995 reorganization) was 395, although the actual number on staff was somewhat less.

The stark contrast is hardly diminished after one takes into account the differences in annual lending. During the period 1990–1993, the World Bank made annual commitments averaging 50 percent higher than those of the ADB Group. Even this factor is somewhat offset when one recognizes that the workload tends to be related more to the number of projects than to the amount of money lent. Because the average World Bank project tends to be bigger, the total number of projects per year was similar in the two institutions. Thus, the World Bank has devoted at least four times as many person-years per project, or almost three times as many person-years per dollar of new lending.

It is true that the World Bank does much more macroeconomic and sectoral analytic work, thereby justifying some of the extra resources at its disposal. But this can become a "chicken-and-egg" argument, since the ADB Group could also do more with more staff. One reaches broadly similar conclusions when comparing the ADB Group with the Asian and Inter-American Development Banks, whose ratios of technical experts to active projects are 1:3 and 1:2 respectively; for the ADB Group it is 1:6.[24] Moreover, the latter is clearly working in the most demanding region.

The contrary position of the EDs is not quite as contrary as it might seem, however. They have argued that the Bank first needs to make more efficient use of its existing wage bill, by redeploying some of its personnel and releasing others before incurring additional expenses. They have also pointed to the difficulties the personnel department experiences in filling the vacancies available. More recently, the declining profitability of the Bank has undermined the feasibility of major increases in staffing. In any event, the board has used its control over the authorization of new person-years as a stick to promote changes in human resource management.

Reform of personnel policies and practices is one of the most difficult areas in any international organization, and perhaps especially in Africa, where anyone released is likely to suffer a huge cut in salary. But in 1990, over 10 percent of the staff was redeployed and, more significantly, some sixty persons were let go. While the majority of the latter group received generous "golden handshakes," this was nonetheless an important step in the right direction. It was probably one of the first fruits of the greater stability that came to the Bank with the reelection of the president earlier that same year.

It was also sufficient to appease the board, which authorized an additional eighty-six positions in 1991 and twenty-eight more in 1992. Since the staff departures and unfilled positions in 1990 had created more than 100 vacancies among already approved person-years at the start of 1991, this gave the ADB Group considerable room to grow. In 1994, it had 1,280 authorized staff positions (plus twenty-four elected officials).[25] However, there remain two approaches to improving the overall staffing situation: increased human resources or lower lending. Though the debate continues, the latter has become the de facto short-term solution. In the long term, it is hard to see how the Bank can play a more substantive role in the continent's development without access to more human resources.

Composition

At least five aspects of staff composition have raised concerns in the recent past: the low share of professionals (especially in operations), the shortage of certain key skills, the underrepresentation of nonregional nationalities, the low number of women, and the proportion of managers to staff. We will deal with the first four here and the fifth later on.

One comparison has already been made with the World Bank in terms of the number of professionals. As a result of the recent spate of recruitment, the share of professionals in total staffing rose from 47 percent in 1988 to 52 percent in 1993.[26] However, most of this growth did not benefit the operations divisions.[27] Their professional complement as a proportion of the total staff remained at a mere 17 percent, while their share of professionals went down from 40 percent to 35 percent. The numbers have not been increased in line with recommendations of the 1989 redeployment report. In 1995, the reorganization called for a significant increase in the share of professionals and a major shift in favor of operations, which was to claim 58 percent of all such positions. If this plan is respected, it will be an important, if overdue, move in the right direction.

With the growing importance of structural adjustment and other policy-based lending in the mid- and late 1980s, there was a generally recognized shortage of macroeconomists. With three economists responsible for as many as twenty-five countries, it was impossible for them to monitor developments in any single country sufficiently.[28] By 1992, the situation had improved so that each country economist had one or at most two countries to cover. However, the total number of economists is still low. The biggest shortage may now be in the project departments, where engineers, agronomists, and other specialists have typically taken the lead. In the health and education sections of these departments, for example, there are several architects but no economists. Including loan officers (most of whom are economists) and project economists, there are now about two economists per country. This pales in comparison to the average of 4.5 economists in the World Bank's African operations. Recent hiring has not improved this ratio. With the growing complexity of development banking, and pressure from the donor community, the ADB Group gave priority to a whole range of other underrepresented fields in its 1992 recruitment drive: environment, population, poverty alleviation, and women in development.[29]

The predominance of Africans among the staff is both striking and noteworthy, given their shortage in all other international organizations outside the continent. Up to 1985, there were virtually no non-African permanent employees. The historical explanation for this situation has already been described. With the arrival of nonregional members, however, it was untenable to prevent their citizens from having access to employment at the Bank. Furthermore, with its growing size and sophistication there seemed to be a need to tap into a wider range of expertise. The number of well-qualified Africans available and willing to live in Abidjan was very limited—and in some specialized fields virtually nonexistent.[30]

As a compromise, the concept of the technical assistant (TA) was developed. Nonregionals funded a few of their nationals to work as regular bank staff, provided they satisfied the usual recruitment procedures. This enabled management to continue reserving long-term staff positions for Africans. It also meant that, in most cases, nonregionals could be offered better financial packages, without which it might have been hard to attract them. By 1988, there were forty-nine such technical assistants—10 percent of the professional staff.

But this compromise did not really satisfy the nonregional members. It limited "their" staff complement to modest levels and effectively ruled out access to management positions, not to mention creating a double standard that was not healthy for everyday work relations. In the late 1980s, a small crack appeared and a few TAs were converted to regular contracts. At last, in 1990, it was agreed to phase out the TA positions over the next few years, and active recruitment began for non-African candidates. By the end of 1993, some seventy-five professional employees were nationals of nonregional member countries, along with eight remaining technical assistants, giving them a 13 percent share of professional staff.[31] Recruitment of regular nonregional staff has only just kept ahead of departing technical assistants.

Thus, the African character of the Bank's personnel remains intact thirty years after its inception. There seems to be some difficulty in attracting non-Africans,[32] but there is also a continuing ambivalence toward the new open-door policy. The ADB Group stands alone among the major multilateral development banks in its protective approach to staffing. Serving as it does the most challenging continent with the smallest pool of local professionals, it must come of age and reap the advantages of more widespread sourcing for its positions. There is every reason to believe that Africa's sons and daughters will continue to hold the majority of posts, while benefiting from the new ideas and perspectives of their nonregional colleagues.

But Africa's daughters, and those of the other member countries, may need some special attention. Women are very scarce at the professional and managerial levels, accounting for 19 percent of the former category and only 11 percent of the latter.[33] Apart from straightforward equity considerations, a greater presence by women should help incorporate gender issues into the Bank's activities. While various steps have been taken to respond to this set of issues, change is clearly going to take just as long as in most other parts of the world. It is to be hoped that the arrival of the Bank's first woman vice-president in 1992 (and its first woman ED in 1993) will accelerate the process.

Quality

How does one evaluate the quality of more than 1,000 staff? Other than the summary results of one comprehensive study in 1989, we are restricted to somewhat impressionistic evidence from those who have worked inside the Bank or closely with it. That 1989 study, commissioned by the Bank, reported that roughly 80 percent of the staff were well suited to their positions, about 10 percent should be redeployed (in some cases after appropriate training), and the remaining 10 percent did not meet minimum requirements and should be replaced.[34] This study provided some of the background for the changes made in 1990 as outlined above.

Most other writers on the ADB Group have commented on staff quality in a less quantitative but often more evocative way. On the one hand, it looks good when compared to other African international institutions: "With its pin-striped economists, sophisticated capital-market presentations and no-nonsense attitude, the Bank has given the business world a new picture of Africa."[35] On the other hand, even the ADB Group's official twentieth anniversary publication acknowledged in 1984 that "in the past it has proved difficult to attract and retain African staff of high calibre at the professional level."[36] Jerlstrom has suggested that the 1989 recommendation of dismissals on the order of 10 percent should in fact be doubled.[37] The Knox Report "was impressed greatly by the calibre of some managers and staff but could not help but notice that they are surrounded by much deadwood."[38]

There is considerable variability within the staff, a fact that creates its own problems. Some of those working virtually at the bottom of the professional ladder as project officers have had extensive experience as senior government officials, even heads of ministries, prior to joining the Bank. Unfortunately, there are others who no longer meet today's standards, particularly some who were hired in the early days when the recruitment process was much looser and the Bank was less attractive to top candidates. In those days, the World Bank was the obvious choice.

By 1990, however, some Africans were voluntarily leaving the World Bank to join the ADB Group. The recent spate of hiring, amounting to some 200 new staff members, appears to have brought some well-qualified, new blood into the institution.[39] These new staff are contributing some much-needed enthusiasm and rigor, but a lot will depend on the examples set and demands made by their managers. The plans for another round of early retirements and layoffs in the context of the 1995 reorganization will be critical to the institution's long-term health.

Middle Management

There is a good amount of corporate memory in the middle management at the Bank. With very few alternative employment opportunities in Africa that would offer similar levels of remuneration,[40] and a quality of life in Abidjan that is comparatively good, there has been fairly low turnover. Such stability has important advantages; it also brings its problems. The recruitment and promotion process was less consistent in the early days of the organization and the management style less demanding. Some of those who climbed up the corporate ladder benefited from the former or were unduly influenced by the latter.

Added to this is the usual pressure to ensure a certain balance among nationalities that any international organization faces. In a continent of some fifty, typically small, countries at low levels of human resource development, this is a serious constraint.

Weak managers create more problems than weak staff because they provide poor models, undermine morale, and are more likely to hire weak subordinates. The problem was diminished with the early retirement program of 1990. New recruitment from outside the Bank, the opening up of management levels to a few nonregional candidates, and judicious promotions have also made a difference. The placement of weaker managers in less strategic positions, while suboptimal, is a well-worn approach that has also been applied. Unfortunately, recent upheaval has resulted in the departure of some of the best managers. The 1995 reorganization will succeed or fail largely by the extent to which the right people are retained for the remaining management positions.

Other aspects of management have shown less progress, in particular its overall size and its hierarchical nature. In 1988, managers accounted for 25 percent of the total professional staff (28 percent if the eighteen EDs are included).[41] The corresponding figure for 1993 was down to 20 percent, but as a percentage of total staff it remained unchanged at roughly 10 percent. Many division chiefs have only two or three professional staff. The justification for some twenty deputy directors is not clear, with nonregional board members arguing that these positions do not deserve managerial classification. Finally, in 1995, major cuts were proposed. The deputy director position was essentially eliminated, while the number of departments was reduced from twenty-four to seventeen.

One of the reasons these deputy positions remain is probably the hierarchical structure of decisionmaking. As a minor yet revealing example, all project officers must get approval from both their division chief and their director (or the deputy) for every international phone call, telex, or fax; and all official correspondence has to be signed by the director as well. Travel authorizations are approved by vice-presidents.

The same phenomenon has hamstrung the regional offices, which were led by people at the level of director, but they had very little capacity to take initiative or resolve local problems without referring them to headquarters. Jerlstrom has called them "little more than mailboxes."[42] They have been another bone of contention at the Board of Directors, who refused to authorize the physical decentralization of the Bank until it had a clear indication that authority would follow. In spite of the 1994 decision to close down the regional offices, an alternative, more cost-effective approach must be found. The Bank needs to be more accessible to its borrowing members.

Lack of authority has contributed to lack of responsibility. So much is out of the hands of the individual professional, either controlled by his or her manager or by another department, that only the most dedicated feel personally responsible when things go wrong. As the Knox Report commented, "Many staff feel responsible for nothing and, therefore, take responsibility for nothing."[43]

Delegation of authority is not widespread in large bureaucracies generally, or African ones more particularly, and the president's own management style has followed the hierarchical tradition. The appointment, promotion, and transfer of managers have tended to be driven by the president, and there has been limited delegation on other matters to vice-presidents. However, with the new breed of highly trained professionals coming in, it is important to allow more room for initiative and independence, coupled with responsibility. Many of these recruits have experience in other modern, large-scale organizations, where the trend is toward streamlined management and greater autonomy, and they may soon get frustrated at the ADB Group.

Conclusions

Various suggestions were made in the first half of this chapter in connection with governance. A number of staffing recommendations emerge from the second half, though some will have to wait until later in the book. In addition to the promising directions laid out in the 1995 reorganization, we have the following suggestions:

1.   The Bank must not slip back into the staff-to-project ratios of 1990–1992. If and when lending recovers to similar levels, additional human resources must accompany it.

2.   After the program of early retirements and layoffs, many of the remaining staff will need concerted retraining. This must apply to administrative and support staff as well as professionals, as they also enjoy relatively high salaries that are sometimes unmatched by productivity levels.

3.   The composition of staff must be altered to include more women, and more citizens of nonregional member countries. While the number of professionals is scheduled to increase in the operations departments, special emphasis must be given to the project divisions therein. It would appear that the number of economists remains inadequate, but we will return to this in the next chapter.

4.   The defunct system of external offices must be replaced to strengthen the presence in the field. Some form of country office is probably the most promising option, provided their mandate is clear and a division of labor is established. Consideration should be given to making service in a country office mandatory for promotion to management.

In general, there is a need for more attention to accountability and less on control at all levels in the hierarchy. Staff must be motivated to take a greater responsibility for their performance. Managers must not turn a blind eye to those who are not carrying their share of the load. Senior managers must ensure that only the best are promoted. Vice-presidents should not be political choices; they should have an unequivocal allegiance to their president, who should in turn give them the authority to do their jobs. The board needs to spend less time doing the job of senior management and more time discussing policy and the performance of the institution. The president and executive directors need to recognize the implications of their confrontations and take greater responsibility for building a more constructive atmosphere. In turn, the governors and shareholders must show more concern for the institution they own, not waiting for crises to develop before they react.

There remains one area of governance that has been overlooked so far: the broader accountability of the Bank to the taxpayers who ultimately sustain it. More frequent contacts with member governments and more comprehensive ex-post evaluation of projects will not be enough if the dialogue remains confidential. In donor countries, rising aid fatigue renders the remote multilateral development banks obvious targets for budget cuts. If the Bank is to compete with NGOs and bilateral programs for the extra dollar of support, it will have to reach out more to explain itself and justify its existence. This is especially the case after the Knox Report. Nonregional EDs, who possess a wealth of inside knowledge, should provide more public reporting in their constituencies.

With the spread of democracy and the rise of civil society in Africa, the Bank must be no less sensitive to the needs of African taxpayers. The comfortable First World conditions of its staff are likely to have weakened the support of politicians and bureaucrats in some member states. The contrast with local circumstances will seem more stark to the average citizenry, whose complaints are slowly but surely beginning to be heard. If the Bank is to serve as a model to which others might aspire, rather than as a target of jealousy, regional EDs and Bank staff will have to respond to the new political openness with an outreach program of their own.[44]

Notes

1. As Mingst puts it, "The Bank's legitimacy may be threatened if policies reflect organizational doctrine rather than state needs" (Mingst, *Politics and the African Development Bank,* p. 106). The relatively small role of the United States has also been an important factor (Mingst, p. 169).

2. At the 1994 annual meeting, one executive director kept using the Charter as an excuse for not discussing a proposed new policy.

3. The United States originally refused to share a constituency, although apparently they would now be more flexible if an appropriate proposal were tabled (Jerlstrom, *Banking on Africa,* p. 29).

4. Note that in the case of the ADB Group we are equating regional members with borrowing members, though Libya has not chosen to exercise this right to date.

5. Nonborrowing members had only four of the twelve seats on the board even though they held some 45 percent of the voting shares. In 1994, two more seats were added for them, raising their share to six out of fourteen. Concurrently, their share of subscriptions and voting power was raised to just under 50 percent.

6. The Chadian official has been in office for nineteen years, though the composition of his constituency has changed several times.

7. The Moroccan ED was scheduled to leave in 1995.

8. The Moroccan ED being the exception.

9. Chad being the exception.

10. Shaw, "Par Inter Paribus."

11. ADB Group, "The Quest for Quality," pp. 2, 29–30.

12. To date, all the presidents have been men.

13. A 1988 ADB loan of $108 million to Zaire, primarily to finance oil imports, is one example of a loan that raised many questions about the role of political considerations. Note, however, that we are not suggesting that the total level of policy-based lending is in any way related to the election process. Indeed, the policy-based lending share of total lending fell during the election year of 1990.

14. With this guarantee of a vice-presidency, Nigeria has not, at least until now, contested the presidential elections.

15. When the number of vice-presidencies was reduced to three in the 1995 reorganization, it was unclear what formula, if any, would be applied.

16. In the IDB, the president is always a Latin American; the one vice-president is always from the United States. In the AsDB, the president is always Japanese; the vice-presidents never are.

17. ADB Group, *Agreement Establishing the African Development Bank,* p. 23.

18. Fordwor commented on the same problem in his book *The African Development Bank*, p. 56.

19. "'Chaotic' Bank Threatens Africa Soft Loans," p. 1.

20. ADB Group, "The Quest for Quality," p. 29.

21. Ibid., p. 33.

22. ADB Group, "Operational Programmes and Administrative and Capital Expenditure Budgets: 1994," p. 56.

23. Obtained directly from personnel officers in the World Bank.

24. ADB Group, "Operational Programmes and Administrative and Capital Expenditure Budgets: 1994," p. 19.

25. This figure was reduced to 1,220 in the 1995 reorganization.

26. ADB budgets for 1989 and 1994.

27. The four project divisions and the two country program divisions.

28. Mingst, *Politics and the African Development Bank*, p. 28.

29. ADB Group Office of the Executive Director for Canada, Korea, Kuwait, Spain, and Yugoslavia, *1992 Annual Report*, p. 73.

30. Other less legitimate reasons can also be imagined, but they probably played little role in the debate.

31. ADB Group, *1993 Annual Report*, p. 81.

32. This is undoubtedly a combination of the low purchasing power of the salaries in high-cost Abidjan (predevaluation), the level of insecurity, the difficult climate, and the reputation of the ADB. The 50 percent devaluation of the CFA franc in early 1994 should rectify the first of these constraints, because the purchasing power of ADB salaries, which are denominated in units of account, has gone up markedly.

33. Figures provided verbally by the Human Resources Management Department of the ADB.

34. Jerlstrom, *Banking on Africa*, p. 41.

35. "Third World Hope," p. 1.

36. Gardiner and Pickett, *The African Development Bank 1964–1984*, p. 36.

37. Jerlstrom, *Banking on Africa*, p. 41.

38. ADB Group, "The Quest for Quality," p. 27.

39. This impression is shared by the Knox Report, ibid., p. 27.

40. Everyone above division chief (the first level of management) receives at least $100,000 a year.

41. ADB Group, *Africa and the African Development Bank: 25th Anniversary 1964–89*, Annex 3, Table 2.

42. Jerlstrom, *Banking on Africa*, p. 39.

43. ADB Group, "The Quest for Quality," p. 26.

44. At the end of 1994, bank management proposed the formation of an inspection panel to receive and investigate complaints from outside parties directly affected by a bank-financed project. If approved, this would be a step in the right direction.

4

LENDING A HAND:
PROJECTS AND PROGRAMS

When compared to a development bank, the life of a commercial bank is more straightforward, even if it is riskier. The ultimate goal of a commercial bank is profitability, and this is basically determined by the quantity and quality of loans it finances. The situation is more complicated for a development bank, as profitability is not the only measure of success. While it is expected to remain profitable (or at least cover costs, including potential losses from doubtful loans), its *raison d'être* is to promote development. At best, development impact must be assessed at several levels; at worst, it opens up the debate to conflicting opinions on what development really means. In addition, the development bank will often be confronted with a trade-off between development and financial soundness. This opens the potential debate still further, begging the question as to the appropriate weight to be assigned to these twin objectives.

In this chapter we try to say something about the developmental impact of the ADB Group, albeit indirectly, through an examination of its lending program at many different levels: the continent, the sector, the country, and the project. We acknowledge the parallel need for profitability, but as a secondary issue for the moment. We also avoid a detailed discussion of competing developmental models, essentially accepting those implicit in development banking as well as those made explicit by the ADB Group.

Overlaying this whole analysis is the broader question of the role of any particular institution in relation to the many other actors supporting development in a given region. While this is a theme that permeates, and to some extent transcends, the whole book, it must also be addressed here. We will do so primarily by contrasting the ADB Group with the other development bank active in the continent, the World Bank, under the assumption that such banks play a sufficiently unique role to justify the existence of at least one. Similarity of objectives also facilitates meaningful comparison, though an extensive juxtaposition with the World Bank is beyond the scope of this study.

The picture of the lending program presented here is an aggregated one. It will be supplemented and tested in Chapter 5 through three country case studies—of Kenya, Mali, and Egypt.

Overall Resource Flows

While its importance has sometimes been exaggerated, it has long been recognized that investment capital is a critical input into the development process. For almost as long, the special need for foreign exchange has been appreciated. Virtually all developed countries have relied on external resource flows to break the constraints imposed by limited domestic savings and to accelerate their economic growth at earlier stages of their development. Some still do.

Most observers of the African development struggle conclude that the continent is underfunded. Perhaps the bleakest picture is provided by the UN New Agenda for the Development of Africa adopted by the General Assembly in 1991. There it was estimated that, even if the continent were to grow by 6 percent per annum by the end of the decade, it would need net official development assistance (ODA) of $30 billion in 1992, and more thereafter.[1] This contrasted with actual ODA flows of about $19 billion in 1990–1991. The contrast was only exacerbated in 1992 when actual ODA declined precipitously to $12 billion.

The World Bank, which is sometimes criticized for underestimating the continent's needs, has provided a less pessimistic assessment in its long-term perspective study *Sub-Saharan Africa: From Crisis to Sustainable Growth*. With different assumptions and the more modest objective of "sustained growth," it called for gross ODA flows to grow from $11 billion in 1986 to $15 billion in 1990 for sub-Saharan Africa, and by 4 percent per annum in real terms through the 1990s.[2] While this 1990 target was met, the subsequent decline in aid transfers implies a widening gap today.

There can be no doubt that the ADB Group has played an increasingly important role in this respect. The rapid growth in its loan commitments and disbursements has stood in marked contrast to most other sources of assistance. The consistency of this expansion has added a degree of reliability often missing elsewhere. Rising disbursements have kept ahead of repayments, thereby maintaining a positive net official flow of resources (see Table 4.1).

Table 4.1   Net Official Flows to Africa, 1985–1992 (in billions of dollars)

	1985	1989	1990	1991	1992
Total[a]	14.9	21.4	24.5	27.4	22.4
OECD countries	9.8	13.7	13.1	17.3	12.2
Multilaterals	4.7	7.3	8.2	9.0	9.7
World Bank	2.0	2.2	2.4	2.0	2.0
ADB Group	0.4	1.3	1.6	1.8	1.8
ADB Group as percentage of total	2.7	6.1	6.4	6.6	8.1

Sources: ADB Group, *1989 Annual Report*, p. 30; *1993 Annual Report*, p. 33.
Note: a. Total net disbursements from all sources (gross disbursements minus repayments of principal).

The ADB Group has become a significant player, as Table 4.1 reveals. Its share of total net disbursements to Africa grew from a rather marginal 2.7 percent in 1985 to 8.1 percent in 1992. In comparison with the World Bank Group, the ADB had moved from a level one-fifth the size to one approaching equality by this measure. Indeed, its net transfers to the region, after repayments of interest and other charges, had become larger.[3] This should not be confused with gross commitments, however, which remained significantly greater at the World Bank ($5.3 billion in 1991/92 compared to $3.0 billion at the ADB Group in 1992). The difference is explained by the much larger repayments returning to the World Bank due to its longer record of lending at significant levels.

The ADB Group's role is decidedly modest if one concentrates on concessional resource flows to sub-Saharan Africa. As Table 4.2 shows, the ADF is tied only for ninth place with Sweden on the list of donors and is well behind the World Bank's IDA, the European Development Fund, and especially official French aid. Even allowing for the fact that some bilateral aid has a significantly lower grant element than ADF funds, the Fund is clearly a small player.[4] Needless to say, the ADB Group's share of total resource flows and concessional flows suffered with the drop in lending in 1993 and 1994.

The size of total resource flows from the ADB Group has been a critical variable in its evolution, arguably the single most controversial one. Bank management, led by President N'Diaye and supported by the regional executive directors, has pushed hard for steadily rising lending targets. This has translated into continuing pressure on the nonregional members to authorize higher borrowing and to provide larger capital subscriptions and Fund replenishments. Inside the Bank it has meant relentless pressure on the staff to meet ever higher lending targets each year.

Table 4.2   Gross ODA to Sub-Saharan Africa, 1990–1992 Average

	Billions of Dollars
Multilateral agencies	
World Bank IDA	2.01
European Development Fund	1.85
ADF[a]	0.64
Bilateral donors	
France	3.35
Germany	1.92
United States	1.36
Japan	0.95
Italy	0.87
United Kingdom	0.70
Sweden	0.64

Sources: Global Coalition for Africa, 1993 Annual Report, p. 88; ADB Group, 1993 Annual Report, p. 10.
Note: a. Total disbursements. This includes North Africa which probably accounts for less than 10 percent of the total.

This has been motivated by both the concern to increase total flows to Africa and a desire to establish the ADB Group as a leading actor in the continent's development. Influence comes with financial clout. As the only one of over thirty multilateral and bilateral agencies controlled by Africans, it seemed obvious that this institution should not remain simply another funding source "in the middle of the pack." By the early 1990s, this was no longer the case. Although the ADB Group may be only ninth (Table 4.2) in terms of net disbursements both concessional and nonconcessional to the region as a whole, it was probably in the top five in 1992.[5] What this has meant in terms of institutional influence is a question we shall return to later.

The other motivating factor—providing more resources to Africa—requires further discussion here. Do the now impressive lending levels of the ADB Group actually represent a net addition? On the side of the Bank, which accounts for about two-thirds of gross disbursements, there can be little doubt that the answer is affirmative. Only the North African countries, Nigeria, Côte d'Ivoire, and one or two others have had regular access to international capital markets, and their number has declined in recent years. The ADB has served as a creditworthy intermediary in which international creditors had confidence; the Bank could then on-lend these nonconcessional resources to a wider range of African governments. The key ingredient was, of course, the guarantee provided by nonregional callable capital.

As concerns the Fund, the argument is more complex. Nonregional members might have provided just as much through bilateral channels and/or through enhanced contributions to the World Bank's IDA or its Special Program of Assistance (SPA) for sub-Saharan Africa. There is probably some truth to this. However, bilateral flows are notoriously fickle, fluctuating in overall amount (and between recipients) depending on the latest domestic political priorities. U.S. ODA to sub-Saharan Africa fell by 43 percent between 1985 and 1989, but doubled again in the next two years. The comparable Canadian figure more than doubled between 1989 and 1990, only to fall right back the very next year. Italian aid to sub-Saharan Africa fell by 45 percent in 1991.[6] Funding through the ADF has therefore probably served to help stabilize concessional flows.

Thus, at this most general level, the ADB Group has made a contribution to the region. As we have seen in Chapter 2, however, its role as resource mobilizer will be less prominent in the immediate future. The Board of Directors, backed by the governors, has decided that it is time to slow down and even reverse the growth path.[7] For the first time in the Bank Group's history, commitments fell for two consecutive years, in 1992–1993, a trend that continued in 1994. The debate became so heated in 1994 that the board was unable to settle on a single figure for the ADB indicative lending program. Instead, it opted for a fairly broad range, the final level to be determined following a midterm review of the Bank's performance (see Table 4.3). Nonregional members had pushed hard for the lower end of the range, and their position finally held in 1995, returning the ADB to lending levels last seen in 1986. As already explained, there were no new commitments by the Fund in 1994. The prospects for the near future were unclear but promised at best a stagnation in annual lending.

Table 4.3 Indicative Lending Programs, 1989–1995 (in billions of dollars)[a]

	1989	1990	1991	1992	1993	1994	1995
ADB							
Planned	1.64	2.13	2.25	1.93	1.65	1.1–1.6	1.2
Actual	1.86	2.16	2.25	1.87	1.61	1.42	
ADF							
Planned	0.90	1.08	1.13	1.11	1.15	n.a.[b]	n.a.[b]
Actual	0.97	1.09	1.16	1.10	0.89	0	
Total actual[c]	2.84	3.28	3.45	2.99	2.52	1.44	

Source: ADB Group, "1995–1996 Indicative Lending Programme" (ADB/BD/WP/94/102), October 7, 1994, p. 6.

Notes: a. Indicative lending programs are set in BUA but have been converted into U.S. dollars for convenience. Note that the exchange rate for 1993 was used for 1994 to reflect better the intentions at the time, which were based on comparisons with 1993.

b. Not applicable.

c. Including the NTF.

The debate continues over the appropriate growth path for the ADB Group in the face of growing demands from the continent. We will return to this issue in Chapter 6. But clearly, in the near future, the institution will have to look beyond the augmentation of resource flows to make its mark. So we turn to the questions: for what purpose and to what effect?

Geographical Distribution

The ADB Group is certainly not apolitical, but in terms of allocating its resources by country the process is relatively transparent and consistent compared to that of bilateral donors. The institution maintains the principle of trying to approve at least one loan for each borrowing member in any given year, providing those members are not under sanctions due to their repayment record. Thus, forty-seven different members benefited from the ADB Group's resources in 1991 alone. In this way, the Bank Group can serve to counterbalance the prejudices of bilateral donors. Ethiopia, for example, has been a regular customer in good standing even while the United States refused it all but humanitarian assistance.[8]

This has also meant that the ADB Group is particularly prominent in the smallest countries. As shown in Table 4.4, it has provided more resources than even the World Bank in eight of its smallest members, usually by a factor of two or more. This is probably explained by the more prominent role of such countries in the ADB governance structure.

There is no predetermined allocation of Bank resources by country, and all borrowers have been eligible—a point that has become very controversial, as already discussed. Fund resources have been

Table 4.4   Cumulative Lending to the Smallest Borrowers (in millions of dollars)

Country	ADB Group[a]	World Bank[b]
Namibia	32	0
Seychelles	129	11
Equatorial Guinea	99	45
Cape Verde	172	45
Djibouti	108	52
São Tomé and Principe	158	59
Comoro Islands	78	73
Swaziland	211	84

Sources: ADB Group, *Compendium of Statistics 1993;* World Bank, *1994 Annual Report.*
Notes: a. To the end of 1993.
b. To the end of June 1994.

allocated at the time of each replenishment according to a formula based on population and level of poverty (measured by GNP per capita). At the time of the sixth replenishment in 1991, it was agreed that economic performance should also play a role. Part way through the three-year replenishment period, strong performers were to be eligible for a 25 percent increase in their allocation; weak performers could expect a potential 25 percent drop. In practice, this process was used primarily to reassign country allocations that could not be used due to sanctions, as well as for some supplementary contributions by donors. It is expected to become more widely applied in the future, though it obviously poses some problems for management. It is not easy to establish performance criteria, and the board representatives of members classified as weak may well take exception. The current reliance on World Bank/IMF standards is unlikely to be convincing.[9] Nonetheless, this offers a potentially useful tool for the efficient allocation of resources that is seldom found among bilateral donors.

Geographical allocation is also guided by country groups. Countries have been classified into three categories according to their per capita income levels, as shown in Table 4.5. This is particularly important in determining the use of ADF resources, which are targeted at the poorest countries. Thus, the richest, category C members are excluded from access to ADF funding, with the exception of a little reimbursable technical assistance (for feasibility studies) or multinational projects. Only 10 percent is generally reserved for category B.

In the second five-year operational program (1987–1991), Bank resources were allocated 30:50:20 among categories A, B, and C, respectively. No similar targets have been set for the current five-year

Table 4.5   Country Categories for ADF VI, 1991–1993

Category A (GNP per capita of $510 or less):
  Benin, Burkina Faso, Burundi, Central African Republic, Chad, Comoro Islands, Djibouti, Equatorial Guinea, Ethiopia, The Gambia, Ghana, Guinea, Guinea-Bissau, Kenya, Lesotho, Liberia, Madagascar, Malawi, Mali, Mauritania, Mozambique, Niger, Nigeria, Rwanda, São Tomé and Principe, Sierra Leone, Somalia, Sudan, Tanzania, Togo, Uganda, Zaire, Zambia

Category B (GNP per capita between $511 and $990):
  Angola, Cape Verde, Congo, Côte d'Ivoire, Egypt, Morocco, Namibia, Senegal, Swaziland, Zimbabwe

Category C (GNP per capita above $990):
  Algeria, Botswana, Cameroon, Gabon, Libya, Mauritius, Seychelles, Tunisia

Note: Namibia is treated as a category B country even though its per capita income is estimated to be above the maximum.

program. As Table 4.6 indicates, both the Fund and the Bank were close to their targets, although the Bank had some trouble placing its funds in the poorest countries. This trend continued in 1992–1993, with an average of 16 percent of Bank lending going to category A countries while 40 percent went to category C. In fact, in 1993 there was only one category A public sector borrower from the Bank: Nigeria.[10] On the other hand, this trend was entirely consistent with the growing concern of some nonregional members over the credit-worthiness of category A borrowers.

Table 4.6   Country Allocation of Resources, 1987–1991 (percent)

Country Category	ADB		ADF	
	Planned	Actual	Planned	Actual
A	30	20	89.5	88
B	50	53	10.2	8
C	20	25	0.3	0.3
Multinational	n.a.	2	n.a.	3.7
Total	100	100	100	100

Source: ADB Group, "The ADB Group in the 1990s," pp. 17, 18, 171.

In spite of the early emphasis on the role of the ADB Group as an instrument of regional integration, multinational projects have never absorbed more than a tiny fraction of its resources. We revisit this theme in Chapter 7.

Category C represents a very limited market, with one nonborrowing member (Libya) and four other very small countries. Category B is not much bigger. There are, in fact, relatively few countries of sufficient size and income level to absorb regular injections of nonconcessional funds from the Bank, and the number is getting smaller. Whereas over the three-year period 1982–1984 some thirty-four different countries received Bank loans, by 1991–1993 the number had fallen to twenty-four. Indeed, in 1993 only eight countries benefited from Bank credits. This has led to three different and potentially conflicting concerns: the risk of excessive exposure in a few countries, the danger of diversification if it means lending to the uncreditworthy, and the predominance of North Africa. The first two are financial issues to which we return in Chapter 6. The latter is a more political one that we can address here.

The four North African borrowers (Algeria, Morocco, Tunisia, and Egypt) accounted for 51 percent of all ADB lending over 1991–1993, with a share of 64 percent in the last year. The political concern over the North African share stems from the continuing tension that exists between the Arab North and the rest of the continent. Sub-Saharan Africa, with its lower stage of development, sometimes has little in common with its northern neighbors. These member states can be jealous of the relative influence wielded by North Africa in the ADB Group as a result of their large voting share and board presence. North Africans, with their eyes fixed on Europe, sometimes need reminding that they too are Africans. In any event, a bank must give priority to its clients' repayment capacity, and that of North Africa is without a doubt superior. Indeed, the ADB would be stronger if it had more such customers. So long as the Fund continues to compensate by favoring the poorer sub-Saharan African states, there should be no quarrel. Only 4 percent of Fund resources went to the four North African borrowers in 1990–1993.

A very different problem has recently emerged in the context of the dramatic peace process unfolding in the Middle East: the proposal to establish a new multilateral development bank for the region. As this would include North Africa, it raises the possibility that these countries may lose interest in the ADB, with potentially devastating effects for the Bank. Perhaps the two banks can be rendered complementary. One can only hope that these implications are being fully explored before the proposal for a new bank is accepted.

Sectoral Allocation

The distribution of ADB Group lending across different broad sectors is presented in Table 4.7. As one would expect, agriculture has received the most attention. This covers a wide range of projects, including livestock raising, fisheries, forestry, lines of credit, irrigation dams, environmental projects and agro-industrial complexes. It has been followed by the other traditional development banking priorities: public utilities, transport, and industry. There have been some major shifts in emphasis since 1989. As Table 4.7 shows, agriculture has declined considerably, along with transport, while the shares of multisectoral and social sector loans have grown. The multisectoral category consists primarily of structural adjustment loans serving to finance a variety of imports, which often include agricultural inputs.

Table 4.7 also provides recent World Bank data for comparative purposes. Although the categories are not entirely compatible, several interesting observations can be made.[11] Even though the share of agriculture has dropped at the ADB Group, it appears to be no lower than at the World Bank. In fact, World Bank agricultural lending has dropped considerably in subsequent years.[12] On the other hand,

Table 4.7   Sectoral Distribution of Lending (percent)

Sector	1967–1988 ADB Group	1989–1992 ADB Group	1989–1992 World Bank Group
Agriculture	30.5	20.8	16.3
Transport	19.3	13.1	9.3
Public utilities	22.8	21.0	15.9
Industry	13.9	15.3	13.8
Social	8.2	12.4	15.3
Urban	—	—	7.0
Public sector management[a]	—	—	3.5
Multisector[b]	5.4	17.4	18.4
Total	100.0	100.0	100.0

Sources: ADB Group, *1991 Annual Report,* p. 41; *1992 Annual Report,* p. 41; World Bank, *1993 Annual Report,* p. 106, for sub-Saharan Africa, plus calculations from Table 7.4 of various annual reports for North Africa.

Notes: a. Included here is the World Bank category of technical assistance, which generally appears to involve public sector management as well.

b. The World Bank refers to "non-project" lending in its *1993 Annual Report,* but changes to the term "multisector" in 1994 with little effect on the total amounts in question.

social sector lending is more important at the World Bank. This conclusion is reinforced when we consider the emphasis given to urban development, which is largely absent at the ADB Group. Another small but vital sector where the World Bank has taken the lead is public sector management; only a few small projects of this type are included under the multisectoral category of the ADB Group. Finally, one notes the higher shares of the more traditional sectors of transport and public utilities.

In Table 4.8, we contrast the two main branches of the ADB Group and compare their performance to stated targets. There is a significant difference between the Fund and the Bank in terms of sectoral allocation. Agriculture, transport, and the social sector are most important in the Fund; public utilities and industry come ahead of agriculture at the Bank. Further disaggregation within agriculture would show that the Bank tends toward agro-industrial projects, and the Fund toward rural development.

This pattern of lending is the result of a combination of factors: the ADB Group's sectoral targets, the different levels of concessionality involved, the interests of borrowers, and the mix of borrowers from the two windows. There has generally been a presumption, right or wrong, that concessional funds are more appropriate for social sector lending and small-scale agriculture. More developed countries, which dominate Bank lending, also put more emphasis on industrial projects. Thus, the ADB Group takes the nature of demand

Table 4.8   Sectoral Distribution Relative to Targets

	ADB			ADF		
	1987–1991		1992–1996	1987–1991		1992–1996
Sector	Target	Actual	Target	Target	Actual	Target
Agriculture	30	25.6	25–30	40	36.3	35–40
Transport	17	13.5	17–21	25	21.3	20–22
Public utilities	20	28.9	20–22	12	15.1	12–14
Industry	25	26.7	25–28	8	6.7	5–7
Social	8	5.3	5–7	15	20.6	20–25
Total	100	100	100	100	100	100

Source: ADB Group, "The African Development Bank Group in the 1990s," pp. 80, 171.

Note: Actual figures are net of multisectoral policy-based lending, since this was not factored into the percentages for sectoral targets.

into account in establishing its targets; but it must also decide where its own priorities lie. The latter are generally negotiated in concert with the member states at the time of Fund replenishments and in the preparation of five-year operational programs.

The planned shares for the previous and current five-year operational programs are given in Table 4.8. By comparing the planned and actual shares for the first period, it is clear that the ADB Group has had difficulty attaining its goals in agriculture and transport. Public utility lending, on the other hand, has easily exceeded its targets. In the social sectors, a Bank shortfall was compensated by Fund lending in excess of its target. In general, the discrepancies are not surprising under the circumstances. The decision to adopt a targeted range instead of a single figure in the current operational program is sensible.

For the current five-year operational program (1992–1996), the Board of Governors has stressed the need to focus on poverty alleviation. At first, this was interpreted primarily as a call to maintain high targets for agriculture, in spite of past difficulties in meeting them, and to increase the planned share of Fund resources going to the social sectors. The results of the first two years (1992–1993) suggest that the ADB Group will continue to have problems living up to its commitments in agriculture, but not in education and health.[13] This reflects the special complexity of designing bankable agricultural projects, together with the lower priority still attached to this sector by some governments. Management points to the fact that about 30 percent of all ADF technical assistance grants for feasibility studies go to this sector, thereby helping prepare future loans. The Bank Group may have to raise this share if it is to meet its lending target.

A more comprehensive strategy for poverty alleviation has only recently been developed; it is discussed in Chapter 7.

Country Programming

Once the resource limits, country allocations, and sectoral priorities are established, development banks normally prepare a lending strategy at the country level. This involves studying the economic conditions and development plans of the borrower, reviewing the activities of other donors, and, after discussions with the borrower, identifying the areas where the lender will concentrate its resources. In this way, experience can be accumulated in a few sectors where the lender hopes to make a difference. Although an ongoing process, its first iteration should be completed before the quest for bankable projects begins.

Such is the theory. In practice, all development banks are ultimately dependent on what the borrower is prepared to borrow for, not to mention the unpredictability of the external environment. With the typical African government dealing with at least fifteen different financiers, and sometimes as many as thirty, they must be constantly juggling available funding sources to meet their own evolving needs. The ADB Group is in a particularly vulnerable position. Its loans are more expensive than the grants offered by most bilateral agencies.[14] It is probably more demanding than many, since it usually requires project proposals showing a reasonable rate of return. On the other hand, the ADB Group is seen as more flexible because its projects are not tied to any one national source for goods and services, in contrast to most funds from bilateral donors. Nor do its priorities shift as often as those of bilateral donors. Thus, a smart government will tend to direct specific projects to the cheapest bilateral source first.

The ADB Group also suffers in competition with the other major multilateral creditors operating in its region. Both the World Bank's IDA and the European Development Fund have significantly more concessional resources available; in 1990–1992, they each made gross disbursements to Africa three times as large as those of the ADF. Both are also more likely to insist on their own institutional priorities. In order not to jeopardize their access to these funds, most governments are keen to maintain good relations with them by respecting their country programming. This is especially true for the World Bank, in light of the influence it plays within the donor community at large. As if this were not enough, the World Bank, and for that matter the bilateral donors, enjoy a greater presence on the ground through country offices and embassies. Given its governance structure, but also its institutional philosophy, the ADB Group will probably always be more sympathetic to borrower concerns and therefore be seen as more responsive, if not pliable. For many countries, the ADB Group is probably considered the lender of last resort, the one that will pick up what the others turn down.

If there were a surplus of good projects, these considerations would be less relevant. In fact, there is often a shortage of "bankable" projects ready to go, and the competition among donors can be surprising. In such a context, country programming is fraught with difficulties.[15] The Bank has partially overcome this problem by expanding policy-based balance-of-payments lending, where the absorptive capacity is larger. It has also worked to expand the supply of projects by financing more feasibility studies.[16] Ultimately, however, the ADB Group has given a higher priority to placing its resources to reach its annual lending targets. When it came to choosing between a country strategy and a bankable project, there was seldom any competition.

Up to the mid-1980s, there was not much in the way of country strategies. However, the last five years have seen considerable improvements in the process. Revised Economic Prospects and Country Programming papers were produced for all but five countries between 1987 and 1991. They present an analysis of the economic situation, the role of external assistance, a review of Bank Group operations, and a medium-term program for a three-year period. These were then supplemented by shorter country strategy papers that concentrate on a more critical assessment of the relationship with borrowers and, for this reason, were confidential.[17] These have been produced for all forty-nine borrowers, and the intention is to revise them annually.

The EPCP papers have improved and expanded over the years. They now provide a good overview of the economic situation and cover such special issues as environmental policy, gender issues, poverty alleviation, and regional integration. Yet the staff is not able to keep up with the three-year cycle, and papers continue to appear after the programming period in question is already well under way. The proposed programs remain very general and contain few clear statements of sectoral priorities. Virtually no sectoral studies are conducted. One still has the sense that it is the project pipeline that drives country programming. This was confirmed in our country case studies, as described in Chapter 5.

The EPCP papers provide a good source of information for Bank staff and the Board of Directors. They are also useful tools to help country economists understand the economies for which they are responsible and to prepare for policy-based lending. Because they are discussed with the government in question, they have occasionally provided an opportunity to open the policy dialogue.[18] Now it is time for these papers and the accompanying country strategies to become true decisionmaking tools, which define the role that the ADB Group sees for itself in each borrowing member. To this end, it might be wise to spend less time and effort on the EPCP papers, which inevitably involve considerable overlap with similar World Bank reports, and focus more on the country strategy exercise.[19]

Policy-Based Lending

While the ongoing economic crisis has curtailed the number of viable projects across most sectors, there has been no shortage of demand for general balance-of-payments support to maintain the flow of imported fertilizer, trucks, industrial raw materials, and the like. Consequently, such lending, in the context of structural and sectoral adjustment programs, has grown very quickly. It helps explain how the institution was able to continue expanding its operations in the face of Africa's economic hardships. This has led to a lively debate over the limits to be placed on the share of policy-based lending in the total ADB Group program.

At least three factors have motivated the shift toward this type of lending in development assistance to Africa generally. First, it was recognized that many projects were not succeeding because the over-all policy environment was not appropriate. Second, given high rates of past investment and low growth in domestic demand, it was often more important to use current capacity effectively rather than add new sources of supply. Third, there was a sense of urgency necessitating quick-disbursing mechanisms to fill foreign exchange gaps before the situation deteriorated still further. Traditional project-type lending was too slow to have a short-term impact on the balance of payments.

To address the policy deficiencies that were felt to underlie both project failure and chronic balance-of-payments deficits, these loans were made conditional on various policy reforms. For example, higher producer prices for export crops, coupled with a reorganization or dismantling of state marketing boards, might be required to improve foreign exchange earnings and reduce government expenditures. Alternatively, borrowers might be urged to raise interest rates, change credit allocation rules, and restructure local banks in the hope of generating more domestic savings in financial form and improving their utilization.

Unlike the Inter-American Development Bank, the ADB Group was all too ready to adopt policy-based lending. From negligible proportions, it shot up to account for almost one-half of Bank lending in 1987 and over one-quarter of all lending in the three years 1987–1989. The ensuing debate was heated. Did the ADB Group, with its limited number of macroeconomists, have the expertise necessary to design and monitor such projects? Would it have the political will to impose conditionality on member states when they play such a key role in the institution's governance? Should this lending be left to the World Bank? And which approach to structural adjustment was the right one anyway? While the nonregionals pushed for adherence to the World Bank/IMF model, regional members tended to favor an alternative such as that proposed by the UN Economic Commission for Africa in *An African Alternative to Structural Adjustment.*

ADB management responded that it was building its own expertise by working closely with the World Bank and by hiring more economists. It argued that its special position, as the Africans' own bank, would facilitate effective policy dialogue with governments and that it was important to have an African voice among the donors during the critical negotiations that surround structural adjustment programs. Finally, it defended its right to propose modifications to the "Washington consensus."

In principle, one can hardly question the involvement of the ADB Group in policy-based lending. This form of assistance was badly needed in the late 1980s, and the Bank had growing resources at its disposal. Furthermore, the World Bank's approach to this form of lending was defining the development agenda in Africa. Most World Bank programs have been cofinanced with a variety of bilateral donors, so it made sense for the ADB to participate too. Only in this way could it hope to master the critical issues involved. Eventually, it should also be able to contribute an African perspective. The mediocre record of SAPs in the continent has forced the belated admission that such a perspective is essential.

Management probably embraced this new instrument too quickly. The Bank Group did not have the requisite expertise in 1987 even to learn from all the programs it was supporting, let alone supervise them. It also undertook too many without the assistance of the World Bank; in 1987, only 59 percent of its policy-based loans were cofinanced with the World Bank. However, the ADB Group corrected both these shortcomings. The overall share of policy-based loans was quickly brought down to more reasonable levels, and it has stayed there since. During the second five-year operational programming period, 1987–1991, commitments were below the 20 percent ceiling for the Fund and the 25 percent limit set for the Bank. However, one might note that this is still higher than the 18 percent of World Bank support to Africa that went to nonproject lending (see Table 4.7).

The promise to collaborate more closely with the Washington-based institutions was also fulfilled. From 1989 to 1992, only three of its policy-based loans were not cofinanced with the World Bank or the IMF, and one of these was in partnership with several bilateral donors. The others were an agriculture sector adjustment loan to Tunisia in 1991 and a foreign trade and taxation adjustment program for Algeria in 1992. Given the relative strength of these two North African countries to design and implement policies, they would seem to be appropriate places for the ADB Group to launch its own initiatives.

The more difficult question concerns the extent to which the staff have actually been able to influence, indeed improve, the performance of World Bank SAPs. There can be no doubt that the staff capacity in this area has significantly improved. Gone are the days when one economist in the country program departments must cover five countries; now, many are able to focus on a single borrower. The new recruits tend to have a solid background in economics, and many bring valuable experience from the World Bank and elsewhere. They are clearly knowledgeable of the issues. At the same time, these economists tended to be relatively junior when they joined the ADB Group, received limited on-the-job training, and had access to few resources in the form of consultants or in-house technical staff in the preparation or supervision of loans. Furthermore, the World Bank does not typically encourage the participation of other donors in the design of adjustment lending; when they do, it is never easy to influence their prescriptions.

The ADB Group was quite explicit about the need to learn from the World Bank in the early days of its policy-based lending. In this spirit, management commissioned the "Study of the Bank Group Experience in Policy-Based Lending," which was tabled at the Board of Directors in 1993, even though there were still relatively few post-evaluations available.[20] The general sense one draws from this study, as well as subsequent interviews conducted in 1994, is that the ADB Group has made little contribution to structural adjustment lending other than financially.

Staff were not involved in the preparation of the Policy Framework Papers that form the basis of SAPs, or in the Public Expenditure Reviews that play a key role in monitoring their performance. They still lacked the expertise (or the resources to hire consultants) to analyze and advise on many of the issues involved. This is less true of sectoral adjustment loans, where experts from the project departments have sometimes participated as equal partners in preparation and appraisal missions with the World Bank. Such programs draw more easily on the staff's long experience with project lending. But only one-quarter of its policy-based loans were focused on its traditional sectors of activity.[21]

When the staff does identify conditionalities that are not being met, or ones imposed by the World Bank with which they disagree, they often find that management is reluctant to pursue the matter. The most obvious examples of divergence in approach between the ADB Group and the World Bank tend to be instances where the former proceeds to disburse while the World Bank withholds its financing for one reason or another. Sometimes this reflects a higher priority assigned to disbursement targets or the maintenance of smooth relations with borrowers, as opposed to policy reform.

On occasion, the ADB Group's more openhanded approach to disbursements may also demonstrate a greater sympathy for the very real difficulty of adhering to the often unrealistic conditions of many SAPs. The World Bank has sometimes been criticized for insensitivity to the implications of a duly democratic process. In one case in Cameroon, ADB staff argued that it did not make sense to continue withholding disbursements because the main unfulfilled condition related to a new law whose approval had been delayed by the process of political liberalization. Failure to disburse would in effect have penalized the borrower for constructive political reforms.

The ADB's different posture may even complement the tougher stand of the World Bank. Where the World Bank feels it must apply the pressure, it may yet be relieved to see another financier keeping the funds flowing—a case of "good cop, bad cop." In the Cameroon example, some individual World Bank officials apparently felt this way, though the official position was rather different, in particular because of the lack of consultation by the ADB. In another example, the World Bank felt obliged to suspend disbursements to Zambia even though there was concern that the new system of foreign exchange allocation and import licensing might collapse in the process. It was agreed that the ADB Group, along with a few other donors, should continue to disburse.

The more flexible approach of the ADB Group does raise questions. Some of its clients have demonstrated a limited commitment to serious policy reform, and the Bank owes it to both their clients' citizens and ADB shareholders to apply the conditions it feels are necessary for effective lending. On the other hand, the Bretton Woods institutions have often been criticized for the number and severity of conditions they routinely apply in the face of considerable uncertainty as to their appropriateness. The ADB Group must be careful not to aggravate an already difficult situation with further demands, especially if they are not based on detailed analysis of the problem. Indeed, the Bank also owes it to its African members to confront the World Bank on some of its more contentious conditions.

Other more symbolic considerations are also at play. The relationship between African governments and the Bretton Woods institutions has often been a stormy one, particularly in the area of structural adjustment. If it is to preserve its legitimacy in the eyes of its majority shareholders, the ADB Group must maintain a certain distance from the World Bank, even as its nonregional members are often recommending greater conformity. The institution has tended to walk a fine line between the two parties to avoid the appearance of taking sides.

The ADB Group has implicitly endorsed the general direction of World Bank/IMF structural adjustment packages through its numerous cofinanced loans. In so doing, it may have played a role in legitimizing the associated reforms in a way that no non-African organization could. While there is no evidence to support this contention, it would not be a small contribution; it has not been easy to convince most African leaders that many of their problems begin at home.

Occasionally, the ADB Group has exploited its position to become an intermediator. The Bank is uniquely placed as the only African creditor to help bridge the gap that can separate borrowers and their financiers, a gap that is often very wide. It understands, indeed speaks, the "language" of the latter, yet can put itself in the shoes of the former. In the case of two different consultative group meetings, ADB representatives found the way to get the borrowing government to discuss sensitive issues that were of critical importance to the donor community.[22] This is one of the most promising areas for a more active role by the ADB Group.

The ADB Group does seem to be maturing in its implementation of policy-based lending.[23] It has demonstrated a willingness and an ability to contribute to program design, especially in the case of sectoral adjustment. The ADB staff has helped draft a number of Letters of Development Policy, including those for Chad and Togo. In Mauritius, it initiated action on an industrial sector program. In Mali, the Bank Group refused the proposed liquidation of the Mali Development Bank, contributing instead to its successful rehabilitation.[24] And, in at least one case in Zimbabwe, it has actually withheld disbursements when the World Bank did not.[25]

Another indicator of progress is the introduction of institutional support operations, and small projects to deal with the social dimensions of adjustment. Between 1989 and 1992, the ADB Group approved eighteen loans and grants in the first category and ten more in the second.[26] The former try to address the constraints so many

African governments face in designing and executing SAPs by providing such things as technical assistance, training, and small capital investments to one or more central economic ministry. Public investment and debt management are two of the areas covered, though the extent of involvement remains modest.

The "social dimensions" interventions often involve the creation of a special facility to lend to retrenched workers and others adversely affected by adjustment or coincident shocks. Sometimes these programs are implemented in coordination with NGOs to benefit from their experience in reaching the poor. Staff speak with pride of these contributions, noting (with some justification) that the World Bank has tended to devote more of its activities in this field to studies than to action.

The study of policy-based lending experience concludes that the ADB Group is spreading itself too thinly given the resources at its disposal. The need for staff training is highlighted, along with greater in-house supervision by senior economists. The Bank Group is urged to adhere to its own detailed, but inconsistently applied, procedures and guidelines. The study recommends that management make some strategic decisions about where their staff can make a difference. While continuing to support macroeconomic work and policy dialogue, it proposes a concentration on institutional support, the social dimension, and sectoral adjustment lending.

Indeed, the report goes further, suggesting that the Bank Group refrain from further traditional structural adjustment loans.[27] While this conclusion may be well founded on the basis of past experience, it would represent a retreat from one of the most important challenges facing the Bank and the continent. The macroeconomic context will remain a critical factor influencing all the Bank's project and sectoral work. More important still, it is contributing to some of the factors that could undermine the very existence of the Bank, notably through the debt crisis and rising arrears in loan repayments. Furthermore, the dominant players in Washington have not found the answers, and there is a growing consensus that Africans must take greater responsibility for and ownership of structural adjustment programs. It would seem illogical for the Bank to withdraw completely from this field at this time.

The solution would seem to be to concentrate on those countries where the Bank thinks it can make a difference. It has not been able to attract a large number of experienced macroeconomists, and current financial constraints will not make it any easier in the near future. The best of these should be devoted to small, poor countries that are committed to adjustment. The Bank is unlikely to be able to contribute to program design in the countries of North Africa and in

Nigeria, or even in places like Kenya and Côte d'Ivoire. These states have more domestic capacity with more country-specific knowledge. But others, like Equatorial Guinea or São Tomé and Principe, are extremely thin at senior levels of their civil service. They desperately need external advice and a second, informed opinion as they negotiate at the table with the Bretton Woods institutions.

The role of the ADB Group has been very similar to that of most bilateral donors—piggybacking on World Bank programs with little substantive involvement. One might argue that Africans have the same right to sit at the donor table when adjustment is being discussed. However, the bilateral donors may have difficulty justifying their support to the ADB Group if they cannot point to a unique contribution distinct from their own.

Project Lending

Ultimately, it is on its more traditional projects that the ADB Group's record to date must be judged—its irrigation schemes, road rehabilitation programs, industrial lines of credit, education support packages, and the like. This is where it has been working for almost thirty years. This is where it often takes the lead, deciding to put up its own funds without waiting for other donors to confirm the wisdom of their choices. This is where the staff has its greatest expertise—in recognizing a viable idea, contributing to an appropriate design, and monitoring its implementation. By the end of 1993, 1,134 projects had been approved (in addition to sixty-five policy-based loans, and 384 studies).

The ADB Group has now completed some 600 projects. It is not obvious how to assess its performance at this level. The single most valuable tool should be postevaluations, or project performance audit reports as they are called in the ADB, even though these cannot cover the other 600 projects still being implemented. Unfortunately, the Bank had a slow start in this area and, by the end of 1993, reports had been completed for only 146 projects (plus another eight on policy-based loans)—representing about 21 percent of the total possible.[28] Further complicating the picture is the fact that many of the projects involved were approved fifteen to twenty years ago, when the ADB Group was at a much earlier stage in its development. Still, these reports provide many important insights and the most comprehensive overview available.

First of all, fewer than 20 percent of the projects have been judged to be unsuccessful. Of the first ninety-six projects to be assessed, 58 percent were classified as very successful or successful with minor shortcomings. Another 22 percent were considered marginally successful and therefore still worthwhile; only 20 percent were unsatisfactory. After 1989, the classification system was changed to comprise three categories. Some of the performance audits already completed were reclassified under the new system, giving a new database of 116 projects. Under this framework, 24 percent were given the highest rating of satisfactory, 60 percent partially satisfactory, and 16 percent unsatisfactory.[29]

One can debate the reliability of these figures. Certainly the Knox Report on project quality has been notably uncharitable toward the quality of the database of postevaluations—perhaps unfairly. Certainly the sample is small, the quality of reports mixed, the system of classification changing over time, and the initial approach particularly qualitative and subjective. It focused simply on the degree to which stated objectives were achieved and appeared sustainable.[30] However, the newer approach is quite rigorous, adding three quantitative measures for a total of five criteria cast in an explicitly weighted framework.[31] Furthermore, the individual postevaluation reports generally demonstrate an appropriately critical stance; even some of the earliest ones are obviously pulling no punches. The aggregate figures on success are certainly less reliable than the many recurring lessons that emerge on the project cycle. But even at the aggregated level, the process of selecting projects for evaluation seems to have been sufficiently random to generate useful results. These data must be treated cautiously but not ignored.

It is not clear what level of success should be expected. Development banks are called to take some risks, and the African continent is full of them. Often projects may fail through no fault of the lender. As one means of comparison, we turn again to the performance of the World Bank. The change in the ADB Group's classification system renders this more problematic, and the two institutions undoubtedly had different ways of conducting their postevaluations. At least, the two institutions used similar terminology until 1990. Taking the first two categories (very successful and successful with minor shortcomings), and keeping in mind all the above caveats, we obtain some idea of the proportion of successful projects by institution and by sector.

We see in Table 4.9 a striking similarity between the ADB Group results, and those of the World Bank in sub-Saharan Africa. The overall average is virtually identical, and the variations by sector are broadly consistent. Note that the ADB Group figures include North Africa, and if one could incorporate the World Bank figures for this region (shown in the last column of Table 4.9), the World Bank average would be significantly superior. In addition, the periods are

Table 4.9   Comparison of Success Rates for Completed Projects by Sector
(percent)

Sector	ADB Group	World Bank in Africa Sub-Saharan	North[a]
Public utilities	70	74	86
Transport	70	79	93
Social[b]	67	72	67
Industry[c]	50	56	91
Agriculture	43	40	75
Overall[d]	58	59	83

Sources: ADB Group, "Synthesis of Project Performance Results, 1982–1987,"
"Annual Review of Evaluation Results," 1988 and 1989; World Bank, "Effective
Implementation: Key to Development Impact," Annex C, p. 3.

Notes: a. Includes the Middle East, but North Africa dominates.

b. Includes education and health for the ADB but only education for the World
Bank. A separate figure was provided for population, health, and nutrition projects at
the World Bank, but the sample size was very small. Furthermore, education projects
dominated the ADB sample in this category.

c. As this refers almost exclusively to lines of credit to development banks, we have
used the World Bank figure for development finance companies for comparison. The
World Bank provides a separate figure for other industrial lending.

d. Includes population; health and nutrition; other industry; and urban, multisector, and nonsector lending in the case of the World Bank.

somewhat different, with the World Bank data including more recent
projects.[32] Since the World Bank had a higher success rate in the early
1980s, the difference between the two institutions may have been
greater at that time. However, the overall picture is perhaps not surprising, given the greater experience and human resources of the
World Bank.

This table also underlines once more the conundrum facing so
many development banks: developmental priorities often conflict
with banking instincts. While there is a general consensus that the
ADB Group (and for that matter the World Bank) should focus more
on agriculture, a prudent banker would clearly opt for more roads
and electricity-generating projects after seeing these data.

One might next ask what the trend is over time within the institution. Much has been made of the recent Wapenhans Report on the
World Bank, which documented a deterioration in that bank's project
performance.[33] The change in nomenclature clouds the picture for the
ADB Group. One option is to look at the proportion of unsatisfactory
projects, the last category in the two classification systems. This
amounted to 20 percent for the ninety-three projects that were
approved before 1980. Of the sixty-eight postevaluated projects (and
programs) approved since 1980, the corresponding figure was 12 percent. Alternatively, one can concentrate on the harmonized database

of 116 postevaluations. This shows a steady increase in the percentage of satisfactory projects, while the number of unsatisfactory ones dropped noticeably in the early 1980s (by year of approval), thereafter rebounding but still appearing at less than earlier levels.[34]

Again, one must be cautious in drawing conclusions. The samples are small, and conditions in the continent changed over the time period in question. All one should probably conclude is that there is no evidence of a decline in loan quality. It is interesting that deterioration in the general economic environment over the course of the 1980s has not been reflected in project performance; perhaps it has been offset by improvements in the procedures and personnel of the ADB Group.

At the same time, there is plenty of evidence that much needs to be done to improve the quality of loans. The first synthesis of performance results for sixty-four projects, completed in 1988, provides a clear picture of the problems encountered by the ADB Group.[35] Three-quarters of the postevaluated projects revealed inadequate preparation, from proper sectoral knowledge to detailed engineering studies. It concluded that this was the most fundamental determinant of both timely implementation and eventual success. Even where preparation was sufficient, there was little involvement on the part of the Bank Group's own technical staff.

The next most important factor was the institutional and administrative capacity of the borrower. This was often neglected in project design or given inadequate attention during implementation. More than half the projects were hindered by factors beyond the direct control of the projects' managers, such as cumbersome recruitment procedures or an anomalous institutional setup within the government hierarchy. None of the lines of credit to development finance companies comprised institutional building components; funds were simply provided for on-lending. Most investments did not take place within the right supportive policy and institutional framework nor were they employed as instruments to influence existing policies or to effect broad institutional change.

Finally, "the inadequacy of Bank Group's involvement in monitoring and supervision is another important issue raised in all postevaluation reports."[36] Of the fifty projects for which data were available, thirty-nine received less than one technical supervision mission per year; eight of these were never supervised. Consequently, opportunities to take corrective action were delayed or missed entirely, and design modifications were often made without the Bank's knowledge. It was recommended that more financial and human resources be given to this stage of the project cycle without further delay.

There were notable differences between the sectors. Design problems were relatively minor in the case of transport projects, which were largely confined to road construction. Institutional development and training was included in six of the eight public utility loans. However, the conclusion reached for agricultural projects would seem to apply across the board: "In general the ADB Group tended to play a passive role at all stages of the project planning cycle, accepting documents produced by others at face value, and playing little part in terms of project supervision and in solving the problems arising in the course of project implementation."[37]

While this synthesis concerned projects approved before 1981, the same themes reemerge in the shorter syntheses of postevaluation reports that were produced in 1989, 1991, and 1992. For example, in the 1991 report, ten of the twenty-two projects examined did not receive any supervision missions.[38] In other cases, it was noted that there was often little assistance given when missions did take place. Even in the public utility sector, the overall role of the ADB Group was characterized as unsatisfactory.

To get the most recent picture possible, we studied all the individual postevaluation reports available for investment projects approved since 1981. The latest one was approved in 1985, underscoring the length of time required for project implementation and the delays in preparing project completion reports. This resulted in a set of twenty projects—six public utility, five transport, five agriculture, two social sector, and two lines of credit—making for a broad, if shallow, sample. While statistically insignificant, it may nonetheless be representative. Because the postevaluation office is totally dependent on the project departments to finish their project completion reports, of which there is never a surplus, the process of project selection for postevaluation is quite ad hoc. In any event, the details appear revealing.

The two social sector projects (education and health) were either conceived as a straightforward construction project or implemented as such. The education project paid no attention to curriculum substance in the teachers' college built; the institutional strengthening planned for the Ministry of Health was not achieved, and there was no discernible impact on the health of the population.

As with earlier road projects, the physical construction went fairly smoothly in the three examples here, but traffic projections were overoptimistic. Thus, the actual rate of return was less than predicted at appraisal but, at between 6 and 8 percent, was still considered acceptable under the circumstances.[39] External factors were blamed in each case (war in the neighboring country, a collapse in the major commodity export). In one case, it was concluded that the wrong route was chosen when the project was first being prepared and that eventually the other alternative should be developed instead. However, in another case, the executing agency did credit the Bank with contributing to finding a rapid solution to problems and to providing useful advice, in spite of its rare supervision missions.

The two nonroad transport projects (port and airport) should probably be listed as failures. Both were overdimensioned for the effective demand, could not be managed by the parastatal responsible, and were financially unviable. In both cases, the planned technical assistance and staff training were never provided, yet the ADB staff did not react.

One of the two lines of credit was also a failure, though the fundamental reason probably had more to do with the declining economic climate of the country concerned (Zaire). The other line of credit does not seem to have benefited from any greater attention, but because it was in a more robust setting (Zimbabwe), the results were somewhat more favorable. In both cases, the postevaluations point to a long list of unattended problems. Note, however, that the World Bank was also providing lines of credit to the same institutions in the same period.

Two of the public utility projects were large, cofinanced electricity schemes in which the ADB had little chance to take initiative, and did not. By contrast, one of the four water and sewage projects revealed a particularly active role by the ADB Group in resolving problems, in conjunction with regular supervision missions. Even then, two critical loan conditions were never fulfilled, institutional weaknesses were not addressed, and the financial rate of return for the executing agency was negative. Very similar problems prevailed in the other three cases. In addition, there were poor maintenance and underutilization of the installed capacity, due to lack of training for the executing agency and insufficient community education. In other words, the human dimension was neglected.

Finally, the five agricultural projects present a diverse set of experiences, but no failures. One was an emergency resettlement scheme that was almost finished before the loan had become effective. Another was only a first phase, though already it was clear that there were lots of problems, particularly at the marketing end. A third seems to have been moderately satisfactory, in spite of major design flaws, with the output of the principal crop exceeding projections.

The last two were generally successful, even though both were located in the trying environment of the Sahel. Operation Wells II in Mali built on previous investments made by the ADB Group. The Bank had been instrumental in helping launch this well-drilling program in 1974. In phase two, a large training program was provided for the executing agency so that by the end it was judged to be functioning smoothly—and without any expatriate technical assistance. Problems of ensuring maintenance and community education remained but were not considered insurmountable. This project is examined further in our case study of Mali in Chapter 5.

The Kourani-Baria irrigation project in Niger is still more notable given its greater complexity. Rice yields exceeded expectations, costs were under budget, and the economic rate of return was put at 10.8 percent. The project was well supervised, facilitating several design changes during implementation. Marketing had become a concern, due to both legal and illegal imports. However, the recent devaluation in the CFA franc should have improved the project's competitive position. Which is not to say that everything is perfect—more attention needs to be paid to the management of the irrigation system as well as its health implications. But this project and Operation Wells II are two of which the ADB Group can be proud, for they seemed to be succeeding in the most difficult sector and in one of the toughest regions.

The picture then is one of an institution that is capable of good work in a difficult setting, but where this is the exception rather than the rule. More often, the ADB staff are not giving their projects the time necessary to deal with routine problems, while major weaknesses are frequently ignored or not recognized. Supervision missions appear to be somewhat more regular than in the past, but their number and effectiveness are still insufficient. Preparation remains hasty; new projects are accepted and first phases are rolled into second ones without enough hard questions asked. Institutional factors are consistently overlooked. Projects are conceived first and foremost as engineering challenges or simply financial transactions, not as attempts to support human initiative and introduce new ideas.

Africa is a tough place in which to work and no donor has a shining record; but the ADB Group still seems to be at the mercy of its environment. It is not doing enough to reduce the risks and to shift the odds in its favor. There is very little evidence that its special African character is being put to good advantage to do things differently, and better, than other donors.

This conclusion gains further support in the next chapter when we present our country case studies. It was also confirmed through staff interviews in early 1994. Technical specialists in the project departments complained about the selection process for new projects, pressure to appraise projects before they were ready, and continued reluctance on the part of management to give supervision the priority it deserved. Particularly disturbing was the general consensus that nothing much had really changed in the last six years. The problems of the 1980s remained the problems of today.

Quest for Quality

The conclusions of the Task Force on Project Quality were very similar, if a bit more forceful. The Knox Report starts off by saying that "the African Development Bank is facing serious problems of quality of lending. Some of these obviously relate to the difficulties of many African countries; most are peculiar to the Bank."[40]

It is not clear how the task force assessed the quality of the project portfolio. Though the database of postevaluations was examined, it seems to have been dismissed as too small, and the evaluative criteria as too questionable, to permit any conclusions to be drawn. Instead, much weight was given to the quality of the procedures (and databases) in place and the degree to which they are respected. Interviews with ADB staff appear to have been the primary source of information, along with meetings held in regional offices with thirty-one representatives from twenty-one countries. Since the chairman of the task force and one of its members were former senior managers from the World Bank, comparisons with that institution undoubtedly played a key role.

The task force seemed generally satisfied with the policies and procedures in place, although it ended up recommending more. In fact, the ADB Group has made considerable progress over the last seven years in introducing new internal procedures, something the report did not acknowledge. The introduction of the Operations Manual was probably the biggest single improvement. Another important step was the addition of mandatory environmental impact assessments prior to board submission for all projects classified as having significant potential for environmental damage. The enlarged Operations Evaluation Office is now quite active—75 percent of all evaluation reports have been completed since 1987. Most of these reports are quite explicit about project shortcomings and lessons learned. The last 116 postevaluations have been standardized and an impressive database set up to generate information on a wide range of project characteristics for various project categories.

Unfortunately, the task force found that existing policies were not properly applied. It concluded that

> the Bank's economic and strategy papers are weak and sector studies nonexistent. Economic missions are few and far between and, when arranged, are too short with too few people. . . . The Bank takes an inordinately short time for programming, design and preparation, and appraisal. . . . It is disturbing to note how often appraisal is started when there have been no feasibility and other basic studies—or at best incomplete ones. . . . Supervision is, in fact, the weakest part of the Bank's work. . . . The Bank's operational

> manual calls for at least one supervision mission every year. This is
> seldom so . . . many missions are concerned only with loan admin-
> istrative issues compliance with loan conditions and covenants,
> adjustments of final disbursement dates.[41]

At the end of the project cycle, the lessons from postevaluations
rarely find their way back into the appraisal reports for new projects.
In sum, "as borrower after borrower complains, the Bank is absent
when it should be present."[42]

There is one positive, albeit unintended, effect from this absence
that is rarely noted. There should never be any doubt in the minds of
the executing agencies as to who "owns" the project. In the case of
World Bank projects, the controls can be so tight that the national project managers eventually reject responsibility for the success of the
activity. Then, when things go wrong, they are less likely to try to find
solutions and, once the bankers leave, the prospects for sustainability are reduced. The ADB approach certainly promotes the sense of
ownership, which critics have increasingly singled out as a missing
factor undermining World Bank/IMF structural adjustment programs, but which is an important consideration in all projects. That
said, the ADB Group has clearly erred too far in the other direction.
It needs to become more involved if it is to help solve the inevitable
problems of project implementation; and it must make it clear that
the borrower will be held accountable for its performance. The members, as both shareholders and borrowers, expect more.

The Knox Report attributed the Bank's problems to three factors:
lack of resources, a lending culture, and problems of governance. As
explained in Chapter 3, the ADB Group has been constrained in the
numbers it could hire, while it has not used the available person-
years effectively. Too few positions have been assigned to the project
departments; too many weak staff have been kept on across the Bank.
Consequently, good project officers are overworked, with their workload steadily increasing as new procedural guidelines are added to
deal with such issues as the environment and gender. In the programming departments, where significant staff increases have
occurred, the difference is palpable. Though the task force was still
dissatisfied with the quality of work done, significant improvements
have been made, and one senses that more is possible as the young
staff matures. By contrast, the operations departments appear mired
in the same routine.

If one asks project officers what the source of the problem is, their
first response is inevitably "the target." Until 1992, the planned level
of lending increased significantly every year, and management made
it very clear that this target had to be met. This was the single most
obvious measure of the ADB Group's performance. So pervasive was

this culture that, in early 1994, with no ADF funds available due to the stalemate in ADF VII replenishment negotiations, and a backlog of appraised projects left over from ADF VI, some managers were still pushing their staff out on new appraisal missions.

This volume culture is common across aid agencies, bilateral and multilateral. It has been especially important for the ADB Group. With a president who made no excuses for his desire to make it into the big leagues, which his board endorsed while keeping a tight hold on the purse strings, the staff was caught in the middle. The task force states that "too much attention is paid to the quantity of lending and too little, perhaps even none, to its quality."[43] This is probably accurate in terms of the signals given by management, though it is an exaggeration if applied to many of the staff. Certainly the will is there: "Why can't we forget about loan commitments for a year and give project implementation top priority?"[44]

Finally, therefore, it is a question of governance. What are the priorities of the board and senior management? How do they see the Bank Group making a contribution to African development? Can they even agree on a common philosophy in the current antagonistic environment? We have broached these issues in Chapter 3 and will return to them in our closing chapter. But first it will be useful to provide a different but complementary view of the lending program from the vantage point of three country case studies.

Notes

1. "Update on New Agenda for Africa," p. 4.
2. World Bank, *Sub-Saharan Africa: From Crisis to Sustainable Growth*, p. 179.
3. ADB Group net transfers were $1.26 billion in 1992. World Bank net transfers to sub-Saharan Africa were only $0.88 billion. A precise figure is not available for World Bank net transfers to North Africa, but they were clearly negative. ADB Group, *1993 Annual Report*, p. 211; Global Coalition for Africa, *1993 Annual Report*, p. 89; World Bank, *1994 Annual Report*, p. 119.
4. Bilateral aid classifies as ODA as long as the grant element is more than 25 percent, whereas ADF loans have a grant element of about 80 percent.
5. Detailed calculations were not attempted. This is an estimate based on the fact that net ADB Group disbursements in 1992 stood at $2.01 billion. ADB Group, *1993 Annual Report*, p. 33.
6. Global Coalition for Africa, *1992 Annual Report*, p. 60; *1993*, p. 88.
7. At the 1992 annual meeting of the Board of Governors, it was decided that the ADB lending program for 1992–1996 should be around BUA 7.0 billion, which implies an average annual level of commitments similar to that of 1989. ADB Group, Statement of Credit Policy for the Operational Period 1992–1996, Annex to Resolution B/BG/92/13, "Provisional Summary Records of the Dakar Annual Meeting," 1992, p. 217.
8. Officially, this position was taken due to the unfair expropriation of

property owned by U.S. citizens at the time of the 1975 revolution; in practice, it had more to do with the Marxist nature of the regime. Mingst, *Politics and the African Development Bank,* p. 35.

9. Strong performers were loosely defined as those countries successfully implementing a stabilization or adjustment program supported by the IMF or the World Bank, or those not requiring such programs due to their good policy framework and economic results.

10. There were a couple of small loans to the private sector in category A countries, as summarized in Chapter 7. In 1994, this general pattern was repeated, although two regional development banks, the East African Development Bank and the Preferential Trade Area (PTA) Bank for East and Central Asia, also received nonconcessional loans.

11. The World Bank does not allocate its lines of credit between agriculture and industry in the summary tables of its annual report, so we have been obliged to classify them all as industrial.

12. The share of agriculture in its lending to sub-Saharan Africa, for example, was only 11 percent in FY 1993 and 5 percent in FY 1994.

13. The ADF did manage to reach its agriculture target in 1993.

14. Once one factors in the cost of tied aid, there may in fact be little difference between the cost of ADF funds and bilateral resources, though recipient governments may not always recognize it.

15. Philip English participated in one ADB identification mission in December 1987. Thinking that the next year's program had long been accepted, so that the discussion could focus on the following two to three years, he was amazed when the government authorities proceeded to dismiss the entire pipeline for 1988 and propose several new projects instead. At least one of the planned projects had been reallocated to the World Bank.

16. In 1993 alone, fifty-nine studies were supported with grants from the Technical Assistance Fund of the ADF. ADB Group, *1993 Annual Report,* pp. 135–136.

17. Recently they have been made available to EDs.

18. One example was provided by a country economist in an interview with the authors.

19. As one report put it, "Cost-benefit analysis of these [EPCP] papers would probably be unfavourable, since they impose a heavy burden on limited resources without being necessarily influential in the Bank's operations." ADB Group, "Study of the Bank Group Experience in Policy-Based Lending," p. 9. This was also the impression gained by Philip English in interviews with staff.

20. Ibid.

21. Eighteen of the sixty-seven policy-based loans made between 1986 and 1992 were in the fields of agriculture, industry, energy, or education. Ibid., Table 3.3.

22. The instances involved land reform in Zimbabwe and human rights in Equatorial Guinea.

23. This was also the conclusion of the ADB Group's "Study of the Bank Group Experience in Policy-Based Lending."

24. Ibid., pp. 13, 28.

25. The government had failed to honor its commitment to remove old zoning regulations that prohibited small entrepreneurs from operating out of their homes, as they do across Africa. The associated ADB adjustment loan was one of its largest ever, and it was decided that the institution had to be

particularly rigorous in the application of its procedures. The government eventually complied.

26. As calculated from the annual reports for these years.

27. ADB Group, "Study of the Bank Group Experience in Policy-Based Lending," p. 27.

28. A few of the agricultural and public utility projects include cases involving two successive loans; these have been treated as single projects. However, where lines of credit were renewed to the same national development bank, these were considered as separate projects.

29. ADB Group Operations Evaluation Office, "Review of the Results of Operations Evaluation 1992–93," Appendix 2.

30. The ADB argues that this earlier approach was consistent with that pursued by others at the time. ADB Group Operations Evaluation Office, "Revue des Résultats de l'Evaluation des Opérations 1990–91," Annex 10, p. 1.

31. The three additional criteria cover cost overruns, time overruns, and the internal rate of return.

32. Note that this may be offset by the fact that this database also goes back farther than that of the ADB Group. Our source does not provide the distribution over time of the World Bank projects evaluated.

33. World Bank, "Effective Implementation: Key to Development Impact."

34. Dividing the data set into three periods by year of project approval (1969–1979, 1980–1984, and 1985–1991), the share of satisfactory projects in each period rises from 13 percent to 25 percent to 46 percent. The corresponding shares for unsatisfactory projects are 21 percent, 9 percent, and 17 percent. Partially satisfactory projects make up the difference. These results are rather surprising, though it is reassuring to note that the report in question was written by an outside expert from the AsDB. ADB Group Operations Evaluation Office, "Review of the Results of Operations Evaluation 1992–93," p. 3 (corrected to include two projects from 1990 and 1991).

35. ADB Group Operations Evaluation Office, "Synthesis of Project Performance Results, 1982–87."

36. Ibid., p. 13.

37. Ibid., p. 28.

38. ADB Group Operations Evaluation Office, "Annual Review of Evaluation Results, 1989," p. 3.

39. The new postevaluation system allocates a maximum of five points for a rate of return equal to or greater than 10 percent, four points if it lies between 7 and 9 percent, three points for rates between 5 and 7 percent, and so on.

40. ADB Group, "The Quest for Quality," p. 1.

41. Ibid., pp. 13–17.

42. Ibid., p. 2.

43. Ibid., p. 2.

44. Ibid., p. 16.

5

COUNTRY CASE STUDIES: A VIEW FROM THE FIELD

To enrich further our understanding of the ADB Group's performance in the field, we turn to three country case studies.[1] These will permit us to deepen our analysis of project performance. They will also help us assess the institution's approach to programming, its relationship to recipient governments, and the degree to which it has adapted to country-specific conditions. Risky as it may be, a comparison with other donors operating in the same country, notably the World Bank, will be made as well.

With a view to rendering the selection as representative as possible, we have chosen one country from each main linguistic group and geographical region. Kenya was chosen to reflect anglophone eastern Africa. As it was also the location of one of the ADB Group's regional offices, this permitted a look at the role of these offices. To represent francophone western Africa, we opted for Mali, which is also one of the poorest and least developed countries on the continent. Finally, it was important to look at one of the northern Arab-speaking countries with their typically stronger human resource base and higher level of development. Egypt, the largest of these, was selected.

Kenya

Kenya has been associated with the ADB Group from its earliest days. It was one of the initial set of twenty African members that provided the basic capital necessary to launch the Bank in 1964, and it was the very first loan recipient three years later. In 1978, the Bank's first regional office was established in Nairobi.

With a per capita income of $340 (1991), Kenya is classified as one of the thirty-four least developed countries in Africa. The agricultur-

al sector remains the dominant determinant of the country's economic fortunes, accounting as it does for 27 percent of the GDP, in
addition to having considerable indirect impact as a supplier to
industry. However, compared to all its neighbors and most other
countries in sub-Saharan Africa, Kenya has a relatively robust
economy. Its agricultural sector is fairly diversified, and its industry is quite developed, amounting to another 22 percent of the
GDP.

In the first ten years of independence, Kenya enjoyed particularly strong growth. The oil shocks of the 1970s took their toll, but this
was partially relieved by a coffee boom in 1976–1977. Macroeconomic
instability in the early 1980s was followed by a resumption of growth
in the latter half of the decade, permitting Kenya to remain one of the
few African countries to avoid debt rescheduling in the 1980s.
However, a sharp deterioration took place in 1990, triggered by the
Gulf War and exacerbated by the suspension of quick-disbursing
balance-of-payments support in 1991. The latter event was primarily
the result of the deteriorating political climate and represented an
attempt by donors to force democratic elections. Elections were eventually held, but not before the economy had descended into crisis.
Aid flows then resumed and the government adopted an IMF/World
Bank stabilization program.

The ADB Group has played a modest role in financing Kenya's
development. Its share of outstanding disbursements of multilateral
public debt has tended to be about 3–4 percent, although it remained
at or below 2 percent of total public debt. Since 1989, this role has
strengthened to the point where the corresponding ratios have
climbed to 8.4 percent and 5.6 percent in 1992. Cumulative commitments by the ADB Group stood at $296 million in 1988; by 1993 they
had reached $617 million (see Table 5.1).

In the early years of this relationship, lending came mainly from
the nonconcessional Bank window, reflecting the good performance
of the Kenyan economy. In the last ten years, the Fund has predomi-
nated so that now it accounts for 53 percent of total commitments.
There have been a total of thirty project loans, four policy-based
loans, five studies, and two institutional support grants.

The Bank Group's lending strategy for Kenya has undergone
some significant changes, particularly from the late 1980s. For many
years, its main focus was on infrastructure and industry. From the
very first loan, for a road project, transport has been the most important sector of operation for the ADB Group. Up to 1990, it accounted
for 37 percent of all lending, followed by industry (26 percent) and
water supply and sewerage (18 percent). International roads linking
Kenya to its neighbors were prominent, rural roads were not. In the

Table 5.1   Cumulative Lending by Sector by the ADB Group and the World Bank in Kenya

Sector	ADB Millions of Dollars	ADF Millions of Dollars	ADB Group Millions of Dollars	ADB Group Percent	World Bank Millions of Dollars	World Bank Percent
Transport	117.5	79.8	197.3	32	459.6	15
Industry	82.9	32.7	115.6	19	189.4	6
Agriculture	16.8	76.4	93.2	15	848.7	28
Water supply	29.4	56.4	85.8	14	150.7	5
Social	—	56.0	56.0	9	394.1	13
Energy	28.5	1.0	29.5	5	329.8	11
Multisector	—	40.1	40.1	6	433.5	14
Other	—	—	—	—	233.4	7
Total	275.1	342.4	617.5	100	3,039.2	100

Source: Compiled from data from the Kenyan Ministry of Finance.
Note: Data provided to the end of 1993.

industrial sector, lending was concentrated in the form of lines of credit directed to firms producing for import substitution. Additional industrial loans, not captured in Table 5.1, were provided to the East African Development Bank. Thus, in both these sectors, there seems to have been an attempt to honor the ADB Group's initial commitment to regional integration.

On the other hand, agriculture and the social sectors were clearly not priorities. Energy was also neglected, with only one project—in which it joined up with other donors behind the World Bank. While the strategy may not have been very explicit, there appears to have been a clear effort to concentrate in a limited number of sectors.

In recent years, there has been a shift in the strategy. Agriculture, which is the Bank Group's highest priority across the continent, has risen to claim 44 percent of the resources provided to Kenya after 1990. In support of this sector, more emphasis is being given to rural road upgrading in transport. Education has received another 16 percent. Export promotion is taking precedence over import substitution in the industrial sector. The Bank Group's current Economic Prospects and Country Programming paper for Kenya calls for a continued concentration on agriculture and export-oriented industrial development. For Kenya its current stage of development, with a fairly well developed road system but serious employment and balance-of-payments problems, this approach would seem to be most appropriate. It is also quite consistent with the Kenyan government's seventh development plan (1994–1996), which places priority on agriculture, trade and industry, and export expansion and diversification.

Project Performance

Throughout the last thirty years, the government of Kenya has accorded a high priority to transportation, and the ADB Group has responded with fourteen projects. All but one was in road construction; all but three have been completed. Two of the earliest projects have had postevaluations (well after their completion), and in both cases the reestimated rate of return was above the initial forecast. Among other things, this reflects the more buoyant state of the economy. Two others were judged to be partially successful, due mainly to external factors. Generally, implementation has been timely and costs below estimates, leading to savings that were pooled to finance a new project in 1990. It would appear that the ADB Group has been broadly successful in its interventions in this sector.

In marked contrast is the record of the ADB Group's five operations in water supply and sewerage. Although four of them were approved before 1983, only one is completed. The postevaluation has concluded that performance was unsatisfactory. Because of defective equipment and poor management, only 60 percent of the intended beneficiaries are being served, and then only sporadically. There were lengthy delays at every stage, inadequate attention paid to the quality of the executing agency at the time of appraisal, insufficient supervision (a total of 1.6 person-weeks), and major cost overruns.

Other projects in this sector are suffering similar problems. In the worst example, it took almost ten years simply to begin disbursements due to delays in the acquisition of construction sites. Two others are fully disbursed but still in progress as a result of the government's inability to provide adequate funds to cover cost overruns. The most recent project, a large multidonor affair led by the World Bank, has suffered lengthy delays in getting started because the government was unwilling to raise water tariffs.

The ADB Group has also had trouble in the agricultural sector, but it appears to have had the wisdom to pull out in a few cases. Its first two projects were eventually canceled: one because of government failure to meet loan conditions, the other due to poor design. The third one fell behind schedule and got in trouble because the executing agency could not account for some of the funds.

The little information available on the various industrial lines of credit suggests no major problems. The one early project that has been evaluated was judged to be successful, with minor shortcomings. Two others were follow-up loans to the same development bank. However, the most recent intervention has been a controversial sectoral adjustment loan. The postevaluation report concludes that the impact of the policy reforms has been negative. Import liberalization hurt domestic producers, contributing to a fall in industrial production. Price decontrol and currency devaluation fueled inflation, while liberalization of the foreign exchange market impinged on monetary policy. Investment incentives did not work and capital accumulation fell. Because this program was designed and led by the World Bank, the blame was laid largely at its feet; but if the ADB Group is going to commit itself to such programs financially, it must share some of the responsibility for the results.

The problems associated with ADB Group projects point to shortcomings on both sides. Inadequate project preparation by the Bank Group has contributed to delays, cost overruns, and unforeseen risks. Neglect of the institutional capacity of the executing agency has been particularly detrimental. Failure to explain procurement procedures and to process disbursements on time has further slowed down implementation. The shortage of supervision missions has inhibited the detection and correction of problems. Even the regional office in Nairobi has relied primarily on desk review with government officials and has had limited recourse to site inspection.

On the recipient's side, the government has frequently failed to fulfill loan conditions on time. Executing agencies have been hampered by excessive staff turnover and the selection of poor managers. Counterpart funds have not always been forthcoming as agreed. There has been poor coordination between ministries—for example, in the transfer of ADB funds from the Ministry of Finance to sectoral ministries. Its own tendering procedures need to be streamlined.

Comparison with the World Bank

Kenya has been a major beneficiary of World Bank lending, receiving over $3 billion in commitments, or five times the level of ADB Group lending. Two-thirds of this has been on concessional IDA terms, and all new lending is through this window. The volume and cost of its resources therefore combine to make the World Bank a much more significant player.

The World Bank has been particularly active in agriculture, to which it has devoted 28 percent of the resources going to Kenya. The World Bank's focus, together with the attention bilateral donors have, paid to this sector, may explain why the Kenyan government has not traditionally turned to the ADB Group for assistance in agriculture. Other major sectors have been energy (11 percent) and education (9 percent). Thus, there seems to have been a certain division of labor between these two multilateral banks.

Policy-based lending has become an important component in both cases. It has actually accounted for a greater share of ADB Group lending (22 percent) than in the World Bank (14 percent), although all the former's operations have been cofunded programs with the latter.

Both institutions try to play a leveraging role, using their resources to attract additional funds from other external sources. The World Bank has been far more successful in Kenya. The ADB Group has been involved in seven cofinancing operations with other donors. In only two cases—two fairly small projects in 1985 with OPEC—was it the lead agency. With the decline in lending by OPEC and other Arab funds, the ADB is the one being leveraged once again.

This reflects a fundamental difference in the styles of the two institutions: the World Bank is proactive, the ADB Group more passive. This begins at the level of ideas. The World Bank has been very active in pioneering new approaches to development in Kenya and aggressive in selling them. The ADB Group has tended to follow, often with a time lag of several years. In determining lending priorities, the ADB Group generally lets the Kenyan government take the lead. In contrast, the World Bank is seen as less receptive to government priorities.

At the stage of project appraisal, the World Bank approach is deemed to be more intense and thorough. It also circulates its appraisal documents with the recipients, encouraging greater feedback and facilitating early implementation.

The most significant differences come once the project begins. Because the World Bank office in Nairobi is adequately staffed and has a mandate to monitor projects, disbursements and design adjustments can be made quickly. Even when the ADB regional office was still open, all important matters, including tendering, procurement, and disbursement, had to be referred to headquarters. Infrequent supervision missions were launched from Abidjan. As a result, implementation was inevitably delayed.

Such a contrast in approaches should be expected to lead to a major difference in development impact. Surprisingly, this does not appear to be the case in Kenya. Both institutions have been very successful in the transport sector and both have suffered serious problems in agriculture. A 1989 World Bank study found that all but one of its agricultural projects recorded an unsatisfactory performance.[2] The complexity of the sector and the quality of the executing agency appear to be determining factors. Both variables have worked against interventions in agriculture, as well as in the water and sewerage sector. Transport projects, on the other hand, tend to be relatively easy to design and supervise, while the Ministry of Public Works in Kenya has a reputation for competent management. In fact, one may reap rewards from a less interventionist approach when dealing with a sound executing agency. Its admittedly subjective assessment was that the ADB Group road projects were if anything more successful than those of the World Bank.

Overall Relationship

The Kenyan government's overall relationship with the ADB Group has been cordial and without major difficulties. Officials consider the ADB staff to be accessible and competent and appreciate that they do not pretend to have set prescriptions for all problems, nor fixed briefs from headquarters.

The ADB Group demonstrated its special sensitivity at the low point in donor-government relations in November 1991. Just a few days after the Consultative Group meeting of donors in Paris suspended balance-of-payments support to Kenya, the minister of finance was invited to Abidjan to sign an agricultural sector adjustment loan on his way home.

Ironically, the ADB Group's much appreciated respect for borrowing-country priorities may be one of the causes of poor project performance. Most of its projects in agriculture and water and sewerage have suffered from the institutional weaknesses of the implementing agencies. The Bank Group probably should have either rejected the proposals or ensured that changes were made in these agencies before they proceeded with funding. As we saw above, however, the World Bank has had similar problems in agriculture.

While the African character of the Bank Group makes it uniquely suited to establish a fruitful dialogue with the government, it has taken a back seat to the Bretton Woods institutions. Kenyan government officials are keen that the ADB Group should play a more active role in policy discussion, providing new ideas different from those of the other donors. Given the intimate knowledge it has of African development problems and possibilities, this missed opportunity is perhaps the most regrettable of all.

Mali

Mali is one of the poorest countries in Africa, and indeed the world. Located in the inhospitable Sahel, its 9 million people had an average income estimated at only $270 in 1990. With the 50 percent devaluation of their currency (the CFA franc) in 1994, this level is even lower today.

Climate is the biggest single factor determining Mali's short-term fortunes. Rainfall is highly variable and droughts are common, which can be devastating. Combined with the expansion of human activity, these climatic conditions are leading to a process of gradual desertification. The population is spread out over a wide area that is poorly served by infrastructure. Mali's landlocked status further constrains its development efforts. Its human resource base is weak, due to low levels of education and poor health, while the capacity of government institutions is limited. Agriculture and livestock raising are the mainstay of the economy, supporting 80 percent of the population and contributing 44 percent of the GDP.

In spite of this challenging context, Mali managed to maintain a GDP growth rate during the 1980s of about 4 percent, slightly above the rate of population growth. However, the declining price of cotton, the country's principal export, combined with a growing debt burden to create a balance-of-payments crisis and finally a debt rescheduling in 1988. Sectoral and macroeconomic adjustment programs were adopted with some positive impact on internal and external balances. However, their social implications coalesced with demands for political liberalization to produce a period of social instability and the overthrow of the government in 1991. Democratic elections were held, the situation stabilized, and the economy rebounded in 1992.

Mali has been a consistent partner and beneficiary of the ADF, with loans or grants in every year but one since 1974. It has received more ADF loans than any other member, though it is only fourth in terms of commitments. Its low income has, on the other hand, restricted its borrowing from the ADB to two small loans, in 1970 and 1977. Overall, to the end of 1993, Mali had received forty-nine loans and grants for twenty-seven projects, three policy-based programs, three institutional support operations, and eight studies. The total amount provided was BUA 304 million, or roughly $380 million. Mali also participated with its neighbors in another six projects and six studies of a multinational nature. Several of these were also from the nonconcessional ADB window.

The ADB Group has been a significant financial player in Mali. Over the period 1987–1990, it contributed 21 percent of all multilateral aid, putting it in second place behind the World Bank, which provided 36 percent of the total. When bilateral aid is included, the Bank Group's share of all aid flows was still almost 10 percent.

As one would expect, rural development has been the largest sector of activity, claiming one-third of all the ADB Group resources going to Mali. The rest has been fairly evenly divided between the social sectors, transport, public utilities (water supply and energy), and multisectoral adjustment programs, as summarized in Table 5.2. Thus, among the ADB Group's usual sectors of operation, only industry has been neglected.

Table 5.2   Cumulative Lending by Sector by the ADB Group in Mali

Sector	ADB/NTF Millions of Dollars	ADF Millions of Dollars	ADB Group Millions of Dollars	ADB Group Percent
Rural development	—	126.6	126.6	33
Social	—	66.4	66.4	17
Transport	—	53.4	53.4	14
Water supply (urban)	—	42.3	42.3	11
Energy	6.3	12.6	18.9	5
Industry/Mali Development Bank	7.0	1.2	8.2	2
Multisector	—	64.5	64.5	17
Total	13.3	367.0	380.3	100

Source: Case study report for Mali. Data converted from units of account to U.S. dollars at a fixed rate of BUA 1 = $1.25 as an approximated average conversion rate for the period 1970–1993.

Note: Data provided to the end of 1993.

The Economic Prospects and Country Programming paper for the period 1991–1993 envisaged a continuation of this comprehensive range of activities, including operations in industry and banking. In fact, the ADB Group was active in all sectors, though less active than planned in agriculture. The social sector (health and education) became the largest domain of intervention. However, after a good start in the late 1980s, it was unable to develop any new operations in the critically important area of institutional support.

While the historical emphasis on rural development is sensible, since the ADB Group began a more conscious effort to develop a strategy, it has had some difficulty choosing its priorities. Apparently this is due in part to the Malian government's reluctance to restrict its demands to a few sectors. The Bank Group's current strategy for 1994–1996 promises a renewed focus on agriculture and the social sectors, along with multisectoral program lending. These would seem to be judicious choices, consistent with the country's needs and the Bank Group's more general priorities.

Project Performance

Seven projects have had postevaluations conducted to assess their performance: one hydroelectric dam and six rural development projects of various types. The dam project was a cofinancing operation led by the World Bank in which the ADB Group played a passive role. Thus, while the Bank Group can take some satisfaction in the successful outcome registered, it probably cannot take much of the credit.

The other six projects present a mixed picture: three were generally satisfactory, three were not. Once again, several were cofinancing arrangements led by other donors, but these were not necessarily more successful than others. The usual problems arose: the institutional dimension was often neglected, agricultural support services were deficient, farmgate prices were too low, delays in implementation were sometimes long, and ADB Group supervision was typically meager. One has the impression that the ADB projects were basically dependent on the performance of the Malian executing agencies and their immediate context; other donors did not fare much better.

However, there are two stories worth telling in some detail and, interestingly, they begin with the first two loans ever provided by the ADB Group. One concerns Operation Wells, a well-drilling project for both human and animal water supply. The other is the group's only intervention in the industry and banking sector until 1993, involving several small projects with the Mali Development Bank (MDB).

Operation Wells was essentially the Bank Group's largest single project until 1988, if one combines the two phases of support.[3] It was also one for which the Bank chose to take the lead. The ADB Group played a key role in the establishment of this Malian government program in 1974 and was easily the largest financial contributor. Serious management problems plagued the first phase, prompting the ADF to demand and obtain a new project director. A report by the International Labour Organisation (ILO) commented that the financial management of the project by the ADF compared relatively well to that of other external partners.[4] While these donors withdrew their support for a second phase, the ADF persevered with renewed support in 1982.

This commitment seems to have paid off. The second phase was generally successful, resulting in 275 new wells in the arid central and eastern parts of the country. As such, it addressed one of the most critical development needs in this drought-prone region. The project was not without its own shortcomings. However, given the difficult physical and human environment, and the problems so well documented in other ADB Group projects, this one stands out.

The loan for the second phase was declared effective in less than two months, and the first disbursement followed three weeks later. The project was completed on schedule, with only a small cost overrun that was covered by the government. More significantly, in a country where technical assistance is the norm, Malians were responsible for the entire operation. The project included a system of bonuses and a comprehensive training program, which undoubtedly contributed to the good performance of staff and left them in good shape to continue the work after the ADF funding had finished.

The principal deficiencies in the project are also revealing. The project did provide for the establishment of a National Water Fund to look after maintenance and ensure that the wells became self-financing. However, the government had still not honored that commitment at the end of the project. By then, the ADF had little leverage left, and nothing was done other than to signal this shortcoming in the postevaluation report. Still less attention was paid to the problem of managing the use of the wells by both humans and animals, with the consequent risk of eventual pollution. The process of well drilling was approached primarily as an engineering challenge rather than a socioeconomic one.

These problems aside, at least four factors contributed to the project's good performance. First, it was a fairly straightforward engineering project. Second, by continuing with a second phase, the ADF benefited from investments made and familiarity gained on both sides during the first phase. Third, the proximity of Mali to Abidjan facilitated regular visits by the project leader (compensating for the shortage of bank supervision missions). Fourth, the critical institutional dimension received adequate attention, at least at the level of the executing agency.[5]

The case of the Mali Development Bank is a very different one. The bank received a small ADB line of credit in 1970, followed by a larger one from the Nigerian Trust Fund in 1985. However, the ADB's role really became important in 1987 when the MDB was hit with a major liquidity crisis. Mali had rejoined the CFA franc zone in 1984, which resembled in some ways a revaluation of the currency. At the same time, stricter financial management rules were imposed by the World Bank and the IMF. When combined with the fall in the price of cotton (and hence of deposits) and the slowdown in parastatal activity, this led to a generalized liquidity crisis in the country. The MDB, as the dominant creditor, was caught squarely in the middle. Both private and public arrears increased to the point where the MDB was excluded from any further refinancing by the central bank and from access to the bank clearing facility.

The initial reaction of the Bretton Woods institutions was to declare the MDB bankrupt. However, the government preferred to attempt its rehabilitation. It was supported in this choice by the ADB Group, the Central Bank for the West African Franc zone (BCEAO), the West African Development Bank, and the French government. With this backing, the government was able to convince the World Bank and the IMF to pursue this option. It then turned to the ADB Group to play a lead role in completing the operation. It was asked to prepare the background technical dossier, help locate a new management partner, finance technical assistance and equipment, and contribute to the financial restructuring of the MDB balance sheets. It was particularly helpful in facilitating the participation of the Moroccan Bank for External Trade (BMCE) as both manager and financial partner (though political intervention between the two countries was also important).

The operation appears to have been successful. By early 1994, the MDB was registering a healthy profit and the Moroccan executives were scheduled to hand over management to their Malian counterparts by September. Thus, the ADB Group played an active role in finding an African solution to Mali's financial crisis.

A Comparison with Other Donors

The differences begin with the process of selecting projects. The ADB Group tends to be very responsive to the requests made by the central ministries of finance and planning. The World Bank, and other donors with local representation in Bamako, tend to question the priorities established by these authorities. They either push their own priorities or work with the ultimate executing agencies to develop alternative programs. While the ADB Group approach is certainly appreciated by the central planners, it puts the responsibility for project preparation on the Malian side, where the capacity is sometimes weak.

Perhaps to mitigate this problem, the ADB Group has relied extensively on other actors to take the initiative. The majority of its projects in Mali have been cofunded operations begun by others. The ADB Group has seldom been the lead agency; even in the case of the various Arab funds, it has been the Islamic Development Bank that has played the role of leader. However, the ADB Group has sometimes extended the work begun by others, as in the development of second phases for Operation Wells and the Mopti rural development project.

Like the Arab funds, but in contrast to the other larger players, the ADB Group has been willing to take on riskier projects in the more isolated, less developed regions of the country. It has invested in infrastructure, health, and rural development projects in northern and eastern Mali. Where other donors have preferred to focus on the rehabilitation of existing irrigation systems, it has been willing to support the establishment of new ones. Whether it has taken adequate precautions to control the risks through institutional strengthening and close monitoring is less obvious. There has also been little attention paid to the participation of target groups, though this criticism is probably valid for most official funding agencies.

On the other hand, when institutional support has been provided, the philosophy has compared favorably. The focus has tended to be on building the capacity of the local agency involved and strengthening the local staff. On long-term contracts, however, Western donors tend to think in terms of expatriate staff, who become directly involved in executing the project.

The ADB Group has the reputation for being fast at the early stages of project development, including appraisal, negotiation, and approval. The reliance on cofunding probably explains part though not all of this. Problems tend to emerge later. Lengthy delays in declaring loans effective and in completing procurement procedures are due in part to the absence of local representation.

Overall Relationship

In general, the relationship between the central authorities and the ADB Group appears to be good—and notably less conflictual than that with the World Bank. This is not surprising given the more responsive, less interventionist approach to programming. The willingness to consider riskier projects is particularly appreciated, as is the lower level of conditionality. However, in view of the weaknesses of the Malian administration, there is probably a need for greater involvement in the project development process if only to promote a richer dialogue. Something in between the World Bank and ADB approaches would seem ideal.

The Malian executing agencies, on the other hand, express some frustration at the process of project implementation. There is often confusion over the procedural requirements of the ADB Group. When it comes to the procurement process, cost overruns, and the like, the ADB Group has tended to be appropriately firm, but without sufficient effort to help the beneficiaries understand the policies in question and work out solutions. The shortage of supervision missions and the diffusion of responsibilities at headquarters have made it difficult to resolve problems, leading project directors to make regular visits to Abidjan. The organization of a seminar on ADB Group procedures in Mali in 1992 was a welcome initiative, but such activities should become more regular events.

This is all the more true given the recent and profound changes taking place in Malian development policy. The move toward greater reliance on market forces, a reduction in direct state involvement in favor of both the commercial private sector and community participation, and the decentralization of remaining government programs to local authorities will inevitably complicate the process of project development and implementation in the short run. The new institutional partners may be even weaker than their predecessors. The

ADB will not be able to rely as much on central authorities, and it will need to strengthen its understanding of both the policy framework and the socioeconomic context surrounding its projects.

While the African character of the Bank Group should facilitate adaptation to this new environment, the past record of the ADB Group has not been particularly innovative. Responsiveness, flexibility, and patience have been its main strong points. It will have to devote more professional human resources to its relationship with the Malian government and its people if it is to make a major contribution at this critical juncture in the country's evolution.

Egypt

With over 50 million people, Egypt is the second largest country on the continent, after Nigeria. Less known is the fact that, from 1970 to 1988, it was also the second fastest growing economy, behind only the tiny state of Botswana. Egypt's per capita income of $640 (1989) places it at the bottom end of the group of lower-middle-income countries, but in many respects it is ahead of others in this classification. It enjoys a productive agricultural sector, a significant industrial base, a vibrant service economy, a relatively well educated workforce, and a history of stable government. A degree of democracy has been achieved and freedom of speech is generally respected.

The country enjoyed a boom from 1975 to 1981, driven by worker remittances (especially from the Gulf states), oil exports, levies from the Suez Canal, tourism, and foreign assistance. GDP growth surpassed 8.0 percent per annum. Problems arose with the fall in oil prices, which hit both exports and the demand for Egyptian workers, yet annual growth continued at a healthy average of 5.7 percent from 1980 to 1988. However, this was achieved partly through Egypt's recourse to foreign borrowing, raising its foreign indebtedness to alarming levels.

In the late 1980s, unemployment rose (as did inflation), social tensions mounted, and the government had second thoughts about the wisdom of its open door policy of economic liberalization. Since the mid-1950s, the economy has been characterized by protection and an overwhelming role for the state. While the government has experimented with various changes over the last twenty years, there has been a lack of clear direction and decisiveness on its part. The highly concentrated population (Cairo has over 10 million inhabitants) and the threat of Islamic fundamentalism make the government especially sensitive to the short-run social impact of new policies.

The 1990 Gulf War and the debt forgiveness that followed earned

Egypt a welcome reprieve in its burgeoning debt crisis. Nonetheless, the economy has continued to struggle and the government has continued to pursue, albeit somewhat reluctantly, a program of policy reforms with the assistance of the IMF and the World Bank.

Given its size and growth record, it is not surprising that Egypt was the largest borrower from the ADB Group up to 1985. It is now the third most important, behind Morocco and Nigeria. Like these two, but unlike Mali and Kenya, nonconcessional ADB loans have dominated the portfolio, accounting for 91 percent of the total commitments of BUA 1.13 billion (about $1.5 billion). Thus, it has been a particularly valuable partner, absorbing the more expensive resources that generate the bulk of the Bank Group's revenues.

The project portfolio in Egypt is unusual in that it is dominated by one subsector (see Table 5.3). Public utilities account for about 65 percent of total lending, and all of this has been in power generation and distribution. The next most important sector is industry with a 12 percent share. Smaller amounts have been provided for agriculture, the social sectors, and structural adjustment, but not for transport. This exceptional concentration is not a question of strategy, but rather a function of the requests made by the government and the previous experience of the Bank Group in Egypt. The provision of electricity has been a high priority for the government; this is reflected in its share of the portfolio of the World Bank (26 percent) and the European Investment Bank (50 percent).

Eight of the thirty-one projects supported up to 1992 have been cofinanced. Three of these were led by the World Bank, but in the rest the Bank Group teamed up with other bilateral and multilateral

Table 5.3 Cumulative Lending by Sector by the ADB Group, the World Bank, and USAID in Egypt

Sector	ADB Millions of Dollars	ADF Millions of Dollars	ADB Group Millions of Dollars[a]	ADB Group Percent	World Bank Percent	USAID Percent
Energy	993.7	18.2	1,011.9	66	26	10
Industry	172.5	2.8	175.3	12	23	39[b]
Agriculture	71.8	28.7	101.5	7	14	7
Social	22.7	65.2	87.9	6	7	14
Multisector	143.0	3.1	146.1	9	10	12
Infrastructure	—	—	—	—	20	18
Total (millions of dollars)	1,403.7	118.0	1,522.7		4,218	14,206

Source: Country case study report.
Notes: 1974–1992 commitments.
   a. ADB Group figures were converted to U.S. dollars at the exchange rate for the year in which the commitment was made.
   b. Predominantly the Commodity Import Program.

donors, and occasionally took the lead. Thus the ADB Group has shown a fair degree of independence from other donors in its programming.

Project Performance

Though only five postevaluations have been carried out on projects in Egypt, they give us a good idea of the general record. First, they cover eight different projects, because in two cases more than one phase was assessed. Second, the other three projects evaluated were also phases of a longer-term support, so they at least suggest the likely performance of another five projects. Third, the four power projects directly evaluated are probably indicative of others in the same sector since the same executing agency was involved. Thus, we have at least a partial picture for twenty-one of the twenty-six projects approved before 1991.

Seven of the eight evaluated projects were judged to be successful. The eighth was classified as successful with minor shortcomings, and it was the oldest and smallest of them. A power project, it was then followed by three bigger ones, the Shoubra El Kheima series. These were completed ahead of schedule and under budget. Officials of the U.S. Agency for International Development (USAID), which cofinanced the last two phases, describe this project as one of their best anywhere. Indeed, the Egyptian Electricity Authority has a very good reputation as one of the best executing agencies in the country. Whatever the reason for the heavy involvement of the ADB in the power sector, it is clear that it has chosen a strong partner with whom to work (ignoring for the moment the pricing policy framework within which it operates).

In the industrial sector, the ADB has provided four successive lines of credit to a local development bank. The first two phases have been evaluated and judged successful. Thirty-five of the subprojects financed by the recipient had fully reimbursed their loans by the time of the evaluation; six were in arrears. An improvement in the repayment record was observed between the first and second phases. In the late 1980s, after two more phases, the ADB stopped working with this longtime partner. It would appear that this decision was the result of some dissatisfaction with the ADB conditions and procedures. During the last phase, a change in the ADB method of applying the exchange rate to compute the value of disbursements proved quite detrimental to the recipient bank. In addition, the interest rate charged by the ADB was not competitive with that of other funding sources. The local bank opted instead for lines of credit from the World Bank and USAID.

Another industrial project, this time to establish a polyester-fiber plant, was also deemed successful. At the time of evaluation, it was operating at 95 percent of capacity and was supplying downstream weavers and clothing manufacturers. The financial rate of return was estimated at 30 percent, higher than initially predicted at appraisal. A second phase of support was subsequently approved.

The final postevaluation dealt with a health project to control bilharzia. It too met its main objectives, reducing the frequency of the disease and benefiting some 15 million people. A telling remark in the postevaluation report is that the ADB Group should have played a more active role in the various phases of the project. Here again, the credit goes primarily to the executing agency. The ADF funded two more phases of this program; it is not clear if they deepened the nature of their involvement.

The only sector without this sort of evidence is agriculture. Inherently a more complex field, it is particularly so in Egypt, where the government is unusually interventionist. The information available suggests that the ADB Group's first agricultural project was not as successful. Among other things, it took ten years to finish instead of the five expected. Since then, the ADB Group has limited itself to two cofunded projects led by the World Bank. It appears to have recognized that the risks were higher. Preliminary evidence indicates that at least one of these projects has been broadly successful.

Comparison with Other Donors

The World Bank and especially USAID have much bigger portfolios in Egypt and, not surprisingly, they intervene in a wider range of sectors, including infrastructure. However, in both cases energy gets a higher priority than agriculture, which appears to reflect the government's own ranking. The European Investment Bank, with total commitments about half those of the ADB Group, has a very similar sectoral composition—energy first, industry second.

The Bank Group's more lenient approach to recipient governments is once more apparent in the case of Egypt. One of the recurring issues in the power sector has been the appropriate level for electricity rates and the timetable for reducing subsidies. Among other things, it is argued that the low cost of electricity is promoting wasteful use, raising demand unduly, and creating an apparent but unjustified need for more generating capacity. The government has found it difficult to close the large gap between the actual price and economic cost, prompting donors to apply pressure in various forms. The ADB Group has been prepared to approve and disburse power loans when others have been holding back. However, tariff issues have usually figured in its loan documents for this sector, and in at least one instance they were included in the conditions prior to first disbursement.

This approach seems to be the result of at least three factors: less preoccupation with the subsidy issue, an interest in placing its Bank resources, and greater sensitivity to the actual or anticipated reaction by the Egyptian government as represented on its board. It may also reason that its influence in Egypt is so small as to be ineffective on such issues. The ADB Group may not have reinforced donor pressure, but neither is there any evidence that it has undermined it. Other donors have continued to work in this sector along with the ADB Group.[6] The Egyptian government is now committed to reaching tariff levels comparable to international prices by 1996.

At the level of project implementation, there is the usual evidence of a need for a greater presence on the part of the ADB Group. In one of the cofunded agricultural projects, the executing agency has observed that it is easier to deal with the World Bank because of their regular missions to Egypt. Whereas the World Bank tended to visit once every three months, the ADB Group came annually at best.

Overall Relationship

While there is room for improvement, the general impression one has is of a smooth working relationship that suits both sides. The government gets its projects funded with a minimum of negotiation and conditionality. The ADB Group filled a gap left by Arab financiers during the post–Camp David embargo. By the same token, the ADB Group has been content to follow the priorities laid down by the government and to rely on its institutional strength to carry out projects satisfactorily. Indeed, it is striking that when the Bank Group has the benefit of such a strong partner, its project performance is consistently favorable.

Perhaps the biggest issue in recent years has been the Bank Group's overall level of exposure in Egypt. The country's rising indebtedness in the late 1980s became a major source of concern among some members of the board, especially when the Bank Group's biggest loan ever (some $280 million) was presented in 1988 for another Egyptian power project. With its approval, the country accounted for 9 percent of the Bank's portfolio. From the Bank Group's perspective, this was reasonable. Here was a country with an economy that continued to grow, a reliable repayment record, and projects that succeeded. Compared with most other clients on the continent, it looked very good. Furthermore, others such as the World Bank continued to lend to Egypt.

The Gulf War led to a welcome respite two years later, but the general issue of country risk has grown in importance in the board. In the specific case of Egypt, the situation would seem to be under control. Average annual lending has slowed to $134 million in 1991–1993. By contrast, the World Bank's nonconcessional lending accelerated in 1991 and 1992. New World Bank lending from 1988 to 1992 has been one-third greater than that of the ADB. However, the ADB's reduced exposure may be less a matter of policy and more a result of reluctance on the part of the Egyptian government. With the reduction in its debt overhang, the return of Arab donors, and the continued high levels of U.S. aid, the Egyptians informed the Bank in 1993 that they were not interested in further nonconcessional loans. If this persists, it would mark a dramatic change in the relationship between Egypt and the Bank Group, through no fault of either party.

Case Study Conclusions

What can we conclude from this small sample of country case studies? While the database is admittedly thin, some common themes emerge. To start with the positive, the ADB Group is sensitive to government priorities and tends to build on past experience. There is evidence of some concentration, even if it is not the result of explicit strategies. The Bank Group has been particularly active in road construction in Kenya and the power sector in Egypt because past experience was positive. In Mali, its focus on rural development, through both agriculture and rural water supply, is consistent with the obvious importance of the sector. Particularly in Mali, but also in Egyptian agriculture, it appears to have sought out cofinancing arrangements to reduce the level of risk.

Where the executing agency is competent, the results are encouraging. The hands-off approach of the ADB probably contributes to a stronger sense of borrower ownership, with positive repercussions when the owner is competent, especially for the long-term sustainability of investments. This does not appear to have been a well-articulated policy, however, and the costs of this approach where executing agencies were weak may have more than offset any gains to date.

The dilemma is that the ADB Group strikes one as being at the mercy of its environment, and the environment is typically harsh. In most cases, the Bank Group has gone beyond responsiveness to become a captive of its borrowers. It must rely on governments to identify priorities without having the capacity to provide an informed second opinion. In difficult circumstances, it tends to lean on other donors. Its personnel are not present enough to help troubleshoot. When they are, in the form of a regional office, they lack the mandate and staff to do a proper job. Executing agencies are left to sink or swim. If every borrower were like Egypt, perhaps this approach would suffice. Perhaps other, more aggressive donors are not doing much better. Perhaps. But even Egypt could benefit from some independent prodding on the policy front, and it faces difficult challenges in the years ahead. It needs a more active development partner, especially one that emanates from the same environment. This is all the more true for Kenya and Mali and the rest of sub-Saharan Africa.

Notes

1. This chapter draws from three larger case studies prepared for our study by national consultants from each of the countries in question.

2. Lele, *Managing Agricultural Development in Africa.*

3. The ADF provided 15.1 million BUA over the two phases, which was roughly equivalent to the same amount in U.S. dollars at the time.

4. Final report of the ILO support mission in 1978, pp. 19–20.

5. Operation Wells has suffered from a subsequent public enterprise adjustment program intended to encourage a more active role for the private sector. The ADB Group participated in its funding and endorsed its broad objectives, but the government dragged its feet. The Bank Group continued to finance Operation Wells even though it had lost its mandate. In 1994, the service was barely functioning.

6. USAID and the World Bank cofunded another power project with the ADB in 1990.

PART 2

DEVELOPMENT AGENDA

6

MOBILIZING AND
MANAGING MONEY

The ADB Group's record on money matters has been at once its most successful and its most contentious area of performance. Its efforts to mobilize resources have paid off handsomely, elevating it to the status of a major financial player on the world scene, comparable to its Asian and Latin American counterparts. At the same time, weakening income and looming risks have made its financial policies a subject of central concern to the nonregional shareholders. In this chapter, we first explore the Bank's experience in resource mobilization and then turn to various policies related to financial management.

Resource Mobilization

Like most MDBs, the ADB Group has three main sources of development finance: capital subscriptions from the member shareholders, which form the capital base of the Bank; grant contributions from nonregional members, which form the bulk of Fund resources; and borrowed funds obtained mainly through ADB bonds floated in international capital markets.

In addition to the above sources, the Bank Group retains net income that would otherwise accrue to its members in the form of dividends, and administers special funds on behalf of member states or contributing organizations.[1] Such special funds include the Nigerian Trust Fund, the Arab Oil Fund, the Special Relief Fund, and the Special Emergency Assistance Fund (SEAF).

Bank Subscriptions

The ADB's capital subscription is divided into paid-up and callable capital. Paid-up capital represents the shares fully paid for, including payments in the form of notes deposited by members. Callable capital is that portion of subscribed capital stock that can be accessed or "called" by the Bank only as and when required to meet obligations on borrowed funds or guarantees. So far no MDB has had to use its callable resources.

Without the capacity to borrow on financial markets, the amount of paid-up capital determines a financial institution's level of lending. Thus, capital subscriptions were the main source of development finance during the Bank's early years and, because of the poor economic conditions in most African countries, these subscriptions remained small. The ADB's initial subscribed capital in 1967 amounted to $250 million, of which only 50 percent was paid-up.

Since then, there have been four general capital increases plus twelve special capital increases to accommodate new members and make adjustments in existing subscriptions. The third GCI marked the entry of nonregional members and saw the authorized capital more than double to $5.8 billion in 1982. The fourth and last GCI in 1987 was even more impressive, tripling authorized capital to $23.0 billion, of which 12.5 percent was to be paid-up. The next GCI is expected in 1997, though preliminary discussions were being held up in 1995 pending the completion of the Fund's seventh replenishment.

At the end of 1993, the total capital actually subscribed was $21.0 billion, or 94 percent of authorized capital, of which 12.2 percent was paid-up. For the second and third GCIs, regional members had the option of making part of their payment in local currency, an alternative that was used by fourteen member states. As a result, roughly 5 percent of the paid-up capital is not in convertible currencies. This component is not usually considered as part of "usable" capital by credit rating agencies when they determine the borrowing capacity of the Bank, thus effectively limiting that capacity somewhat.

Many regional members have had difficulty remaining current in their subscriptions, at least in part because obligations accepted under the fourth GCI had to be honored in hard currency. By 1991, such arrears had grown to $130 million or 4.9 percent of total paid-up capital. Since arrears in subscriptions have the effect of reducing the voting power of delinquent members, this threatened to upset the 2:1 ratio of voting power between regionals and nonregionals, as called for in the Bank charter.

To rectify this situation, the Bank decided to apply the full force of its Share Transfer Rules for the first time, in 1992. Overdue subscriptions would lead to the forfeiture of shares, which could then be purchased by other members so long as the statutory regional/nonregional balance was maintained. This move had the desired effect, and by the end of 1993 arrears had fallen to $19 million or less than 1 percent of paid-up capital. However, because some of the authorized capital intended for regional members was not subscribed, the voting share of regional members remained at 64.2 percent as compared to the statutory 66.7 percent. A few of the unsubscribed shares were allocated to Eritrea when it joined in 1994, while others were picked up by Côte d'Ivoire when it expanded its subscription in 1995. The rest could be taken up by South Africa, depending on how it chooses to enter.

ADF Contributions and Special Funds

The African Development Fund began in 1972 with $87 million, of which the ADB's contribution was $5 million, while the remainder came from thirteen nonregional members. Since then, ADF resources have increased with the arrival of new members, through special increases made by old members who want to maintain their voting power, and by general replenishments made at regular three-year intervals. The first full replenishment was made in 1978, followed by five others. At the end of 1993, resources mobilized through the ADF amounted to $10.6 billion. The sixth replenishment (1991–1993) suffered a shortfall of $367 million because one member (Italy) failed to honor its pledge.

Two funds were established by oil-rich regional countries following the dramatic increase in the price of their principal export in 1974. The Arab Oil Fund was set up with $20 million from Algeria that same year. However, $5.5 million was refunded to Algeria on request in 1975. The Nigeria Trust Fund was established in 1976 with an initial naira contribution equivalent to about $89 million. It was replenished once in 1981 with an additional $70 million. At the end of 1993, the resources of the NTF had accumulated to $410 million. There is little prospect of further replenishment of either of these funds, since both benefactors have become major borrowers from the ADB Group.

Two other small funds have been administered by the Bank. The Special Relief Fund for countries affected by drought was established in 1974. A similar emergency fund for drought and famine in Africa (SEAF) was created ten years later to respond to another major natural disaster. Together they received contributions of approximately $50 million.[2]

Borrowing from Governments and Capital Markets

Commercial borrowing by the Bank during its early years was constrained by its lack of experience in international financial markets and its weak capital base. From 1975, the Bank made several attempts to raise capital by issuing bonds both within and outside the region. Although most of the bonds were not purchased, the Bank did succeed in obtaining loans from Canada, Sweden, and Austria for a total of $11 million. This demonstration that there was such scope for raising capital helped convince members to open up the Bank to non-African shareholders in 1982.

The arrival of nonregional members improved both the quantity and quality of the Bank's capital base. International creditors were now willing to lend funds by purchasing ADB bonds backed by ADB shareholders' callable capital, including that of the regional members. This meant that the Bank could reduce the share of its capital that was paid-in, making the same cash payments go much farther. The paid-in portion was set at 25 percent when the nonregionals joined. However, at the time of the last GCI in 1987, the stature of the Bank had grown such that creditors were willing to accept a much lower ratio, more in line with the other MDBs. The paid-in portion of that GCI was only 6.25 percent (yielding an overall average of 12.5 percent). Although paid-in capital was increased by only some 50 percent, the authorized capital, and hence the borrowing capacity, was raised by 200 percent.

In an innovative departure from all other MDBs, the Bank issues two types of debt: senior and subordinated. The former has the first claim to full repayment in the event of a call on the Bank's capital and is backed by the callable capital of member states with AA and AAA credit ratings. The latter is backed by the callable capital of all members. The Board of Directors of the Bank has adopted a policy to limit senior debt to 80 percent of the callable capital of its nonborrowing members (nonregionals plus Libya) and total debt (both senior and subordinated) to 80 percent of the callable capital of all members. (It has also decided to maintain a 60:40 ratio of senior to subordinated debt.) Since the industrialized members contribute more than 80 percent of the nonregional callable capital, they effectively guarantee senior debt. Primarily for this reason, senior debt has enjoyed the highest AAA rating from most credit agencies since the mid-1980s, and from all of them since 1990. This has enabled the Bank to raise capital without difficulty and at attractive terms.

At the end of 1994, total borrowing amounted to $9.2 billion, of which 62 percent was senior debt.[3] Senior debt had reached 73 percent of nonborrowing members' callable capital, while total debt remained at only 47 percent of total callable capital. Clearly, total borrowing could be much higher with additional recourse to subordinated debt, not to mention the possibilities if the 80 percent rule for senior debt were relaxed. However, concern over the reliability of regional callable capital and the desire to send a clear message of financial prudence have encouraged nonregional members to insist on a cautious approach. For the current GCI (up to the end of 1996), the Board of Directors has set a limit equivalent to roughly $11.0 billion for outstanding debt, keeping total debt down to 56 percent of callable capital. In fact, the proposed borrowing programs for 1995 and 1996 will keep debt levels well below even this amount. It has been decided to incur total debt no greater than the sum of callable capital from members with at least an AA rating, plus paid-in capital, plus reserves.

While the backing of industrialized member states is undoubtedly the most important factor explaining the Bank's high credit rating, such cautious borrowing strategies also help. So does the 12.5 percent ratio of paid-up to total capital, which is still high compared to that of other MDBs. The set of financial policies discussed later in this chapter also plays a part.

The ADB has learned to make the most of its high credit ratings. In 1991, it was classified by *Euromoney* magazine as the top supranational borrowing institution of the year. In 1993, its $500 million bond issue on the Eurodollar market was judged by the *International Financial Review* to be the most successful dollar transaction of that year. It has also established its own trading room, which has mastered the intricacies of foreign currency markets. This unit has achieved rates of return comparable to the Bank's independent specialized portfolio managers while serving the institution's short-term liquidity needs. If anything, the ADB may have been ahead of other regional MDBs in this regard, at least until 1994.[4]

Future Needs and Prospects

Given the discouraging pace of economic growth over the last thirty years, the need for financial resources will remain at the top of the African development agenda for decades to come. The reconstruction of Chad, Mozambique, Angola, Ethiopia, Eritrea, and Rwanda after periods of civil strife has generated additional demands, as has the democratization of South Africa. These demands will be further enlarged when the situation finally improves in Zaire, Liberia, Sierra Leone, Somalia, and Sudan. Unfortunately, aid flows in the first few years of the 1990s have failed to match even the World Bank's conservative estimates of the continent's requirements, and the immediate future prospects are hardly more promising.

The ADB Group seems destined to reinforce this trend at least in the short run. Since 1991, loan commitments have fallen significantly for three years in a row. The situation of the Fund is particularly worrisome. There was a major shortfall in the actual contributions to ADF VI, 1994 was lost through delays in negotiations, and ADF VII appeared headed for the first decline in a replenishment level in the Fund's history. At the same time, the relative importance of concessional resources has increased with the growing list of low-income countries that are finding it impossible to service their existing debt.

The fundamental problem is that Fund resources cost much more to nonregional members than do Bank resources. They represent grants that must be disbursed dollar for dollar over the few years following a replenishment agreement. On the other hand, only a small amount of capital must be paid up with each GCI, the callable remainder serving merely to access capital markets. As explained above, the cash implications of the last GCI were further reduced by lowering the required paid-in portion. Thus, the nonregional members found it relatively easy to authorize a 200 percent increase in the Bank capital in 1987. In principle, they could fairly easily authorize another, more modest, increase in the Bank's capital in 1997.

In practice, it seems unlikely. For one thing, it will be difficult for many regional members to provide more hard currency as their share of the expanded capital base. This constraint could be relieved if the ratio of paid-in to callable capital were further relaxed, but under the current circumstances at the Bank, international credit agencies would probably find that difficult to accept. The arrival of South Africa could bring a significant new source of capital subscriptions, but it may do little more than absorb the authorized but unsubscribed shares already outstanding. The only other alternative would be to reduce the regional share from the current 66.7 percent, a prospect we have already raised for other reasons in Chapter 3.

However, it is the absorptive capacity of African countries that is most likely to constrict Bank lending. As we saw in Chapter 4, the number of countries borrowing from the Bank has fallen fairly steadily over the years, but most dramatically in the last few. Only eight member governments borrowed in 1993. Some former borrowers are now ineligible due to their arrears on previous loans, an issue to which we return below. More are uncreditworthy due to the continued stagnation of their economies or the heavy burden of the ongoing debt crisis.

The prospects among those who still borrow are not much better. One of the largest clients is Nigeria, even though it is now classified as a low-income, and severely indebted, country. Another is Egypt, whose future interest in commercial borrowing from the Bank is in doubt. CFA countries like Côte d'Ivoire and Cameroon will probably find it more difficult to service their debts now that their currency has been devalued by 50 percent. Even oil-rich Algeria gives cause for concern, due to its civil unrest and high indebtedness. Again, South Africa offers perhaps the only exception, as it will generate some additional demand for nonconcessional resources. But initial indications are that it will proceed cautiously in this regard, and with good reason.

Weak absorptive capacity is one of the reasons the Board of Directors has limited Bank borrowing to levels much below those that could be sustained even by the existing capital base. In fact, the Bank could still raise an additional $6.5 billion in total debt and stay within the guidelines it established earlier. The other reason for resisting this temptation has to do with the Bank's financial health. The nonregional members have been particularly concerned to control the ADB's liabilities and hence reduce the possibility of an appeal to their callable capital. We turn, then, to the financial position and policies of the Bank.

Financial Policies

Financial Performance

Although it is not the primary objective of MDBs to maximize profits, it is important for them to generate sufficient income to be able to both meet their current costs and build sufficient reserves to protect their creditors and shareholders against any impairment of the paid-up capital in the event of severe loan losses. One of the many reassuring features of the ADB for its credit rating agencies has been its consistently healthy net income. Its income after expenses but before attribution to reserves exceeded $150 million each year from 1989 to 1992 (see Table 6.1).

This was also considerable solace to the Bank's management and most of its member states. Some nonregional members, however,

Table 6.1   Evolution of the Bank's Net Income, 1989–1993 (in millions of dollars)

	1989	1990	1991	1992	1993
Total income	447	566	661	775	799
From loans	316	385	440	558	602
Total expenses	291	399	500	613	697
Interest on borrowing	242	328	410	490	544
Administration	34	40	44	51	54
Loan-loss provisions	4	21	28	57	82
Net income	156	167	161	162	102

Source: ADB Group, *Annual Report,* various years.

started to become concerned about the likelihood of repayment from the more distressed African borrowers. In 1993, their fears appeared to be justified as net income fell by 32 percent. This did not pose an immediate crisis, since past profits had been set aside in reserves that totaled $941 million by the end of 1993. It did underline for any who still had doubts that there was a serious problem.

The decline in net income is of concern for several reasons. Banks usually determine the adequacy of their income by comparing it to their major expense category—the financial charges they pay on their borrowings. One frequently used ratio is the interest coverage ratio, for which a level of 1:5 is generally regarded as giving adequate protection. In the case of the ADB, this essentially means that net income should equal at least 50 percent of total borrowing expenses. The interest coverage ratio of the ADB was only about 33 percent even in the relatively good year of 1992. It declined to 20 percent in 1993.[5]

Weak net income also impedes the Bank's ability to build up adequate reserves. While its total reserves might seem substantial, they are far lower than those of the other MDBs. Compared to total paid-up capital, they amounted to only 38 percent in 1992, in contrast to a range of 130–140 percent for the World Bank, the IDB, and the AsDB. Since the risk of having to call on these reserves is probably highest at the ADB, the contrast is all the more marked.

Finally, there is growing interest among the nonregional shareholders in the idea of establishing self-sustaining development banks whose reserves are large enough to support a stable level of lending without further recourse to capital increases. This was the new principle that guided the recent GCI at the IDB. While this option was still a distant prospect for the ADB, the current situation threatens to put it off indefinitely.

The position of the ADF had started to deteriorate earlier, with net income turning negative in 1990 (see Table 6.2). However, since loan income is very modest due to the low interest rate on Fund loans, this had more to do with the division of the overall adminis-

Table 6.2   Evolution of the Fund's Net Income, 1989–1993 (in millions of dollars)

	1989	1990	1991	1992	1993
Total income	63	57	60	69	72
Total expenses	55	79	75	91	85
Administration	51	77	74	85	77
Loan-loss provisions	—	3	21[a]	41	16
Net income	8	−25	−36	−63	−29

Source: ADB Group, Annual Report, various years.
Note: a. Includes other provisions.

trative expenses between the Bank and the Fund (through the payment of management fees to the Bank). Nonetheless, as in the case of the Bank, arrears have become a problem.

The Bank's predicament cannot be separated from the continuing economic distress of the continent, and particularly the huge debt burden that has compromised the ability of an increasing number of countries to honor their debt service obligations. In Chapter 7, we pay more attention to this key piece of the puzzle. Here, we summarize the arrears problem of the ADB Group. We then explore the extent to which the Bank has helped or hurt its cause, through its policies on sanctions, loan accrual, and loan-loss provisioning. We also examine its lending policy, administrative budgeting, and liquidity policy.

Arrears

Arrears due the Bank have grown rapidly from $104 million in early 1989 to $550 million at the end of 1993 to $761 million by February 1995 (see Table 6.3). The bulk of arrears are still concentrated in a few countries affected by political strife or civil wars. Zaire accounted for 47 percent of all Bank arrears by 1995 and Liberia for another 18 percent. In fact, Zaire was responsible for 58 percent of arrears outstanding for more than six months.

What is of greatest concern, however, is that the total number of countries involved is increasing, while the recovery rate (the ratio of payments received to payments due) continues to decline. By

Table 6.3   Evolution of ADB Arrears and the Recovery Rate (in millions of dollars[a])

	1989	1990	1991	1992	1993
Arrears at end of previous period	96.4	131.5	152.5	221.1	349.9
Claims January to June	227.8	295.4	387.5	457.3	512.7
Claims to December	244.5	321.3	420.0	465.6	575.7
Total due	568.8	748.4	959.5	1,144.0	1,438.5
Payments received	447.4	596.9	729.7	793.9	888.0
Arrears at end of period	121.4	151.4	229.9	349.9	550.5
Recovery rate (percent)[b]	78.7	79.8	76.0	69.4	61.7

Source: ADB, *Rating Agency Review,* 1994.

Notes: a. Figures have been converted from BUA to U.S. dollars using the average rate of exchange for the year in question. This explains why the arrears at the end of one period are not usually equal to those at the start of the next. Total may not add due to rounding.

b. Ratio of payments received to total claims due.

February 1995, thirty-one ADB borrowers were in arrears of at least one month, while the Bank's recovery rate had dropped from 80 percent in 1990 to 62 percent in 1993. It is also disconcerting to note that even more countries (thirty-seven) are unable to remain current on the very soft ADF loans. Their arrears totaled some $70 million by early 1995, with a declining recovery rate comparable to that of the Bank.

Sanctions

To discourage countries from falling into arrears, the Bank adopted a series of sanctions divided into three categories, depending on the default period. Prior to 1991, category I sanctions, covering arrears due for over three months and up to six months, involved the suspension of signing new loans; category II sanctions, for arrears of six to nine months, carried the suspension of disbursements on the specific loans in arrears; category III sanctions, for arrears over nine months, led to the suspension of disbursements on all loans, including those of the ADF and NTF.

In the face of growing arrears, the Bank has tightened up its penalties. In 1991, the above sanctions were reviewed and the grace period for imposition reduced in all categories. The new time frames became: category I, one to three months; category II, three to six months; category III, over six months.

When this failed to alter behavior, the sanctions were further strengthened in 1994. Now the ban on signing new loans, as well as the suspension of disbursements on loans in arrears, takes effect thirty days from the due date. After sixty days, the cross-effective rule is applied, stopping disbursements on all loans and the approval of new loans by all three institutions of the Bank Group. With this latest reform, the sanctions policy is close to those of the World Bank and the IDB. It is actually tougher than that of the AsDB, but then that bank does not have an arrears problem!

The principle behind these changes is sound. In practice, it is not clear if they will make a significant difference in light of the overall economic performance of the region, coupled with the serious political problems faced by countries with substantial arrears. The reluctance of regional members to endorse the recent changes suggests that the pinch will be felt. There seems little on which to fault the Bank from the point of view of sanctions policy.

Nonaccruals Policy

The nonregional members have had greater concerns about the Bank's nonaccrual policy. When loans fall into arrears, every financial institution must decide at one point it will no longer count that expected revenue in its income statements. Until 1994, the Bank waited for one year before placing an overdue loan in nonaccrual status. This, it was argued, inflated the Bank's income figures inappropriately.

At the end of 1992, four countries (Congo, Liberia, Somalia, and Zaire) were in nonaccrual status accounting for $120 million, or about 78 percent of the outstanding arrears on principal and about 1.7 percent of loans disbursed and outstanding. By the end of 1993, the number of countries in nonaccrual status had doubled, with arrears amounting to $199 million or about 87 percent of total arrears. This represents about 2.4 percent of the loans disbursed and outstanding.

This policy was also reinforced at the start of 1994, so that Bank loans would henceforth acquire nonaccrual status after only six months. As a result, the number of ADB borrowing countries in this position increased to seventeen by mid-1994. In the cases of the ADF and the NTF, where the policy remained unchanged, the number of borrowing countries classified in a nonaccrual position was twelve and five, respectively.

Loan-Loss Provisioning

Loan-loss provisions are amounts that are specifically charged against current income and accumulated as loan-loss reserves. If a loan write-off becomes necessary, it is first charged to those reserves. Provisioning involves not only the loss of revenue in the calculation of income, but also a deduction from net income to cover the possibility that even the loan principal will not be repaid. As such, it can have a dramatic impact on the level of profits.

Until the end of 1993, the Bank set aside specific provisions equal to 10 percent of the outstanding principal amount or arrears on principal (whichever was greater) for loans in arrears for more than twenty-four months. The first such provisions were made in 1988 for loans to the Comoro Islands and Liberia. The evolution of these provisions is shown in Table 6.1.

Along with the reforms introduced to sanctions and nonaccrual policies at the end of 1993, the Bank decided to adopt a general provisioning policy. Starting that same year, provisions were set aside so that the minimum reserve available equaled 2.5 percent of total outstanding loans. This was to be increased to 3.0 percent in 1994. The old policy was retained for the ADF. Consequently, the Bank had accumulated provisions for loan losses of $208 million at the close of 1993, while another $75 million had been so allocated by the Fund.

The combination of greater provisions, lower revenues due to the tougher nonaccrual policy, and a fall in investment income threatened to eliminate net income for the first six months of 1994. Adjustments in liquidity investment averted this possibility. Nonetheless, over the next few years, it seems unlikely that the Bank will achieve even the pessimistic results it projected for its rating agency review earlier that same year and summarized in Table 6.4.

Table 6.4   Actual and Projected ADB Net Income, 1992–1996 (in millions of dollars)

Year	1992	1993	1994	1995	1996
Net income before provisions for loan losses	219.8	184.0	146.8	146.0	150.4
Provisions for loan losses	57.5	82.2	70.8	80.8	86.6
Net income for the year	162.3	101.8	76.0	65.2	63.8

Source: ADB, Rating Agency Review, 1994.
Note: Figures for 1994, 1995, and 1996 are projections. Converted from BUA using the 1993 average exchange rate.

Debt Reduction/Relief Facilities

The Bank has proposed several mechanisms to help borrowers deal with their arrears problem and has had limited success with at least one. Bilateral arrangements have been made with several donors to help members reduce or eliminate their arrears to the Bank. The Central African Republic, Niger, Uganda, and São Tomé and Principe have already benefited.

In 1994, the Bank undertook three portfolio restructuring operations linked to bridge financing for Cameroon, Congo, and Côte d'Ivoire. Arrangements were made for these countries to borrow from commercial banks in order to repay their arrears to the ADB, with the assurance that it would immediately make new disbursements enabling complete repayment to the commercial source in a matter of days. Then, by canceling the balances on some existing project loans and recasting them in the form of new balance-of-payments support, it was able to meet the borrowers' short-term resource requirements without increasing their debt. It is too early to tell how successful this approach will prove.

Recently, the Bank has broached the use of "workout programs" similar to those of other MDBs. This involves freezing a debtor's accumulated arrears and establishing a performance period over which the country will clear its stock of arrears, while remaining current on debt service falling due. The weakness with this arrangement is that new disbursements can resume only after the arrears have been cleared, and it does not really address the basic obstacle posed by an unmanageable debt overhang.

Ultimately, refinancing will be the only permanent solution for many heavily indebted member states. Bilateral arrangements will have to be formalized through the establishment of a Fifth Dimension facility similar to that of the World Bank. The ADB has proposed using resources from the ADF VII replenishment to convert existing ADB debts to ADF terms, in effect an interest subsidy. It would be reserved for member states that are in good standing and pursuing adjustment programs. Such a mechanism is particularly appropriate because it rewards good performers and deals with problems before they become crises.

For countries in chronic arrears, another approach is needed. In the course of the ADF VII negotiations, Bank management also proposed the creation of a trust fund to acquire and hold a portfolio of ADB loans in arrears. Repayments would be due the trust fund and no new lending would occur to the country in question until the arrears had been settled. This would be most useful in terms of clearing the Bank's balance sheet of nonperforming loans, though it would not mitigate the members' debt overhang. Discussions continued on the appropriate mix of funding options: within the replenishment, via the reallocation of unsigned and undisbursed ADF loans, and/or grants from bilateral donors.

Liquidity Policy

All MDBs have a significant proportion of their asset portfolio maintained in liquid form. The basic explanation is twofold: first, to meet anticipated cash requirements, which include scheduled disbursements on loan commitments, debt service payments on borrowed resources, and operational and administrative expenses; and second, to minimize risks associated with sudden fluctuations in exchange and interest rates. The ADB has aimed to ensure that the level of liquidity held did not substantially exceed net available paid-up capital, and that liquid assets were properly invested so as to contribute to net income.

Up to 1992, the ADB's policy was to maintain liquid assets equivalent to twice the amount expected to be disbursed the following year. As a result, it maintained liquidity ratios far above those of other MDBs between 1987 and 1991. In the mid-1980s, the ADB's investment record on liquid assets was also poor, with a negative average spread between yields and the cost of funds over the period 1984–1988.[6]

The Bank has since rectified both issues. The introduction of the trading room in 1989 led to a significant improvement in the average spread, which has been positive since 1990. The Bank has also lowered its liquidity level to 1.5 times the forecasts of following year's gross disbursements, which will control financial charges and the growth of outstanding borrowings.

The liquidity level of the ADF was fixed during the sixth replenishment at a level of roughly $500 million. Given the large losses experienced by the Fund since 1990, management has recommended raising liquidity levels. This proposal has been resisted by the nonregionals on the grounds that investing liquid assets would raise income only marginally, and that there is limited rationale for using scarce concessional resources for the purpose of earning income.

Lending Rates

The enhanced volatility of global interest rates has presented a challenge to all MDBs. Borrowing at rates that could change monthly created the potential for a serious mismatch with MDBs' long-term lending at fixed interest rates. Therefore, in 1990, the ADB followed other MDBs and adopted a variable lending rate policy. Although quite reasonable in its own right, it is worth noting that this change has rendered the Bank's loans even more costly for its clients. In effect, it transfers the risks associated with interest rate volatility to the borrower.

While no decision has yet been made, there has been discussion of increasing the spread used in calculating the appropriate Bank interest rate to be charged on its loans. Regional members have objected that the Bank already has the highest interest rates of the MDBs.

There has also been a suggestion that the ADF interest rate (referred to as a service charge) be increased from its long-standing, fixed level of 0.75 percent. It has been calculated that even a modest rise to 1.0 percent could eliminate the persistent deficit the Fund suffers in its net income. While the Fund must be careful not to overcharge its members for funds it receives in grant form, it should also be required to carry its own weight. As it now stands, donated resources are being used to help cover administrative expenses rather than to finance development projects. Because the terms of Fund loans would still remain highly concessional, with a ten-year grace period and fifty years to repay, this slight increase would not seem out of line.

Administrative Expenses and Cost Sharing

The debate over the Fund's net income position turns on the management charges it pays to the Bank as its share of administrative expenses. Since the Bank and the Fund use the same personnel and facilities, a formula had to be devised to allocate a share of operating costs to each entity. Fund projects tend to be much smaller than those of the Bank, even before including the growing number of studies that actually outnumbered its loans in 1993. Consequently, the total number of Fund loans and grants has far surpassed those of the Bank, and it was on this basis that over 60 percent of administration was annually charged to the Fund. (See the relevant line items in Tables 6.1 and 6.2.)

At the same time, the value of Bank lending was almost double that of the Fund, so it was felt that it should bear a greater share of the operating budget. Finally, in 1994, a new cost-sharing formula was accepted to be phased in over five years. This will have the effect of shifting some of the administrative burden back to the Bank, further depressing its net income. It is not clear if this will obviate the need for other actions to balance the Fund's budget. If not, the modest interest rate hike discussed above may be warranted.

As can be seen from Tables 6.1 and 6.2, the total administrative budget of the ADB Group has grown by about 50 percent between 1989 and 1992. This would appear to offer some scope for increased efficiency, especially with net income stagnating over the same time period and new loan commitments returning to the 1989 level by 1992. Certainly many nonregional directors have seen it that way. However, the picture is a little more complex.

For one thing, loan income actually increased faster than administrative costs over this interval (again see Tables 6.1 and 6.2). This reflected the earlier growth in lending, and to some extent administrative costs were simply catching up. If we extend the reference period back three more years to 1986, and stop at the peak year of 1991, we find that the administrative budget grew by 74 percent while lending increased by 110 percent. This helps explain why the human resources available per project still seem small compared to those of other MDBs, as discussed in Chapter 3.

What appears to have happened more recently is that management and the board did not interpret the fall in lending in 1992 as a long-term phenomenon, and therefore continued with a significant (17 percent) increase in operating expenses. By 1993, the seriousness of the situation was better understood and the operating budget was actually reduced by some 6 percent.

Without going into the details, it would appear that the budget is probably within reasonable limits once one takes into account the additional work to be done to improve loan quality, as outlined in Chapter 4. Further increases will certainly be impossible to justify in the current financial state. If extra resources are to be found for the operations departments of the Bank, they will have to come from a reallocation of the existing budget. This process was in fact begun in the 1994 budget, notably with reductions in the budgets of the Board of Governors, the Board of Directors, the Office of the President, and the Office of the Secretary-General.

In fact, it may be possible to achieve further savings without major cuts by taking advantage of the recent 50 percent devaluation of the local currency in Abidjan, the CFA franc. Since staff are paid in units of account, their purchasing power has increased dramatically. If, as seems to be the case, local prices are not allowed to rise to offset the devaluation, staff might be expected to accept a modest decrease in their salaries under current circumstances. However, they should not be targeted until the Board of Directors has made a more significant effort to reduce its own costs. At 9 percent of the total administrative budget, their share of expenses seems well beyond the usual norms.

Lending Policy and Country Risk

There was a time back in the 1970s when many people at the ADB Group and elsewhere probably thought that there was basically no risk associated with lending to sovereign nations. After all, nations, unlike businesses, could not go bankrupt. Perhaps, in the light of earlier historical experience elsewhere, that was naive. In any event, there is no such illusion any longer. Only frequent debt reschedulings and various other emergency measures have prevented many African countries from effectively declaring bankruptcy.

A multilateral development bank must therefore go beyond developmental considerations when preparing a new loan and assess the degree to which a country can be relied upon to repay that loan; in other words, it must assess the country risk. In addition, the significance of that risk will depend on the size of the loan and the number of other loans already outstanding in the borrower country. The first one may cause relatively little concern, especially if it is small, since any eventual loss could be fairly easily absorbed by reserves. As the loans add up, a bank must consider the possibility that the borrower may default not simply on the latest loan, but on all previous ones as well. It must evaluate its country exposure.

Finally, the risk associated with a bank's overall portfolio must be addressed. If too many of its total assets are concentrated in high-risk countries, their combined default could threaten the very existence of the bank. Portfolio concentration is the third and most important financial issue in the lending policy.

With a concept as uncertain as risk, there is much room for debate and disagreement. For the individual borrower under scrutiny, it is likely to be a very sensitive issue; when linked with lending policy, it can be explosive. However, it is also sensitive for bank management. Confined to a continent where country risk is widespread, a careful assessment of the matter could point to lower lending and hence a smaller bank. Fewer managers anywhere consider smaller to be better.

It is probably for these reasons that the ADB has been reluctant to develop explicit guidelines or to apply them rigorously. It was only in 1992 that the Exposure Monitoring Committee was formed, and its country review process remained quite flexible. On the other hand, Bank lending has been restricted to a smaller number of countries, and total Bank lending has dropped. However, the former is partly due to sanctions and decisions taken by borrowers, while the latter has been strongly influenced by nonregional pressure. We return to the issue of overall lending limits after reviewing some of the components of portfolio risk.

The loan portfolio of the ADB is not in fact heavily concentrated when compared to that of other regional development banks (see Table 6.5). The five largest borrowers (Nigeria and the four North African borrowing members) account for a significantly smaller share of total outstanding loans than in either the AsDB or the IDB. This is thanks to the large number of borrowers the ADB has served in the past. Nor is the Bank exceptionally exposed in its largest single borrower, Morocco.

ADB lending concentration is not much worse than that of the much larger IBRD. In fact, the World Bank is actually more concentrated if we look only at its lending to Africa. The same top five countries accounted for 81 percent of IBRD loans to the continent from

Table 6.5   Loan Portfolio Concentration of Selected MDBs

	AsDB	IBRD	IDB	ADB
Total number of borrowers	15	91	24	46
Largest borrower	36%	12%	18%	14%
Five largest borrowers	82%	46%	66%	49%
Seven largest borrowers	95%	52%	75%	59%

Source: AsDB, *Review of the Bank's Major Financial Policies*, November 1992.

1989/90 to 1992/93.[7] This is not surprising given the size and relative strength of these economies.

Two factors suggest a note of caution. First, the trend at the ADB does appear to be one of increased concentration. The four North African borrowers and Nigeria accounted for 63 percent of all new loans in 1992, rising to 78 percent in 1993. Second, the ADB's "top five" are probably a riskier group than the top five of the AsDB (Indonesia, the Philippines, India, Pakistan, and China), though perhaps comparable to the corresponding group in the IDB (Mexico, Brazil, Chile, Colombia, and Venezuela), at least in terms of recent history.[8]

However, it would seem preferable to concentrate on these countries than to return to poorer and more fragile economies in sub-Saharan Africa in the name of portfolio diversification. This has been the approach of the World Bank. It was clearly the implicit conclusion reached by the nonregional members as they pressed for restrictions on Bank lending in the course of negotiations for the seventh Fund replenishment in 1994. But then, country-risk assessment becomes all the more important for the remaining clients (and for guiding the eventual reentry into other markets).

Among major borrowers, one—Nigeria—has a relationship with the ADB quite different from that it has had with the World Bank. The ADB has continued to lend substantial sums to this country, amounting to 13 percent of all Bank loans in 1993 and 22 percent in 1994. In contrast, Nigeria's borrowing from the IBRD has steadily declined in recent years, stopping completely in 1992/93; it was classified as IDA-only in 1993/94.[9] The IBRD is still much more exposed in Nigeria as its cumulative lending had reached $4.6 billion by 1994, as compared with some $2.6 billion for the ADB. This reflects the fact that Nigeria stopped borrowing from the ADB Group between 1974 and 1986. Since the ADB is in a much weaker position to absorb defaults, however, it will have to monitor the situation in countries like Nigeria very closely.

The Bank must learn from past experience. Three of its five largest borrowers in 1985 now account for the bulk of its arrears (Zaire, Liberia, and Congo). In retrospect, its decision to persist with major loans to Zaire through 1990 was probably a mistake; the World Bank, by contrast, made its last nonconcessional loan to that country in 1986. Unfortunately, it is often political rather than economic factors that create the biggest problems in a client's capacity to repay, and these are particularly difficult to quantify, or to apply, in an institution where political factors are not supposed to intervene.

The 1992 country exposure policy did establish an indicative limit of 18 percent of the total Bank portfolio for any single borrower, but only "indicative." It also stipulated that preferred creditor (i.e., multilateral) debt service should not exceed 20 percent of a borrower's total debt, and that the ADB's share of this preferred creditor debt service should be no more than 35 percent. Finally, debt service to the ADB should not exceed 5.5 percent of export earnings. This was a start, but one not likely to have much immediate impact on lending practices.

Thus it was that the negotiations for the ADF VII replenishment stalled largely on the definition of creditworthiness. Nonregional shareholders insisted on controlling country risk in the Bank portfolio by imposing internationally recognized measures of external indebtedness. In essence, the proposition was to exclude from Bank lending those countries classified by the World Bank as both "low income" and "severely indebted"—with the notable exception of Nigeria.[10] This was actually more liberal than the World Bank's approach to determining IDA-only countries, but at the end of 1994 it was still being resisted on principle by some regional members. They argued that it was a fundamental right of all members of the Bank to have access to its loans, even though they had already accepted more stringent limitations to World Bank lending. In practice, it only represented what had already happened in 1993 and what management had committed itself to continuing in 1994. Indeed, while anyone may have the right to apply for credit, a bank must not be obliged to lend regardless of risk. A compromise based on the World Bank model was finally reached in April 1995.

The Bank Lending Program—the "Target"

Finally, one must ask how much total nonconcessional lending the Bank should attempt to conduct. This is a complex question. It depends to some extent on the demand emanating from borrowers, but also on the capacity of the Bank to prepare loans, the borrowing implications, the need for further revenue, the effect on the level of portfolio risk, and the combined impact on the Bank's financial situation. Inevitably, targets are set on the basis of the Bank's plans and constraints, under the assumption that the demand is unlimited.

This can sometimes lead to efforts to stimulate demand or to an exceptional willingness to respond to demand in order to meet stated targets. With the universe of potential borrowers diminishing rapidly, this danger increases. Furthermore, beyond a certain point there is a trade-off between the quantity of lending and its quality. As detailed in Chapter 4, the latter is in need of greater attention. Thus, it becomes especially important to set realistic targets at the start of each fiscal year.

This issue became unusually controversial in 1994. Bank management proposed the same target as in 1993, equivalent to roughly $1.65 billion. Although this was well below the 1991 peak of $2.25 billion, several nonregional directors pushed for an even lower figure. They were concerned about the impact on the Bank's financial position and the need to shift the culture of the Bank from its emphasis on quantity toward quality considerations. For the first time in the Bank's history, the Board of Directors was unable to settle on a single figure, opting instead for a broad range and agreeing to review the lending target at midyear.

Although, as we have seen, the Bank still had some leeway for further borrowing, there was a concern that an aggressive lending target would send the wrong signal to credit rating agencies. There was also undoubtedly an interest in controlling the growth in Bank liabilities at a time when the nonregional callable capital began to appear exposed. As it turned out, the Bank's AAA rating was reconfirmed in the summer of 1994, in spite of the disastrous annual meeting in May and the fallout from the Knox Report.

The preoccupation with the Bank "culture" was certainly well founded. However, there too the immediate problem dissolved somewhat—due to the failure of the ADF negotiations. Without any concessional resources, the staff had plenty of time on their hands to deal with the implementation of ongoing projects.

In the longer term, the issue remains very pertinent. The capacity of the current staff complement will depend on the eventual size of the Fund replenishment. Above and beyond that question, however, several factors call for a cautious approach. If the lending market is reduced to some ten members in any one year, there is a very real danger that the Bank will be tempted to go looking for projects where "bankable" ones cannot be found. The Bank should probably avoid further growth in its lending for the next few years and also move away from the notion of specific annual targets. A generous range could be used instead. Then, decisions could be made on an individual project basis, combining measures of project quality with careful assessment of country risk. This should not unduly complicate borrowing operations, since most liquidity needs in any one year depend primarily on previous commitments. If it turns out that lending is too low to justify the administrative budget, the latter should be the one to adjust.

Conclusions

The Bank Group has enjoyed major success in mobilizing development resources for Africa, despite the constraints it faced in the early years of operation. In the last fifteen years, paid-up capital has grown by a factor of six, ADF subscriptions by a factor of eight, and borrowings by a factor of eleven. This success can be attributed to many factors: the strong commitment of the founding members even as their condition worsened in the 1980s; the admission of the nonregional members; the staff's capacity to master the complexities of the international money markets; and management's ability to respond, albeit sometimes reluctantly, to each new crisis.

Unfortunately, the Bank's growth has made it more difficult to deal with shocks from the external environment, even as that environment has deteriorated. Large foreign borrowings make the opinions of unknown credit rating officials critically important. Large annual flows of concessional funds make it harder for the nonregional members to maintain their commitment when fiscal pressures build up back home. Large levels of Bank lending make it harder for the founding members to respect their obligations.

In response to these problems, the Bank has made significant efforts to strengthen its financial policies, often with the constructive prompting of nonregional members. It has tightened its sanctions and nonaccrual policies by reducing the grace periods involved; increased loan-loss provisions; enforced the share transfer rules to reduce arrears on capital subscriptions; reduced liquidity levels to control borrowing requirements and hence financial charges; strengthened asset/liability management by establishing an in-house trading room; changed to a variable lending interest rate to protect its income from interest rate fluctuations; and reduced its administrative budget. It has cut its total nonconcessional lending and stopped it completely for low-income, category A member states, other than Nigeria. The ADB's financial policies now approach those of other MDBs.[11] It is not simply the presence of nonregional callable capital that explains the continuing AAA rating of the ADB.

If the Bank has seemed systematically more optimistic and hence less cautious than the nonregional members, perhaps it is not surprising. One who lives in difficult conditions has to believe that they are going to improve; otherwise, there is no purpose. Certainly the Bank's majority shareholders would expect no less. The most important point is that the ADB has generally adjusted its policies appropriately, while walking that fine line between regional hopes and nonregional fears.

Nonetheless, the Bank cannot escape its operating environment. Its arrears continue to accumulate and no amount of cajoling will make its weakest members more solvent. Only the nonregional members live outside that environment, and finally they must provide most of the funds to refinance the debt. They have already extended the same assistance to the much stronger World Bank; there is now no justification for not offering the ADB the same treatment.

Ideally, the nonregionals should also help the ADB Group shift the bulk of its lending from the Bank to the Fund windows, through a higher ADF replenishment. Without that, it will be very difficult to maintain positive net flows from the Bank to its members. This will jeopardize both the Bank's developmental impact and the borrowers' capacity and incentive to repay. The nonregional members argue that their environment has also deteriorated, and that they must choose between different channels for their support. While a case could be made for the relative efficiency of multilateral institutions like the ADF over bilateral ones, recent events have not strengthened this argument.

And so the ADB Group must do its best in a second-best world. It should eliminate further nonconcessional lending to severely indebted low-income countries and continue to restrict such lending to the few remaining creditworthy clients. Nigeria may be the exception, but one calling for greater prudence and close monitoring. In short, the Bank must minimize the danger of aggravating the continent's debt problem—a fundamental consideration, but one that can be overlooked in the day-to-day work of the Bank. By respecting this criterion, the Bank's long-term health can only benefit.

Notes

1. Retained dividends form part of the capital base of the Bank.

2. The precise amount depends on the exchange rate used. An amount totaling BUA 40.8 million is shown in the ADB Group's *1993 Annual Report,* pp. 95, 120.

3. ADB Group, *1993 Annual Report,* p. 76.

4. The performance of the trading room appears to have declined somewhat in 1994, possibly as the result of some key staff departures.

5. Calculated from the Bank's income and expenses statement as given in ADB Group, *1993 Annual Report,* p. 88.

6. ADB Group, *Audited Financial Statement,* 1985–1988.

7. Of course, the IBRD's overall level of concentration across the Third World is much lower.

8. The contrast between the AsDB and the other two regional banks is more marked when one looks at the rest of its nonconcessional customers. Its sixth and seventh borrowers are the eminently creditworthy Korea and Thailand, compared with Argentina and Bolivia for the IDB, and Côte d'Ivoire and Zimbabwe for the ADB.

9. It is now treated as IDA-only.

10. Low-income countries are those classified as category A by the ADB Group. Severely indebted countries are those for whom the present value of debt service is greater than 80 percent of GNP or 200 percent of exports. One

more criterion was added: that scheduled debt service not be above 30 percent of export earnings.

11. The debate over policies on country exposure and net income management continued in early 1995, but past experience suggests that they too will be resolved in due course.

7

CROSSCUTTING ISSUES:
A FULL AGENDA

Every organization has its subtext, a variety of interests and objectives that sometimes enrich, sometimes impede its principal function but always complicate day-to-day life. A development bank is particularly affected by this situation. It is rightly viewed as a powerful instrument that can address other public concerns in addition to sound public investments, both directly through those investments and indirectly through the authority it commands as a leading development actor. These concerns often involve the promotion of certain types of projects or different ways of designing and implementing them. But they also entail raising the profile of an issue, perhaps even introducing a new one into the public and political consciousness.

The significance of this subtext in development banking has grown considerably in recent times. With increasing experience, a more active and vocal civil society, and the accelerating pace of change in the world, the introduction of new ideas seems to have accelerated as well. This process has been especially fertile in the debate surrounding African development due to the failure of the traditional models to make much headway. In fact, while new priorities have cascaded one on top of the other, old ones have been reintroduced under a new guise or have simply refused to go away.

Thus, the African Development Bank Group, struggling to master the basic elements of effective project lending in the world's toughest environment, has been called upon to address a growing list of related concerns simultaneously. At least one, regional integration, was there at the founding of the Bank. Another, democratic development and good governance, is very much a theme of the 1990s. Poverty alleviation is a theme of then and now, but in quite different ways. Most of the others gathered steam in the mid- to late 1980s: gender, the environment, the private sector.

However, the one we begin with is the external debt crisis. This is a truly crosscutting issue, though perhaps *undercutting* would be an even more appropriate term. As we have seen in the previous chapter, the survival of the Bank is potentially threatened by the inability of its borrowing members to honor their obligations. This is fundamentally attributable to the ongoing debt crisis confronting most of the continent. It is an issue that some are tempted to write off, or at least overlook; with the recent major improvements in the Latin American situation, the global dimensions of the crisis have dissipated. For Africa and the ADB Group, unfortunately, nothing could be more important. Consequently, we give it pride of place, and space.

The African Debt Problem

The costs of Africa's debt burden are enormous. They go well beyond the direct costs of higher interest on short-term commercial credits, beyond the opportunities foregone while devoting scarce foreign exchange and fiscal revenues to external debt. In the face of severe balance-of-payments and budgetary constraints, the reduced imports of real goods and services that are the inevitable consequences of debt service payments have meant multiple setbacks: reduced capacity utilization in both the private and public sectors, hence reduced levels of income and fiscal revenues; increased inflationary pressures arising from budget deficits; reduced capacity to save and invest; and weakened prospects for future growth and employment.

Failure to meet debt service obligations has compounded the problem. The unpaid interest and charges on existing debt add to the "overhang" of the debt burden, which in itself undermines economic recovery. A large and growing debt stock, like that of Africa, generates strong disincentives for both domestic and foreign investors. Meanwhile, repeated rescheduling negotiations preoccupy the few senior economic officials who should be devoting their time to improving the policy environment and implementing a coherent long-term development strategy.

A new associated problem is the creation of huge domestic debt arising from governments' heavy borrowing in domestic money markets and their reduced capacity to raise tax revenues to service it. High domestic debt makes it difficult for governments to service external debt even when a country has adequate foreign exchange reserves. Although an important phenomenon, and one with implications for external debt management, we shall not address it here. This section is confined to a brief review of Africa's external debt, measures that have been undertaken to address it, and the implications for the ADB Group.

The Nature of African Debt

The African debt burden is heavier today than it was at the onset of the international debt crisis in 1982, or even at the end of the "lost decade." Total debt for the region more than doubled, from $111 billion in 1980 to $248 billion in 1987, and reached $282 billion in 1993.[1] While debt service payments as a percentage of exports have fallen somewhat since the late 1980s, this is largely because a growing number of countries are simply unable to keep up with their payments. Thus, the stock of arrears has jumped from $3 billion in 1980 to a staggering $47 billion in 1992.[2] Now the capitalization of interest on rescheduled arrears continues to add to the stock of debt.

Both North and sub-Saharan Africa have suffered from the debt crisis, but in different ways. North African debt has been more onerous in the sense that a much higher share has been contracted at commercial rates of interest and payback periods, but their stronger economies have made it easier for them to survive the crisis. Egypt was also greatly assisted by debt reduction as a reward for the role it played in the Gulf War. In 1992, Morocco and Algeria were still classified by the World Bank as severely indebted. Morocco seems to be succeeding in its long adjustment process, but Algeria continues to have one of the world's highest debt service ratios—77 percent in 1993.[3]

It is in sub-Saharan Africa that the crisis is proving truly intractable. Table 7.1 summarizes its relentless evolution. One should not be fooled by the declining debt service ratio, as it reflects actual rather than scheduled payments. Its reduction is largely due to the incapacity of many countries to maintain the high repayment rates of the mid-1980s and is directly related to the rapidly expanding arrears. Debt service due as a percentage of export earnings was almost twice as high at 28 percent in 1993.[4]

Twenty-four sub-Saharan African nations were classified as severely indebted low-income countries (SILICs) in 1994, along with Egypt; three others—Angola, Cameroon, and Congo—were considered severely indebted middle-income countries (SIMICs), along with Morocco. Public and publicly guaranteed debt has always tended to account for roughly 75 percent of total debt and over 90 percent of long-term debt. While bilateral debt remains the largest component, the share of multilateral debt has steadily risen to reach 23

Table 7.1   The Evolution of Sub-Saharan Africa's Debt, 1980–1993 (in billions of dollars or percentages)

	1980	1987	1990	1993
Total debt	$84	$166	$192	$200
Debt service	$9	$13	$15	$12
Arrears	$1	$13	$27	$49
Debt/exports	92%	253%	230%	254%
Debt/GNP	31%	75%	73%	73%
Debt service/exports	10%	19%	18%	15%
Multilateral as percentage of total debt	9%	17%	19%	23%

Source: World Bank, World Debt Tables, 1994/95, p. 216.

percent of total debt. This is partly because there is no mechanism for rescheduling or forgiving this type of debt, a characteristic that now makes it one of the main problems.

There are significant differences in the debt burden among the SILICs. The ratio of total debt to exports varies from 250 to 300 percent for Nigeria and Kenya to over 1,000 percent for Tanzania, Uganda, Mozambique, and Burundi (and still higher for exceptional cases like Sudan and Somalia).[5] The debt service ratio varies even more widely, from virtually zero in countries that have essentially stopped all payments (e.g., Liberia) to an incredible 121 percent in Uganda, which continues to make a valiant effort to honor its engagements.[6] Scheduled, as opposed to actual, debt service equaled or exceeded 100 percent of export earnings for at least a half-dozen countries.[7] This picture is especially grim when one realizes that some of these countries have been struggling with some form of structural adjustment for close to ten years.

Debt Relief Initiatives

Various steps have been taken toward finding a solution.[8] Official creditors have shifted away from nonconcessional forms of financing so that 97 percent of official flows to SILICs were on concessional terms by 1993, compared to 65 percent in 1982. There has been some cancellation of ODA debt for low-income countries by individual creditors, debt rescheduling on increasingly easy terms, and progressively greater debt relief within the framework of the Paris Club. Finally, there has been both multilateral and bilateral support for buybacks of commercial bank debt.

With $100 million from its IBRD profits, the World Bank established a debt reduction grant facility in 1989 for the purchase of private debt in IDA-only countries. This has been supplemented with bilateral funds and a further $100 million from the World Bank in 1993. Until 1993, only two countries in sub-Saharan Africa benefited (Mozambique and Niger), but in that year another five were able to use this facility to retire their commercial bank debt. These buybacks take advantage of the low market value of private debt—on average 10–15 percent of the face value.

Bilateral debt represents by far the largest share of debt and debt service obligations for African countries. Bilateral donor governments initially provided new funds and cash flow relief through rescheduling operations. When this failed to suffice, limited debt forgiveness was arranged on a bilateral basis. For individual IDA countries following structural adjustment programs, official donors began to cooperate through the Paris Club. In 1988, they agreed to apply a menu of three options that would have the effect of reducing the present value of debt service by 33 percent. However, this was offered only for debt contracted during a certain consolidation period. These became known as the "Toronto terms."

This too proved inadequate. Eighteen of the countries so handled returned for further reschedulings, sometimes as many as seven times (Madagascar and Niger). Thus, in 1991, the Paris Club agreed to implement "enhanced Toronto terms." Under these conditions, debt relief of 50 percent was offered for the consolidation period, along with a "goodwill" clause in which creditors agreed to consider, some three to four years later, a similar reduction of the remaining debt stock. By March 1994, seventeen African countries had benefited from these terms. Cameroon and Côte d'Ivoire were given similar concessions before they became IDA countries in 1994.

Since 1990, some observers have recognized that these measures would be inadequate. British Prime Minister John Major proposed "Trinidad terms" to effect a one-time reduction of the total eligible debt stock by 66.7 percent, including an initial five-year period of interest capitalization and an extension of the repayment period by as much as twenty-four years. The Dutch suggested total forgiveness of official bilateral debt to SILICs. The United Nations has called for a three- to ten-year moratorium on all bilateral debt servicing and a rescheduling using only IDA terms. All were intended to be pursued in conjunction with acceptable adjustment performance and not to divert funds from existing ODA commitments. None has been implemented.[9]

Since multilateral institutions have always insisted that their debt cannot be rescheduled, let alone forgiven, there has been less discussion of this component of the debt problem. These agencies have been strong advocates of debt reduction by private and official creditors. In addition, the World Bank has earmarked a portion of repayments on IDA credits to assist eligible SILICs in meeting their interest payments on IBRD loans they received when they were middle-income countries, the so-called Fifth Dimension facility. Bilateral donors have also contributed.

IMF debt is particularly burdensome because much of it has been short-term and nonconcessional, yet countries must remain current to qualify for debt relief and other external finance.[10] Such loans have proven quite inappropriate to the long-term nature of Africa's problems, resulting in a steady negative net transfer out of Africa to the IMF. Critics have urged the IMF to sell some of its substantial gold reserves, employing the proceeds to freeze or, better still, eliminate its most onerous claims on low-income countries.[11] To date this advice has fallen on deaf ears.

The ADB Group Response

The ADB Group has put forward several ideas to deal with the debt problem[12] and taken measures to deal with the impact on the Bank Group itself, as reviewed in Chapter 6.

Debt Securitization Plan

In 1987, the Bank proposed a refinancing plan to convert all private and bilateral nonconcessional debt into long-term bonds. Interest payments were to be set according to a country's demonstrated debt service capacity so as not to undermine its recovery and future growth. All payments were to go to a debt redemption fund. While the proposal provided a number of options for creditors, it maintained the principle of comparability of treatment. This proposal was well received when presented at a special Organization of African Unity (OAU) meeting of heads of state but received little attention from creditors.

Debt Management Unit

In 1990, a specialized unit was created within the Bank to coordinate the monitoring of developments concerning Africa's external debt; formulate initiatives to address the problem; assist regional members in the verification, management, and renegotiation of their debt as well as the preparation of debt-reduction strategies; maintain close relations with international agencies; and establish and maintain a database on Africa's debt. Eventually, the unit was also expected to provide consultancy services on debt questions.

The debt management unit (DMU) did not materialize as planned because it failed to attract the necessary additional financing from the nonregional members. They felt that the Bank was extending itself too far and was in danger of duplicating facilities already existing at the UN Conference on Trade and Development (UNCTAD), the Commonwealth Secretariat, and the World Bank. Despite this setback, the DMU is operational, though at a much reduced capacity with only one professional. Its main function was to collaborate with the above organizations in the provision of debt management training, though recently the emphasis has shifted to coping with arrears owed to the ADB.

Bridge Financing

In at least one case (Cameroon), the Bank has provided bridge financing to help a borrowing member clear its arrears to another agency and thereby gain access to the next disbursement of a structural adjustment loan. This provided only a short reprieve and Cameroon was back in arrears the following year. Later the Bank tried combining commercial bank bridge financing with a portfolio restructuring exercise to clear arrears that Congo, Côte d'Ivoire, and (again) Cameroon owed the Bank (see Chapter 6). However, in both instances, it was dealing with the symptoms, not the causes of the problem.

The debt securitization plan was perhaps the boldest attempt ever by the Bank to contribute to the conceptualization of African development strategies. Without judging the details, the principle was clearly ahead of its time. In light of the subsequent proposals for more fundamental relief put forward by Prime Minister Major and others, this plan may not have been as unrealistic as originally suggested. Both this and the DMU were hampered by the lack of support from the Bank's nonregional members. Now they are being called upon to provide additional funds for various facilities to assist both the ADB and the World Bank.

While frequent debt reschedulings have helped maintain a positive cash flow to the region, the debt stock is still rising, debt service continues to drain valuable foreign exchange, and repeated negotiations divert the scarce time of senior economic officials. The World Bank estimates that even with the comprehensive application of enhanced Toronto terms, combined with continued bilateral cancellations and commercial debt buybacks, there would still be eighteen

African SILICs with unsustainable debt loads, with most of the others barely reaching the threshold.[13] It rightly argues for deeper debt reduction and additional concessional funding to reduce the debt overhang to manageable levels.

For its own future as well as that of the continent, the ADB Group should contribute in every way possible to end the African debt crisis. At the most general level, it must ensure that the problem is not ignored, keeping it on the international agenda by highlighting the severity of the problem. Adding its voice in support of proposals like that involving the sale of IMF gold reserves could help enhance their credibility.

At its level, the Bank must take care not to aggravate the problem. As discussed in the previous chapter, some already approved ADB loans to SILICs in good standing should be converted to ADF terms, with a Fifth Dimension–type facility. It should also refrain from further lending at nonconcessional rates to all SILICs (with the possible exception of Nigeria).

For their part, the nonregional shareholders should rethink their position on the debt management unit and encourage it to play a more active role. The assistance it could provide in strengthening national DMUs would be particularly welcome. These units are typically understaffed, enjoy low status, and are preoccupied with routine functions of debt recording rather than the more important issues of debt analysis and the linkage of debt to a country's overall economic policies. While the Commonwealth Secretariat and UNCTAD are making important contributions, there is more to be done. In particular, it is necessary to provide similar services to francophone Africa and to establish a capacity within the continent to provide technical assistance to debt management units.

In eastern and southern Africa there is already a promising regional initiative that the Bank should support: the Eastern and Southern African Initiative in Debt and Reserves Management (ESAIDARM) based in Harare, Zimbabwe. Established in 1992, it is collaborating with UNCTAD and the Commonwealth Secretariat to create a regional center of expertise. It intends to foster the exchange of debt and reserves management information and train regional specialists to service the needs of the ten member countries.

A similar initiative is planned for West Africa, and the ADB Group would be well placed to help it get started. The International Development Research Centre (IDRC) and CIDA of Canada have been developing an assistance program for francophone countries, which is now in need of an institutional home in the region. The ADB Group could either offer that home or, probably better, help establish an independent agency along the lines of ESAIDARM. In the domain of external debt, which often seems overwhelming in its magnitude and complexity, this would be one very concrete and practical contribution.

As G. K. Helleiner stated in 1992, "Reducing the current external cash flow obligations and payments on debt account . . . will thus probably be the most cost-effective form of official external resource transfer to Africa in the 1990s. Debt reduction must constitute a major element in any serious externally-supported effort to restart African development."[14] The ADB Group has no choice but to persevere in its attempts to help resolve this crisis.

Regional Integration

Regional integration is decidedly unique among the special issues treated in this chapter. It has figured among ADB Group priorities since the very beginning, the impetus for its promotion generally emanates from within the Bank, and it enjoys significant support inside Africa. This is an area in which the Bank has always said it wanted to make a difference, without any prodding from the nonregional members. Indeed, the foundations of the Bank rest in no small measure on recognition of the importance of regional integration; in a very real sense, the ADB Group itself is a regional integration initiative.

The concept of regional integration commands high priority among African leaders. Early ideas of a continental political union in the late 1950s gave way to the development of regional groupings. These have included market integration schemes (e.g., East African Community), project-oriented institutions (e.g., SADCC, now the Southern African Development Community), and more narrowly focused cooperative arrangements (e.g., African Regional Standards Organisation). Two francophone groups have gone as far as sharing a common currency, the CFA franc (e.g., West African Economic Community, or CEAO in French). Overall, there are more than 200 organizations created to foster regional cooperation in Africa.

Declarations by African heads of state in the Lagos Plan of Action and in the 1991 Abuja Treaty have reaffirmed their commitment to the principle of regional integration. African states remain terribly small by world standards, while much larger nations in Europe and North America continue to broaden their economic ties. The combined economic output of sub-Saharan Africa (including Nigeria) is comparable only to that of Austria.[15] Thus, the Abuja Treaty established the African Economic Community and called for the strengthening of regional blocs as part of the process of building an African Common

Market by the year 2025. The OAU is spearheading this ambitious initiative with the assistance of the UN Development Programme (UNDP) and the African Capacity Building Foundation (ACBF), and in collaboration with the UN Economic Commission for Africa and the ADB Group.

While there are many ways in which the Bank can and does promote regional integration, the most visible one has been the financing of multinational projects that are jointly undertaken by two or more countries or by a regional institution. The largest such loans have been to the West African Development Bank in 1987 ($40 million), Air Afrique in 1990 ($53 million), and the Muela Hydropower project, benefiting Lesotho and South Africa, in 1992 ($54 million). The Bank also identifies a second category of projects, which are national but serve to increase complementarity among countries, such as ports or roads improving access to a border. The regional benefit of this project type is sometimes difficult to assess and not always the main reason for the investment. However, it has been estimated that their 2.3 percent share of Bank Group lending over the period 1969–1989 was equal to that of multinational projects.[16]

The ADB Group has attached a high priority to multinational projects, to the extent of stipulating in its 1982–1986 Operational Program that 10 percent of its resources would be channeled in this direction.[17] In practice, it has proven impossible to honor these intentions. Lending of this type for 1982–1986 amounted to only $126 million, or 2.4 percent of total commitments.[18] Equally disconcerting, the share of multinational projects has been dropping to the point where they accounted for less than 1.0 percent of total lending in 1991–1993.[19] In 1993, the Bank was essentially confined to supporting feasibility studies (see Table 7.2).[20] The ADB Group has stopped setting lending targets in this area.

The difficulties encountered in promoting multinational projects reflect the poor performance of regional integration schemes more generally and share similar causes. The deteriorating economic picture in so many African countries has diverted the political leadership from broader programs to domestic concerns. In some cases, the links between neighbors are extremely weak, especially when they had different colonial masters. Most countries have been at such an early stage in the process of nation building that they have been reluctant to cede their sovereign powers. There have also been major political differences between neighbors, from wars to divergent ideologies to forced repatriation of non-national workers. Even when these obstacles have been overcome, the technical and political problems in apportioning the costs and benefits of such projects complicate the allocation of responsibility for loan repayment between

Table 7.2   Multinational Projects and Studies, 1992–1993 (in millions of dollars)

Year	Countries/ Organizations	Project/ Study Name	Loans[a]	Grants
1992	Lesotho	Muela Hydropower	54.1	
	Namibia	Trans-Khalagadi Road	11.4	
	OMVS[b]	Right Bank Dyke-Diama Dam	6.6	
	ECOWAS	Floating Weeds Control Study		2.8
	Francophonie	Université Senghor–Institutional Support		1.2
	Various	Kankan-Bamako Road Study		2.8
	Various	Trans-Caprivi Highway Study		2.8
	Various	Power Interconnection Study		3.1
1993	Mali/Côte d'Ivoire	Power Interconnection Study		1.5
	Burundi/Tanzania	Regional Electrification Study		0.8
	Guinea/Cape Verde	Madina-Oula Agricultural Study		0.9
	PTA	Telecommunication Master Plan		0.9
	OMVG[c]	Electrical Energy Integration Study		1.4
	Various	African Research Institutes Support		4.4
	Various	African Institute of Re-adaptation		0.5

Source: ADB annual reports for 1992 and 1993.
Notes: a. ADF except for the Lesotho loan, which involved a blend of Bank and Fund resources.
b. Senegal River development authority.
c. Gambia River development authority.

partner states, discouraging them from seeking loan financing. For all these reasons, the lofty pronouncements of African leaders have not yet been translated into commensurate action through regional groupings or on the ADB Group balance sheets.

Nonetheless, the ADB Group continues to pursue this elusive goal. Indeed, consonant with the renewed political interest, it has raised the issue's profile in a variety of other ways. It has participated in the recent review of the Economic Community of West African States (ECOWAS) Treaty, and has collaborated with the UNECA in the establishment of a small CINERGIE office at the Bank to promote regional trade in West Africa. Anticipating the new opportunities to arise from a democratic South Africa, the Bank commissioned a major three-volume study on economic integration in southern Africa in 1991.[21] The following year, it commissioned a group of prominent Africans to advise it on how to accelerate the process of regional integration. The theme of its *African Development Report 1993* was economic integration and structural adjustment.[22]

But the largest single initiative in this direction has been the establishment of the African Export-Import Bank (AFREXIMBANK). The shortage and high cost of trade financing, insurance, and guarantee facilities have been important factors constraining the growth of trade within Africa as well as beyond. The president of the ADB

Group and the advisory panel saw this as an area where the ADB Group could usefully intervene. When the feasibility study proved encouraging, but the nonregional directors did not, the proposal was carried to the Board of Governors, where just enough support was obtained to pursue the idea further. Finally, in June 1993, management received approval for a 5 percent equity participation of $25 million, though there was still very little support for the idea among nonregional directors.

In contrast to the lukewarm reception from nonregional members and non-African commercial banks, African governments have enthusiastically endorsed the proposal. Twenty-eight African countries signed the official agreement, along with four African institutions (ADB Group, BCEAO, African Reinsurance Corporation, and the PTA Bank). The initial authorized capital of $500 million was fully subscribed by early 1994. Egypt has been particularly supportive, pledging 20 percent of the total, but the private sector response was less than expected.[23] Depending on whom one listens to, this could be a major contribution to trade and integration in the continent—or another losing investment. The launching of yet another regional institution seems ill-advised to some, given the number already existing and the difficulties experienced by so many. However, African countries desperately need to improve their trade performance. Their share of world trade has been steadily falling, while trade links between neighbors are unnaturally low. This initiative responds to a specific need of the growing African private sector. Provided its promoters learn from the mistakes of past efforts in regional cooperation, it should be worth trying.

Genuine regional integration is clearly an area in which political, economic, and intellectual leadership within Africa is critical to success. The shortage, especially of political will, has undermined most past efforts, generating considerable skepticism over future prospects. This is no longer a new idea full of promise. While most donors continue to support the principle, and some are active in practice as well, others have demonstrated a pragmatic ambivalence. They prefer to work on general trade liberalization with the "induced integration" it generates, or wait until concrete proposals emerge. The World Bank endorsed this issue only in 1989 after much internal struggle, and its approach tends to shy away from the proactive.[24]

The ADB Group, as Africa's most successful regional institution, is a logical standard-bearer. Most reports on the Bank's mandate conclude as much. Bank management appears to be trying to meet this challenge, even though the everyday reality of borrower demand for project financing argues against it. Institutional innovations like AFREXIMBANK may be more significant than individual investment projects, and national integrative projects more promising than multinational ones. In grander integration schemes, the Bank's African character suggests a special role in addressing the inevitable political obstacles, while its practical bent should aid in the definition of realistic agendas. The Bank must continue these efforts, but with its eyes wide open and past experience squarely in view.

The Private Sector

Amid the trials and tribulations of the 1980s, there were a few positive signs. One was the emergence of a widespread recognition of the key role private enterprise can and must play if long-term economic growth is to be achieved. The reasons are many: the poor performance of most state enterprises, the inability of government to continue subsidizing such entities in the face of large budget deficits, and the central place assigned to private sector development in World Bank adjustment programs. On a more positive note, greater awareness of the contribution made by the private sector in other countries, notably East Asian, has played a role as well.

On the other hand, many governments remain somewhat ambivalent when it comes down to the details. The indigenous African entrepreneurial class is often quite small and dominated by foreigners and resident non-Africans. Officials and politicians worry about the risk of transforming state monopolies into private ones, the willingness of private agents to service isolated regions, and the social and political consequences of assisting non-African elites—not to mention the potential challenge to their authority any healthy business class can represent. While local business groups are becoming increasingly organized and vocal, the principal impetus for change has been the donors and the Bretton Woods institutions, which inevitably elicits some suspicion that foreign remedies are being transposed without sufficient understanding of the local context.

From its very beginning, the ADB Group has supported the private sector through loans to development finance companies for on-lending to small and medium enterprise. By 1989, it had committed $1.63 billion to sixty-five such companies.[25] However, most of these intermediaries were state-owned, which contributed to bureaucratic inefficiencies, political interference, and a neglect of profitability. When combined with the weak economic situation, this has led to generally poor performance.

Of course, much of the Bank's infrastructure support has provided indirect assistance to the private sector, while many of its agricultural projects targeted private smallholders. But in the late 1980s, the Bank joined the move toward a more active focus on private sector development. Perhaps its most important instruments were the policy-based loans, generally cofinanced with the World Bank and therefore strongly private sector–oriented. In this way it provided at least tacit, but often explicit, endorsement of this new theme in development assistance.

The ADB Group has also made a conscious effort to promote the capacity of African suppliers to participate in the implementation of its projects. It assisted in the establishment of the Federation of African Consultants, which is housed at its headquarters. Local suppliers have been given a slight cost advantage in the comparison of tenders, and procurement from regional members has consistently accounted for about one-half of total disbursements. This is significantly higher than at the World Bank, where African countries captured only 37 percent of total disbursements to the region in fiscal years 1993 and 1994.

The Bank has gone further to begin direct support to private entrepreneurs. It started in 1986 with the launching of the African Project Development Facility (APDF) in collaboration with the International Finance Corporation (IFC) of the World Bank Group and the UNDP. This facility helps African entrepreneurs develop their project ideas, locate investment partners, and arrange financing. By the end of 1993, financial packages had been completed for 163 projects representing an estimated total investment of $270 million.[26] Although the IFC is the executing agency, the ADB Group is the regional sponsor and sits on the advisory committee.

Since 1991, the ADB Group has also been in a position to provide the follow-up financing for some APDF dossiers, among others. The Private Sector Development Unit (PSDU) was established in that year to provide loans and occasionally equity investment for private enterprise without government guarantees.[27] About $210 million was earmarked for an initial four-year period, to be allocated in amounts between $140,000 and $15 million per project. The PSDU has as an explicit objective to encourage cofinancing, so its contribution to any one project cannot exceed 30 percent of the total investment (25 percent in the case of equity participation).

Similar initiatives at other regional development banks have had a slow start, and this one was no exception. By the end of 1993, fifteen projects had been supported for a total ADB investment of approximately $63 million (see Table 7.3). Thus, more than halfway through its first four-year phase, only 30 percent of PSDU's resource envelope had been committed. The very problem the unit is meant to address—the weakness of the African private sector—renders it

Table 7.3   PSDU Approved Projects, 1991–1993 (in millions of dollars)

Year	Country	Project Name	Project Cost	ADB Investment Loan	Equity
1991	Morocco	Locust bean processing	4.6	1.3	
	Regional	Meridien Bank	75.0		7.5
1992	Côte d'Ivoire	Paper production	1.0	0.3	
	Cameroon	Fertilizer plant	2.1	0.6	
	Nigeria	Yarn production	18.7	5.0	
	Senegal	Fish processing	15.7	4.7	
	Swaziland	Pharmaceuticals	7.0	2.3	
1993	Guinea	Pineapple plantation	8.4	1.8	0.1
	Guinea	Flour mill	7.1	2.0	
	Côte d'Ivoire	Instant-coffee production	22.9	6.4	1.2
	Ghana	Particleboard production	8.1	1.7	
	Mali	Food complex	3.1	0.7	
	Cameroon	Shrimp fishing	10.8	3.6	
	Nigeria	Oil field development	72.0	10.0	
	Egypt	Car assembly plant	52.0	14.0	

Source: ADB Group, Annual Report, various years.

difficult to identify sound proposals and to find suitable partners, even with some help from the APDF. The PSDU has also had diffi-culty getting letters of assurances from African governments. These are required to protect bank investments from restrictions, seizure, or foreclosure, as well as to grant tax exemptions on earnings from equi-ty investments by the Bank.

The PSDU seems to be gathering speed, and once it is running at full steam it should make a useful contribution to private sector development. Its intervention will be especially welcome in many smaller countries where local financial markets are too thin to handle large private sector financial needs. Several of the countries where it has already been involved (Guinea, Mali, Senegal, and Ghana) would seem prima facie to fall into this category. At the same time, some larger loans, like those in Nigeria and Egypt, will be necessary to defray administrative costs and reduce portfolio risk.

The total resources of the PSDU remain very small, so they will have to be used strategically. The unit must resist the temptation to concentrate on the easier, more developed countries where it may simply crowd out other sources of financing. It must maximize its leverage, using its funds and good reputation to attract other foreign financiers. And its experience must be exploited elsewhere in the Bank. In particular, the lessons learned could be well worthwhile if applied in the context of structural adjustment programs. The record of such policy-based lending has been particularly disappointing in the area of privatization and financial sector reform.

The Bank may have a special advantage in promoting foreign investment. Such private resource flows are again playing a big role in other parts of the Third World but have been very slow to enter Africa. Both investors and host governments are wary, if not positively suspicious, of each other and cognizant of past experiences that turned sour. With the improving policy environment, there is greater potential for mutually beneficial investment, but there may be a need for an intermediary, such as the ADB, that enjoys the confidence of both sides and can intervene when necessary to smooth out problems. Indeed, the Bank has already been called on to fill this role. When a government changed its regulations after an investor had committed himself to a PSDU project, senior management succeeded in working out a compromise with the appropriate minister.

The PSDU's ability to offer equity financing could be very important, since this is especially scarce in Africa. However, the Bank's past experience with equity investments in the public sector has not been encouraging, so some members of the board are pressing for a more thorough policy review on this form of financing before it is expanded. The extra risks of lending to the private sector without government guarantees give cause for concern, especially in view of the Bank's current financial status. This point was soon brought home when the largest beneficiary of the unit's equity participation, the Meridien Bank, went bankrupt in 1995. The PSDU will also have to avoid the very problems that so many ADB-supported development finance companies have suffered over the years. In particular, it will have to think and act like a successful private bank, minimizing bureaucratic process and avoiding political interference.

Given the different nature of private sector lending, it may well be more appropriate in the long run to have a separate, independent agency dedicated to this end, in place of the PSDU. In fact, in 1994 the Bank launched a feasibility study on the creation of an African Finance Corporation. This would presumably be a separate institution dedicated to private sector needs, an African version of the IFC. The IFC's activities in Africa remain modest and, in fact, have been declining in value over the last three years.[28] The feasibility study will have to examine its experience and determine if there are grounds for the establishment of a similar organization focused on Africa.

Another original contribution by the ADB management has been the creation of the African Business Roundtable (ABR). Initially convened to help formulate the Bank's private sector strategy, the ABR was then formally established as an independent, nonprofit organization in 1990. By 1993, it comprised over seventy-five business leaders from across the continent. Its main objectives are to publicize the profitable business opportunities opening up in Africa under economic liberalization; to attract foreign investment; to promote intra-African trade and investment; to encourage government policies conducive to private enterprise; and to project a positive and forward-looking image of Africa abroad. Promotional missions to industrialized countries have been conducted, resulting in several joint ventures. Its secretariat is located at the ADB Group headquarters, but all operating expenses are covered from membership fees.

At the other end of the size spectrum, the ADB Group is poised to provide more active support to microenterprise with the help of local NGOs. A position paper has been accepted as part of the negotiations for the seventh replenishment of the Fund. This will enable the Bank to build on its limited experience with microcredit schemes obtained in the course of its poverty alleviation projects. However, Bank management has been asked to move slowly with several pilot projects in the first instance.

The private sector, both in agriculture and in industry, will inevitably be the engine of growth in coming years. The public sector's capacity to absorb new funds is limited and unlikely to expand significantly under current fiscal constraints. Furthermore, if major additional foreign capital inflows are to materialize, they will have to come from the foreign private sector. Given the ambivalence of many African governments and the weak state of the commercial banking sector in most countries, there is undoubtedly a role for the ADB Group in private sector promotion. The Bank's unequivocal move into this field has surely helped raise the sector's legitimacy in the eyes of African officials. But with the extra risks involved, the relatively small size of most potential loans, and the sobering lessons from development finance companies, the Bank and Fund will have to make a careful assessment of their comparative advantage. It may be that their greatest role lies in the development of an enabling policy environment, including a vibrant commercial banking sector and viable capital markets. Perhaps a separate AFC is the most suitable instrument for expanded lending to the private sector, from oil field development to small enterprise promotion.[29]

Environment, Gender, and Poverty

The three emerging priorities in development assistance—environment, gender, and poverty alleviation—are closely related. Most environmental degradation in Africa is fundamentally linked to poverty. The poor are compelled, not through ignorance but as a matter of survival, to overexploit their limited natural resource base. A disproportionate share of the poor are women. Particularly in sub-Saharan Africa, women constitute the backbone of smallholder agriculture, as well as being the primary fuelwood gatherers. Thus, there can be no major improvement in environmental conditions without the active participation of women.

The manner in which these three themes have risen to the top of the agenda also recommends their joint treatment. All three have been primarily driven by the donor community. All three have found their strongest proponents among Western NGOs, whose well-organized lobbying based on grassroots support has played an important role in convincing Western governments to take up the challenge. The environmental cause has been the most successful in this respect, but a similar dynamic has been at work in the other two. Again in varying degrees, these NGOs have built on initially domestic concerns to focus attention on what were considered to be similar problems in the Third World.

The impetus has therefore been largely derived outside of Africa. In many cases, it has taken root within the continent among the burgeoning local NGO community and civil society more generally, as well as at the UNECA. However, these themes have rarely found strong advocates among African governments. Sometimes there has been outright animosity as proposals are judged to be ill informed of the domestic reality and based on inappropriate Western experiences. Poverty alleviation might seem to be the exception, since all governments attest to the high priority they attach to this obvious social goal. But even here the manner in which the issue is understood and pursued is generally very different from the model current proponents have in mind.

Thus, we have three related but distinct themes that have originated outside the continent, and certainly outside the Bank management. The nonregional executive directors, backed by the Western governors, have become the principal advocates within the Bank. Given the prevailing tensions on the board, this has presented Bank management with another challenge: how to address concerns for which the regional member states show little interest, and which at least some of their representatives consider to be nothing more than the latest donor fads, if not downright irrelevant.

In the following sections, a brief description is given of the evolution and current status of the Bank's initiatives under each heading. Since most of our questions or critiques are generic to the three topics, and often relate to other themes in this chapter, they are gathered in a separate concluding section.

Environment

Perhaps no other issue has so influenced the development agenda as that of the environment. Western NGOs have built on growing concern for domestic conditions in industrialized countries and the impact of global forces on them. From sometimes simplistic beginnings, they have elaborated an increasingly sophisticated and convincing argument that no development can be sustainable if the physical environment is being undermined in the process. In Africa in particular, they have shown how poverty is inextricably connected to environmental degradation.

While some of the earliest pressure seemed to focus more on Africa's wildlife resources than on its human poverty, there can be no doubt that the continent suffers from a fragile environment. Its soils are largely sandy and poor, not just in the extensive arid regions, which are themselves gradually spreading through a process of desertification. The mountainous terrain in the eastern and central parts of the continent is increasingly eroded. Forested areas are being depleted with dangerous consequences for both local soil fertility and regional climatic patterns. Rapid population growth together with widespread, often increasing, poverty have created a potent combination. The search for new agricultural and grazing land and the demand for fuelwood are putting incredible pressure on the rural resource base, and accelerating urbanization is adding a whole new set of problems. Such factors are raising serious concerns about the sustainability of food production and traditional energy supplies, as well as about some industrial and export activities in a growing number of countries.

The Bank Group's response started slowly, with the hiring of a Scandinavian technical assistant in the mid-1980s to serve as environmental adviser. The Socio-Environmental Division (later the Environment and Social Policy Division) was established in 1987, but as of 1990 there was still only one regular staff environmentalist, plus two technical assistants. Bank management was probably constrained by at least two different factors: the lack of demand from African member governments for what was clearly a donor-driven agenda, and the difficulty of finding African professionals to work in this new field.

However, an environment policy paper was finally approved by the board in 1990, with sectoral and procedural guidelines following a year later. By the end of 1993, there was a significant contingent of environmental specialists on staff: eight in the policy group and four in operations. The majority of these were Africans.

The central element in the Bank's environmental strategy is its project screening process. Beginning in 1992, every project in the lending program is classified in one of three categories:

I Significant environmental impact requiring detailed field review and an Environmental Impact Assessment (EIA) study

II Limited environmental impact or impacts that can be mitigated by applying specific measures or changes in the project design

III Not expected to result in adverse environmental impacts

Any project located in an environmentally sensitive area is automatically classified in the first category. Structural and sectoral adjustment programs, initially grouped in the third category, are now considered to fall into the second one. Where an EIA study is necessary, it must be completed and a summary sent to the board 120 days before the presentation of the request for loan approval. In 1992, twenty-six projects were included in category I, increasing to thirty-three in 1993. Over these two years, this represented about 18 percent of the total number of projects in the lending program.

A few projects, and more studies, specifically designed to improve the environment have also been approved. The Bank began by cofunding in 1992 the Madagascar Environmental Programme with a large consortium of donors. In 1993, it took independent action in the Mozambique Forestry and Wildlife Resources Development project and the Bazega Natural Resources Management project in Burkina Faso.

Environmentalists now regularly participate in project preparation and appraisal missions and are starting to join the programming missions where country strategies are established. The Economic Prospects and Country Programming papers must include a section on environmental issues. Staff are gradually being trained in environmental management. Studies have been completed on topics such as the management of mangrove ecosystems, and chemical hazards and toxic waste. A separate forestry policy paper was approved by the board in 1993. Work has started on the preparation of Environmental Country Profiles, eventually to be conducted for all regional members, and some staff are being trained in the use of geographical information systems (GIS) for environmental assessment.

In addition, the ADB Group helped launch the Network for Environmental and Sustainable Development in Africa (NESDA) in 1991, in collaboration with the World Bank and the UN Sudano-Sahelian Office (UNSO). Based at the Bank in Abidjan, it is managed by three African experts. This is a regional program to assist countries in designing strategic frameworks for sustainable development, including National Environmental Action Plans.

There is every reason to believe that the Bank is now committed to the environmental agenda, within the various constraints that it faces. A significant number of EIA studies are being conducted each year, at considerable expense. Projects are occasionally redesigned or even stopped as a result.[30] The policy division is now well staffed and engaged in a broad range of activities. This is probably the best example of the Bank's capacity to incorporate new issues into its normal operations.

Gender

The struggle for women's equality is much older than that for environmental protection, and it began to influence the development debate somewhat earlier. However, its impact has been more gradual, largely because it has not enjoyed the same strength within the Western NGO community. It could be argued, though, that the more basic reason was that both within that community and in the development institutions and Third World governments beyond, this movement represented a more fundamental challenge to the power of predominantly male leadership.

Whatever the explanation, the relevance of the topic in its broadest sense to African development cannot be disputed. Women dominate food production in sub-Saharan Africa and make important contributions to export crops. Sometimes they are the principal rural labor force, as men spend much of their time working (or looking for work) in the cities or mines. Especially in southern Africa, significant numbers of men are outside the country for extended periods. Important segments of urban informal activity also depend on women entrepreneurs. In many West African cities, the marketing system for local food supplies essentially rests on the shoulders of the famous "market mamas." Small and microenterprise credit schemes consistently show higher rates of repayment among female borrowers.

The economic role of women in North Africa is somewhat different, but still important. The need for social emancipation is, if anything, still greater. The situation is most serious in Algeria with the rise of Islamic fundamentalism, but generally women are less free to circulate in public and much of their economic contribution must take place in the household. As is true across the continent, the health and education of the next generation lie in the hands of women.

Explicit women in development (WID) activities began at the

Bank in 1985 with a seminar. Two years later, a senior adviser to the president on WID issues was appointed and a WID policy unit was established. An official policy paper was approved in 1990, followed by guidelines and checklists for operations staff to use in incorporating WID dimensions into projects and programs. A gender screening process was initiated for the 1992 lending program, with the objective of monitoring proposals as they pass through the various stages of the project cycle. Twenty-four projects were singled out in 1992. Although the process is less rigorous than that for the environment, some projects are delayed for board presentation pending a special mission to examine WID issues.

There have been several specialized projects devoted to women's needs. A Skills Development Project for Women was approved for The Gambia in 1989. In 1991, the board approved Strengthening of Women's Promotion Groups (Senegal), which were followed by others: Strengthening of Women's Institutional Capacities for the Promotion of Income-Generating Projects (Senegal) and Green Zones Women in Development (Mozambique). There were, however, no comparable projects in 1993.

In spite of this project activity, and considerable effort on the part of some nonregional directors, the WID issue has not been integrated into the Bank's operations and thinking to the same extent as the environment. The senior adviser on WID did not stay long enough to make a major impact, and the position was subsequently eliminated. The first members of the WID unit were special UNDP-funded technical assistants and not regular staff. It has been difficult to get staff to attend training sessions. The unit still had only four professional staff in early 1993 and no specialized WID counterparts in the operations departments. Consequently, there have been fewer strong advocates outside the unit.

WID sensitization and program implementation have been constrained by a shortage of extrabudgetary funding (through donor technical assistance funds), as well as the quite legitimate decision to work with existing operations personnel through training and the designation of WID representatives. However, this slow progress is perhaps not surprising for an institution that, in 1989, still had only one woman among its top sixty-four managers and professionals, and no women on its Board of Directors until 1993.[31]

Poverty Alleviation

The alleviation of poverty is at once the oldest and the youngest of the three issues under review. One could argue that it was the poverty of Africa that underlay the original establishment of the Bank. It was certainly an explicit preoccupation when the concessional Fund window was created in 1972 to better serve the Bank's least developed, less creditworthy member states. On the other hand, there was no particular strategy to measure the Bank's performance on this front or target the needs of the poorest citizens until October 1992.

Africa is significantly different from Latin America, where major segments of society approximate First World conditions. Income inequality is a problem in Africa, but the groups at both ends of the spectrum are smaller and less conspicuous. Poverty is so ubiquitous and development needs so all-encompassing that the notion of targeting the poor can strike some as superfluous. This can be particularly true for a development bank that is perforce called upon to concentrate on large, import-intensive infrastructure investments. Thus, the ADB Group tended to operate under the belief that all its projects, if well conceived, would contribute to poverty alleviation directly or indirectly.

Over time this approach was refined somewhat by focusing more Fund resources on the poorer countries and in certain sectors. By 1987, 90 percent of Fund financing was to go to category A members, while on a sectoral basis 40 percent was earmarked for agriculture and another 15 percent for education and health. Given the predominance of smallholders in most of rural Africa, and the neglect that the agricultural sector had suffered, this was an appropriate step in the right direction.

Policy in the area of the social sectors was more explicitly equity-oriented. The 1986 education sector policy paper made it quite clear that primary and nonformal education would be priorities, while rural areas and women would be particularly targeted. The 1987 health sector policy paper reiterated similar concerns, emphasizing primary health care, access for all, and preventive medicine. It even promised not to finance new "sophisticated hospitals."[32]

However, as conditions worsened in the 1980s, and the need for tough economic reforms could no longer be ignored, there developed a growing concern outside the Bank for the most vulnerable groups who were least able to adjust, or simply survive. The Bank joined the UNDP and the World Bank to launch the Social Dimensions of Adjustment (SDA) Program in 1988. While clearly a junior partner in this initiative, the ADB appears to have played a useful role by highlighting the need for some direct action when the World Bank was putting the highest priority on data collection and analysis. To this end, the ADB funded projects that targeted retrenched workers and microenterprise promotion, starting with The Gambia in 1988.

However, by 1990 the aid community began to conclude that the SDA Program was insufficient. With the stagnation of most economies, and the concomitant rise in the number of poor, the prevailing philosophy of development came under increasing scrutiny. For an institution that eschews explicit statements of its development model, it was nonetheless time to pay closer attention to the links between its projects and its ultimate goal.

The 1992 Poverty Alleviation Strategy and Action Programme lays out a comprehensive vision of the challenge at hand and an impressive array of changes in bank policy and procedures in response. It is clearly recognized that an integrated approach is required, covering the full range of instruments, from macroeconomic conditionality to procurement policy. While targeting the poor is a central feature, other key elements include an enabling policy framework, major sectoral priorities, private sector promotion, environmental sustainability, the involvement of NGOs and grassroots groups, participation by beneficiaries and women in particular, greater use of local resources, and expanded donor coordination. Reforms are proposed for the process of country programming as well as in every step of the project cycle through to postevaluation. A process of monitoring and reporting is to be established and various potential indicators are discussed. Once again, a screening mechanism is proposed. The idea is to identify projects with strong poverty reduction potential so that special attention is paid in the design stage to issues such as targeting, participation, labor intensity, and poverty indicators.

To date, the Bank's activities in this area have been largely confined to project funding and the preparation of a few country poverty profiles. The first formally titled "poverty alleviation" project was approved for Zambia in 1992, followed by three more in 1993—for Burundi, Uganda, and Equatorial Guinea. All involve microcredit schemes managed by NGO intermediaries directed to vulnerable groups, including women, refugees, widows, orphans, the disabled, school dropouts, retrenched civil servants, and demobilized soldiers. A total of $29.5 million in ADF loans was provided for these four projects.

The first two country poverty profiles, for Sierra Leone and Malawi, were completed in 1994. These profiles delineate the characteristics of poverty in a country, with the intention that they serve as an input into the preparation of Economic Prospects and Country Programming papers as well as a reference for individual project work. These would normally be complemented by country poverty assessment papers that review the policy environment from a poverty perspective. None had yet been completed by the Bank in 1994, though similar documentation was being collected from other organizations, notably the World Bank.

While the ADB team was in Sierra Leone preparing its first

poverty profile, it recognized the need for a supplementary document, which it called a Framework for a National Action Plan.[33] The idea was to assist governments in ensuring effective coordination of all external and internal efforts to alleviate poverty. It was concluded that two sets of strategies would be needed: one for the social, economic, and political transformation of society; the other to generate higher, more secure, and more equitable incomes. Practical mechanisms for the coordinated implementation of projects were also suggested. This innovation, which has since been repeated in Senegal, should be a welcome contribution in an increasingly crowded field.

Few of the other proposals in the ambitious strategy have yet been pursued. This is partly because staff resources have been severely constrained. Whereas the strategy called for eighteen additional professionals spread across the Bank (an admittedly unrealistic figure), there was still only one social policy specialist working on poverty alleviation in 1995. With the worsening financial situation of the Bank, it has not been possible to go any further.

This theme could be the most complex of any under review here. If one attempts to break down the population by income levels, target the poorest groups quite specifically, and then track the distribution of costs and benefits, the data requirements alone could be extremely challenging. The analysis of different policy options would be even more demanding, involving macroeconomic models and not a few brave assumptions. Meanwhile, the systematic adoption of truly participatory approaches could turn the Bank inside out, with uncertain consequences.

But it may not be necessary or appropriate to make things so complicated in the short term. For one thing, the data are often simply not available or else not reliable. For another, the poor are often quite uniform and widespread across certain regions or sectors. And third, a development bank is not usually the best vehicle for meeting the needs of the truly destitute. The ADB Group could do a lot simply by ensuring that it focuses on key sectors, favors the most equitable forms of intervention in those sectors (e.g., smallholder food production or basic education), and works hard at improving the effectiveness of these operations. (The latter might well include community participation.) If this were coupled with policy dialogue with governments, many of whom continue to pay only lip service to this theme, the results could be significant.

Governance

The latest, and possibly largest, wave to break onto the shores of the ADB Group is that of good governance. Perhaps it would be more accurate to describe it as a series of waves, representing democratization, human rights, and governance in its narrower sense. Like so many of the previous waves, it has been pushed by strong winds from the West, but there is much more to it. It is also a wave sweeping across Africa on the basis of local breezes and not a few gales. As such, it is a force that the ADB Group cannot ignore.

Historically, issues of good governance have been associated with state sovereignty and therefore have not been an overt factor in aid relationships between donors or bankers and recipients. The pressure for change emanated from many sources. Structural adjustment programs were inevitably drawn into issues like the functioning of economic institutions, the role of the state, the size and relationship of that role to the private sector, and the allocation and management of budget resources. When these programs failed to live up to donor expectations, the international community was forced to look farther afield for explanations. The UNECA, in its critique of conventional SAPs, called for greater attention to governance issues, notably the role of the military, the size of defense expenditures, and the respect of human rights.[34] Meanwhile, the collapse of the former Soviet Union shifted the focus of development assistance from Cold War concerns, clearing the way for more attention to long-standing problems of dictatorial regimes and human rights abuse.

Within Africa, deteriorating standards of living, economic mismanagement and corruption, widespread human rights violations, and the absence of institutional arrangements for the orderly change of governments generated a demand for change. Finally, by virtue of its high dependency on external aid, sub-Saharan Africa is more amenable than other Third World regions to pressure from donors.[35] It has therefore been easier to introduce noneconomic considerations into policy dialogue.

Governance defies tight definition. Some would limit it to a notion of corporate governance—the framework of laws, regulatory practices, and reporting requirements. The more widely accepted understanding of the term incorporates at least three aspects: the nature of the political regime; the process by which authority is exercised in the management of a country's economic and social resources; and the capacity of a government to design and implement policies and discharge functions. Thus defined, governance covers a broad spectrum of national life, from economic management to democratization and participatory development to human rights.[36]

The Charter of the ADB, like that of most other multilateral development banks, discourages the institution from applying political considerations in the course of its lending decisions.[37] Given the diverse nature of the regimes represented among its shareholders, such a restriction seemed essential to avoid divisive ideological debates that would distract it from its true mandate. It was also assumed that economic development could be promoted more or less in abstraction from "politics." While the former point remains a very real concern, the latter has been generally dismissed as simplistic.

The World Bank was the first multilateral bank to raise the issue of African governance explicitly, if somewhat reluctantly, starting with its 1989 Long-Term Perspective Study.[38] It has chosen to concentrate on improving the performance, accountability, and transparency of economic management in recipient governments. The ADB Group, which is more responsive to the will of its borrowing members, has even less room for maneuver than the World Bank. With both the presidency and the vice-presidencies essentially determined by these members, senior management is naturally reluctant to push too hard. It has already been seen, in the Kenya case study in Chapter 5, how the Bank was a reluctant participant in the 1991 donor sanctions intended to advance the democratization process in that country.

Thus, the ADB Group is now called upon to walk a fine line between the promotion of good governance and political interference. To date, the main avenue for addressing governance issues has been policy-based lending operations. Here the ADB Group has by and large adopted most of the World Bank proposals for reform in areas such as civil service administration, privatization, decentralization, budget transparency, expenditure management, and accountability. However, there is as yet no evidence of a strong leadership role in this respect.

In its poverty alleviation strategy, the Bank has recently promised a variety of changes that in effect represent a wider involvement in governance issues. These include an emphasis on participatory approaches to development, a greater role for women, and more collaboration with NGOs. In fact, the decision to promote a poverty focus, including the monitoring of governments' performance, is an important new entry point in the promotion of good governance. It could have significant implications if, as indicated in the strategy, a government's willingness to pursue poverty-reducing measures is used as one criterion in adjusting ADF lending targets.[39] Once again, not much can be said about the track record to date.

These tentative contributions are unlikely to satisfy many member states and observers, outside Africa or within. Indicative of the topic's high priority, the newly established ADB African Advisory Council chose as its first theme "the democratization process and governance." This council is intended to be a permanent revolving body of eminent Africans whose function is to advise the Bank on critical areas of development policy. In their first report, submitted in early 1994, they justify their choice on the grounds that "the success of the development enterprise itself is dependent on the consolidation of democracy, as well as on the existence of good governance" and that "the Bank, although primarily a financial institution, has, of necessity, to be involved in these two sets of issues."[40]

The council offers a wide-ranging set of recommendations for Bank involvement in promoting democracy, which can be summarized as greater attention to employment generation and poverty alleviation, education, the private sector, political and economic integration, the establishment of an endogenous science and technology base, and research. To foster good governance, the council proposes comprehensive policy advice to regional members, projects, and programs that address the issue in a more integrated and direct manner than the ADB's traditional adjustment programs, research, and training activities to develop principles consistent with African values and norms and better coordination and harmonization by the Bank of the international development community's efforts in this field. The council rejects the idea of "negative conditionalities" as a means to promote their objectives, opting instead for the provision of additional resources to reward positive performance.

Thus, at a time when the Bank is already grappling with a full slate of issues new and old, its African advisers have added a few more. Furthermore, its declining concessional resources constrain its flexibility to shift priorities, let alone adopt new ones. This also implies that any move to link country allocations to good governance is likely to appear as one based on penalties rather than rewards.

But this issue cannot be ignored. It is as important to many average Africans as it is to the Advisory Council. It is also an area in which many non-Africans are becoming increasingly involved, even though the potential role for imported solutions has rarely been smaller. The Bank must find a way to respond and to contribute its African perspective. Somehow, governance issues will have to be factored into its country allocations, perhaps through the lens of their impact on country risk. The issues will need to be considered in specific projects and programs, particularly via adjustment lending. The World Bank may have a headstart in this field, but they have found few solutions so far. The past experience of many ADB staff inside African governments should give them an advantage in introducing appropriate institutional changes.[41]

Ultimately, this may be an issue Omar Kabbaj chooses to take on as his own. It is so complex, so delicate, and yet so fundamental to long-term development that it calls for leadership from the top. There will also be great pressure to hide behind the Bank's charter.

An Emerging Pattern

For each new theme, the Bank has demonstrated a willingness to embrace issues of interest to the donor community even though most of its borrowers attached a low priority to them at the time. Policy papers have been developed, new staff recruited, old staff trained, specialized projects funded, and new procedures adopted. In this way, the Bank has undoubtedly helped promote an awareness of issues within Africa and, indeed, their very legitimacy. When only Northern donors are pushing such agendas, it is easy for recalcitrant governments to dismiss them as just another foreign fad. When they are not just a fad, the ADB Group is in a special position to cut through at least this initial prejudice, obliging governments to deal with the issues on their merit.

The Bank should also be well placed to translate these sometimes delicate issues into a language that African counterparts better understand. The environmental movement has long created consternation, not to say outright hostility. For some it appeared to place the needs of animals above those of people; for others it prevented African countries from exploiting the same development path Western nations enjoyed. The Bank has been careful to stress the link between the environment and poverty, as did so many Third World nations at the UN Conference on Environment and Development in Rio de Janeiro in 1992. It is a link that Northern agencies still sometimes overlook when setting their priorities.

The same applies to gender issues. African women generally occupy a social status from which Western women escaped many years ago. This should not be surprising, given the respective levels of female (and male) education, female labor force participation in the formal sector, urbanization, and fertility rates. Obviously, judging from Western experience, it will take a long time for this to change, though probably not as long. The Bank may be more sensitive to the realistic pace of change.[42] And yet, there is something unsettling about all this new activity. For one thing, one wonders how much of an impact is actually being made. The EPCP papers now carefully include general sections on environment, women, and poverty in the country in question, but when it comes time to outline the Bank's lending program and priorities, they scarcely surface. At best, they are three more variables in a long list.

The environment, and to a lesser extent WID, have also benefited from a significant share of new professional hiring, but most of it has been concentrated in the central policy division. With the exception of the two managers involved, the staff has been recruited from outside the Bank, therefore having little feel for the conditions under which their policies and guidelines must be implemented. Meanwhile, project officers have complained that these new considerations exacerbated their workload at a time when high lending targets (and the resultant mass of ongoing projects) made it difficult for them to execute their existing responsibilities. Such conditions are hardly conducive to a serious treatment of the issues.

The Private Sector Development Unit also represents a significant diversion of staff resources. It enjoyed a professional staff of twelve in 1993, but could only generate loans totaling $40.3 million that year (see Table 7.2). Indeed, it was considered to suffer from a shortage of personnel.[43] Private sector lending, like most of these other issues, is clearly human resource intensive.

The centralized nature of the Bank has further impeded its capacity to follow up on its declared intentions. In such areas, where it is actively promoting new priorities and a change in government behavior, its typically responsive approach to project development is unlikely to be adequate. To be convincing, its staff must be in more regular dialogue with national officials and possess a stronger understanding of the local conditions. They must also have more opportunities to meet with NGOs, women's groups, community organizations, and the like. Certainly, the commitment to enhanced poverty alleviation through a more participatory approach to programming and project design cannot be fulfilled when all the decisionmaking authority rests in Abidjan. Nor will it be easy to make small private sector loans efficiently and effectively long distance. The 1994 decision to close all the Bank's satellite offices only exacerbated the situation.

One also has to be concerned about what has happened to the Bank's process of planning and prioritization. It is striking that policy papers, country profiles, training seminars, and even some staff are funded through special agreements with various donor agencies. USAID financed the poverty alleviation strategy, UNDP paid for WID staff, Canada supported the production of WID monographs, and Norway covered the cost of the first environmental country profiles. The Bank is committing itself to courses of action without having the requisite budget. Management has been encouraged to lay out ambitious programs and then go out and try to raise the additional resources necessary. This process can be very time-consuming for staff, while the final results depend greatly on the priorities of individual bilateral agencies.

More important, the institution's core budget, its managers, and its operations personnel are being pulled in many directions. The Bank seems to be constantly scrambling to meet new donor expectations, while last year's commitments are still filtering down to the staff. If supervision missions and disbursement procedures have been neglected, part of the explanation probably lies in the plethora of new issues that have emerged year after year, each one perfectly legitimate in its own right, each one suggesting a variety of exciting new initiatives, but all distracting from improvements in basic functions.

The current era of financial cutbacks will ease some constraints but aggravate others. Existing staff will have more time to incorporate some of the new ideas and procedures, though there will be less room for hiring new staff. The recent strategy for poverty alleviation is particularly out of proportion to the additional human resources likely to be available. It will have to be scaled back to match the new fiscal reality.

There will also be fewer of the concessional Fund resources that are used for specialized projects in most of these areas. Borrowing members may be reluctant to use their allocations for environmental or women's projects if it means squeezing out public utility or agricultural ones. If this encourages the Bank to integrate such issues into "traditional" projects rather than developing stand-alone actions, this may be the more appropriate long-term approach. On the other hand, if an increasing share of declining resources is devoted to a donor-driven agenda, the very legitimacy of the Bank may be called into question for some of its borrowing members.

One is struck by the fact that the ADB Group always seems to be trying to catch up with the World Bank. A new issue gains prominence at the World Bank, and the next year it must receive special attention in Abidjan. This is probably because the nonregional board members tend to look to the World Bank as the leading institution in the field and an example to follow. Some ADB managers likely feel the same way, often with good reason. But it seems impossible for the ADB Group to replicate everything the much larger and richer World Bank decides to do. More fundamentally, if it is to make a strong and original contribution, it must focus on themes that are more "homegrown," ones about which the management and staff can get truly excited.

It seems that the ADB Group is caught in the turbulence created by the confluence of waves from many different directions: the debt problem, regional integration, private sector development, women, the environment, poverty alleviation, and now governance. One could add the role of NGOs, participatory approaches, AIDS, and population.[44] All are eminently worthy in their own right. Yet one wonders if the Bank, especially in its weakened condition of 1995, might be overloaded and in danger of capsizing. Bank management and the shareholders must ultimately decide what they think can be accomplished given the resources available. Nonetheless, in the following, concluding chapter we offer a few ideas based on our assessment of the Bank's performance to date.

Notes

1. World Bank, *African Development Indicators 1994–95,* p. 172.
2. World Bank, *World Debt Tables 1994/95,* vol. 1, p. 216, for sub-Saharan Africa; vol. 2 for individual country tables for North Africa.
3. Ibid.
4. There has been little change in this ratio since 1989, the first year for which such data are available. Ibid.
5. These are nominal values for debt as opposed to present values. Ibid.
6. World Bank, *World Debt Tables 1994/95.*
7. Uganda, Tanzania, Mozambique, Guinea-Bissau, São Tomé and Principe, and Madagascar. Ibid.
8. World Bank, *Reducing the Debt Burden of Poor Countries.*
9. A slightly revised version of the Trinidad terms, labeled the Naples terms, was adopted in January 1995. Perhaps it will have more success.
10. The IMF did introduce more lenient terms under its Structural Adjustment Facility (SAF), which was subsequently enhanced as ESAF. However, normal interest rates still apply to its traditional standby and compensatory finance facilities and to SDR use.
11. G. K. Helleiner, "External Resource Flows, Debt Relief and Economic Development in Sub-Saharan Africa," in Cornia and Helleiner, *From Adjustment to Development in Africa.*
12. For more information see an ADB staff memorandum to the Board of Directors dated June 15, 1994, entitled "Arrears Situation and Perspectives on Recovery Efforts."
13. The threshold for a sustainable debt load is defined as present-value-of-debt to exports equal to 200 percent. World Bank, *Reducing the Debt Burden of Poor Countries,* pp. 61–62.
14. Helleiner, "External Resource Flows," in Cornia and Helleiner, p. 16.
15. Excluding South Africa. The GDP for all of Africa is comparable to that of Austria and Sweden combined. Calculations based on 1990 GDP figures in the World Bank's *World Development Report 1992.*
16. ADB Group, "Regional Development Finance Institutions and Economic Integration," p. 18.
17. ADB Group, *African Development Report 1993,* p. 185.
18. Calculated from various ADB Group annual reports.
19. Calculated from various ADB Group annual reports. Including the $25 million equity investment in the African Export-Import Bank would raise this figure to 1.2 percent. The cumulative share of multinational projects from 1965 to 1993 is 1.8 percent.
20. There was also a grant involving a program of support to seventeen research institutes, but this had little to do with regional integration.
21. ADB Group, *Study on Economic Integration in Southern Africa in a Post-Apartheid Period.*
22. ADB Group, *African Development Report 1993.*

23. To maintain the agreed public-private balance in the capital base, the authorized capital was increased to $750 million and a special effort made to ensure that much of the additional capital came from private sources. See "Africa's New Trade Bank 'a Living Reality'," *Africa Recovery* 7, no. 1 (1992): 34. By 1995, at least the minimum private capital sought had been attracted.

24. The topic has a very low profile in drafts of the World Bank's latest strategy statement on sub-Saharan Africa, "Africa's Development Strategy Revisited."

25. ADB Group, *1989 Annual Report.*

26. International Finance Corporation, *The African Project Development Facility*, p. 5.

27. Joint private-public enterprises can also be considered, provided the government has a minority share of the capital and the firm enjoys managerial autonomy.

28. IFC lending and equity investments in sub-Saharan Africa declined to $157 million in FY 1994 from $193 million in FY 1993 and close to $290 million in FY 1992. Note, however, that the number of projects increased from forty-five in 1993 to fifty-seven in 1994. No separate figures were available for North Africa. IFC, *1994 Annual Report*, p. 31.

29. The IFC already operates the Africa Enterprise Fund specifically for small and medium-scale firms and planned to launch a new initiative for microenterprise in FY 1995. Ibid., p. 30.

30. A road project in Cameroon was redesigned and the most controversial section excluded, albeit after considerable pressure from a Canadian NGO. Another road project in Côte d'Ivoire was stopped at least temporarily pending further analysis.

31. The 1989 figure is derived from Annex 2 of the Policy Paper on Women in Development. The first woman ED was a Canadian, followed shortly by the new ED from the United States.

32. It did leave the door open to consider the rehabilitation or extension of such facilities. ADB Group, *Health Sector Policy Paper*, p. 25.

33. ADB Group, "Poverty Alleviation Policy and Experience," p. 6.

34. UNECA, "African Alternative Framework" and "The Khartoum Declaration," both published in 1989.

35. ODA accounts for about 10 percent of GDP in sub-Saharan Africa, compared to 1.5 percent for all low- and middle-income countries.

36. See, for example, OECD, *DAC Orientations in Participatory Development and Good Governance* (Paris: OECD, 1993).

37. The most recent addition to this group, the European Bank for Reconstruction and Development, is somewhat different in this respect.

38. World Bank, *Sub-Saharan Africa: From Crisis to Sustainable Growth.*

39. ADB Group, "Poverty Alleviation Strategy and Action Programme," p. 22.

40. ADB Group, "The Democratization Process in Africa, Governance, and the Role of the African Development Bank," p. 1.

41. Their greater penchant for using local consultants, many of whom are former senior government officials, will also help.

42. In one cofunded rice irrigation project, the other financier was pushing hard to prevent men from capturing some of the benefits from the rising yields in a crop traditionally grown by women. ADB staff countered that one could not isolate rural Muslim women from their social context. The women were benefiting from the improvements generated by the project, but they could not be expected to monopolize them; indeed, they did not want to.

43. ADB Group, "Status Report on Implementation of the Private Sector Development Program," p. 4.

44. A policy paper on population was discussed by the board in 1993 but sent back for revisions.

8

THE WAY AHEAD

The African Development Bank Group must persevere. It must continue to struggle with the problems that surround it, both within and without. If there is one defining feature of African underdevelopment, it is the lack of indigenous capacity to master the crises that continually beset it. The ADB Group represents one key effort to build capacity within the continent, and on this score it has been successful—an impressive capacity has been built. The Bank Group is arguably a critical link in the struggle to build capacity in borrowing member countries as well. The nonregional shareholders must continue to support the institution if they are serious about helping Africans help themselves. Regional shareholders must rise to the present challenge if they are serious about taking charge of their own destiny.

In these days of constant change, capacity building is a never-ending process. Nowhere is this more true than in Africa, which is still so far behind most of the world in economic and institutional development, a world that now evolves at incredible speed. Some shareholders appear frustrated that the job is not yet complete. Some others on the board and the staff seem to think that the task is largely accomplished. Both groups must rise to the new challenges facing the institution, demonstrating their capacity to grow and to contribute to the difficult process of qualitative institutional growth, regardless of what happens quantitatively to either the lending target or the staff size.

But capacity building is only a means to an end. After thirty years, the ADB Group must be able to point to the impact it is having on the development of the African continent and, more fundamentally, on the lives of ordinary people. We have argued that there is some such evidence. Significant financial resources are being channeled to the region, roads are being built and used, agricultural yields are improving, and new ideas are emerging. However, it is still very difficult to pinpoint the extra and unique contribution the ADB Group is making.

In this final chapter, we draw together the various strands presented over the course of the book and look ahead to how the ADB Group might enhance its contribution and justify this long capacity-building exercise. While the primary purpose of this study has been to evaluate the institution's historical record, no evaluation is complete without some lessons for the future. Furthermore, the past always serves as one reliable guide in a forward-looking discussion. In this perhaps ambitious endeavor, we begin modestly at the level of project lending and gradually build up to some final thoughts on the role of the ADB Group in Africa's development. Along the way, we touch on the financial status of the Bank Group, its governance structure, and the people who make it run.

The Basic Building Blocks: Projects and Personnel

It is worth repeating that projects are the foundation on which the ADB Group is built. This is partly because of their role in absorbing and replenishing the resources of the Bank. It is also because through projects one gains an understanding of how development succeeds. Even though policy reform may sometimes take priority, its ultimate importance lies in the fact that it facilitates success at the project level. This is worth repeating because project work has been rather neglected over the last ten years. In the excitement of expanding lending targets, worldwide resource mobilization, administrative reform, program lending, and emerging development issues, project lending was treated as one area where the house was generally in order.

Yet the Task Force on Project Quality has emphasized that the house's foundations are not in good shape. This is also our own conclusion, if in somewhat less apocalyptic terms. The project departments have not been given adequate resources to do their job properly. In the face of rapidly rising targets, they have not had sufficient professional expertise of the type and quality they need. Staff from a previous era have been kept on without retraining while there were few opportunities to bring in new blood. Insufficient supervision missions and inadequate field offices have deprived staff of essential information to guide project implementation. Lack of time and encouragement from management has detracted from efforts to draw lessons systematically; lack of coordination with the programming departments has discouraged the informal process of feeding past experience into future project selection.

The reorganization approved in early 1995 attempts to respond to some of the deficiencies identified here and in the Knox Report. The project departments are to receive a greater proportion of available staff, some older or underperforming staff will be released, and new staff will be hired. The board has wisely resisted the temptation to impose major cuts in overall staff levels in spite of the fall in lending. The project and country programming departments are to be combined in five subregional groups, with teams established for each country. Management has been streamlined, with a promise that more authority will be delegated. Finally, a commitment has been made to change the culture of the Bank to one that focuses on quality.

This reorganization is very promising. However, it can be judged only by its implementation: who is let go, who fills the new management positions, and how principles like "delegation of authority" and "a focus on quality" will be interpreted. There are also other issues that cannot be addressed through such an exercise. At the risk of some repetition, we would make the following additional recommendations:

1.   The project operations component of the new subregional departments must be given special priority in personnel policy. A special effort should be made to increase the number of women and to supplement scarce skills through greater recruitment of non-Africans. The difficult process of removing weak employees must be pursued vigorously, and subsequent rewards of salary, promotions, and training should be more closely tied to merit in order to derive the maximum from the many good people on staff.

2.   One way or another, more attention must be paid to supervision missions. Executing agencies are generally weak and unstable and require regular contact with experts like those at the ADB Group. Those same experts need the on-the-job training that comes only from such on-the-ground experience. In the face of serious resource limitations, this will probably mean ignoring the fortunate few projects with strong institutional homes or good supervision from other cofunders. But even in weaker settings, this does not mean hands-on interference that effectively undermines local ownership of projects and programs.

3.   A permanent local presence is essential in as many countries as possible. If all the regional and country offices have been closed, it is because the model was defective, not the principle. As the Task Force on Project Quality has emphasized, the borrowers crave a greater presence by the ADB Group. That task force is probably right to promote the concept of country offices rather than regional ones. But new country offices must be given high-quality staff with both

responsibility and accountability. Such postings must not be seen as career-limiting moves. Perhaps they could be made a prerequisite for anyone aspiring to an eventual position in management. All managers could certainly benefit from a refresher course in the "real world" beyond Abidjan. The Bank would do well to start with some of the smallest countries where it plays a relatively large role and where it could do much more.

4.   More attention should be paid to analytical sector work to improve understanding of policy and other limitations projects face, facilitate the selection of good projects, and feed into sectoral adjustment lending. This would build on the Bank's extensive project experience better than does structural adjustment lending. It would require more economics expertise, but at least some of this could come from the programming departments.

5.   Greater sectoral work will probably have to come at the expense of macroeconomic policy-based lending. The Bank has been trying to increase its macroeconomic expertise for several years now, but it is still not able to contribute more than money to many of the programs it is supporting. In part, this is because it is competing head-on with the IMF and the World Bank. It should focus on those cases where it can make a difference and offer ideas and knowledge of its own, especially in light of the declining finances at its disposal. Its best economists should be assigned to the smaller countries that are serious about reform but lack national expertise comparable to that at the Bank. For the time being, this should still be pursued jointly with the Bretton Woods institutions and other donors, not in isolation. Indeed, the ADB could make a major contribution by providing a second opinion to that of the Washington-based institutions, where local officials do not yet have that capacity—and ultimately by building that capacity.

6.   The results of postevaluations must be incorporated more effectively in new project lending. These reports have been raising warning flags for years with little apparent impact. The recent decision to have the Operations Evaluation Office report directly to the Board of Directors may help, but only if the directors decide to use the information. Economic Prospects and Country Programming papers are now supposed to include data from postevaluations, but this policy is not yet being honored systematically. A similar policy should be adopted, and enforced, for project appraisal reports.

7.   Until 1994, there was one other crucial factor hindering improvements in the quality of lending, and that was the quantity of lending. With targets rising rapidly until 1992, it was virtually impossible to devote more time and effort to the different stages of the project cycle. Nor could managers afford to lose much staff to retraining.

Finally, the pressure has been removed, at least temporarily. Management should view this not as a crisis but as an opportunity; project staff certainly do. With complementary reforms along the lines described above, a real change could be made. If and when resources become available again, the temptation to make up for lost ground through future expansion of the lending program should be avoided until it is clear that the reforms are taking hold.

The Engineers and Architects: Management and the Board

To achieve these changes, a revitalized management will be required, together with a new understanding between them and the Board of Directors, and among the directors. The recent reorganization contains some of the elements. Empowering senior managers to appoint their immediate subordinates, and so on down the hierarchy, could work if the right precautions are taken. The move to reduce the number of vice-presidents from five to three and to decrease the size of the president's office are also promising. This should help build a cohesive senior management team. However, other measures should also be considered:

1.   The vice-presidencies should be made career positions appointed by the president. Without this, the president will inevitably have lingering doubts about vice-presidents' loyalty, undermining other team-building efforts. If vice-presidents wish to compete against their president for that position, they should be required to resign one year beforehand to avoid internal conflict.

2.   A clearer division of labor is needed between the president and the Board of Directors. The president should be allowed to manage, but ways must be found to judge the results more effectively. If the Bank is mandated to take on new tasks, the necessary resources should also be approved. The board needs to focus on Bank policies, define a more coherent strategy, and then assume that management will respect its decisions (with regular progress reports). Such confidence probably requires that both the board and management be more realistic in what is accepted.

3.   Somehow, the Board of Directors must learn to achieve greater consensus in its deliberations. In particular, the wall between regional and nonregional directors must be torn down once and for all. There is no guaranteed solution here. Term limits of six to eight years are probably part of the answer, as some of the regional members are too close to the past problems of the Bank and too far from

the current problems of their constituencies. In contrast, an increase in the normal term to say four years may be helpful for both nonregional directors and those regional representatives who regularly rotate. This will help them develop greater familiarity with the Bank and each other.

4.   It would also be preferable to have a smaller board. Besides the fact that is may be impossible to develop consensus on a regular basis among eighteen members plus the president, the cost of the current arrangement is too onerous as a share of total administrative expenses, especially given the tight financial situation. The AsDB and the IDB each had only twelve members until 1994 (when the IDB added two more).

5.   The regional member states must be encouraged to take a greater interest in the health of "their bank." More frequent participation by some governors, through a subcommittee of some kind, would be a good start, as would more extensive contact at a technical level between senior management and government officials. Perhaps nothing would work as well as the regular presence that comes from small country offices.

6.   At long last, it is time to clarify the relationship between the president and the Board of Directors. He or she should be appointed and, when necessary, dismissed only by the Board of Governors. The power of the Board of Directors in the latter regard has dogged the Bank's history for too long.

7.   The imbalance between the voting shares of regional and nonregional members is no longer tenable. Nonregional callable capital is sustaining the AAA rating of the Bank; grants from nonregionals have always been the essence of the Fund. Now there is an urgent need to increase the proportion of concessional Fund resources available, but one cannot expect these to be forthcoming under current circumstances. A fifty-fifty split in the voting shares of regionals and nonregionals would better reflect reality, especially if the boards of the Bank and the Fund were combined, as they are in all other multilateral banks. Such a change might also guarantee that all nonregional members would view the Bank as theirs too, bringing subtle but significant changes in their behavior.

8.   There remains the broader accountability of the Bank to the taxpayers who ultimately sustain it and the citizens it ultimately serves. If the Bank is to compete with NGOs and bilateral programs for the extra dollar of support, it will have to reach out more to explain itself and justify its existence among nonregional members. Their EDs should do more by way of public reporting in their constituencies, representing as they do a wealth of inside knowledge. With the spread of democracy and the rise of civil society in Africa,

the Bank must be no less sensitive to the needs of African citizens. If the Bank is to serve as a model to which others might aspire, rather than as a target of jealousy, regional EDs and Bank staff will have to respond to the new political openness with an outreach program of their own.

Paying the Bills: Mobilizing and Managing Money

The investment climate in which the ADB Group must operate is terribly difficult, hardly attractive to foreign capital. The Bank Group has the advantage of being able to spread its risks across the continent, but it is still confined to the poorest continent in the world. In the eyes of international finance, that is not much of an advantage. Fortunately, the Bank has had the backing of the world's strongest economies, in the form of the nonregional shareholders, which counts for rather more in the money market.

The nonregional members have been generous in mobilizing resources for the benefit of the ADB Group, and those resources have grown at an impressive rate. One must remember that nonregionals have been the ultimate source of this growth, even if many African members have gradually increased their capital subscriptions as well. The Bank's borrowing operations and its financial policies have generally been two of its stronger elements, even though they have lagged behind those of the World Bank. The growth in resources has been due neither to the Bank's lending practices, which have been more liberal, nor to its financial results, which have been very modest. Now, the nonregional members are becoming less generous, while the economic environment has yet to improve. Under some pressure from these same members, the Bank has recently made important improvements in its financial policies. In order to maintain the crucial support of nonregionals, as well as that of the international capital markets, the Bank will have to go further still. But when it does, the nonregional members should be prepared to hold up their share of the bargain.

In our view, the Bank should take the following steps:

1. As a prerequisite to at least some of the necessary changes, management and the regional members of the Bank will have to take a greater interest in its financial health. In general, they have shown a remarkable complacency about the problems facing the Bank, with the pressure for reforms coming almost exclusively from nonregional executive directors—the representatives of the minority shareholders. Both must recognize that their stake is greater still. While the

nonregionals may risk their callable capital, the borrowing members risk their reputation as bankable prospects. A financial crisis at the ADB Group will make it even more difficult for them to attract loans and investment capital in the future. Management risks its careers.

2.   While there are many financial indicators to track, none has quite the same impact as the level of net income. This is particularly important in the case of the ADB Group because of the need to build up reserves to cover problem loans. The Bank must take whatever measures are necessary to reverse the decline in its net income, including various incentives and penalties to encourage timely loan repayment. Borrowing members must be encouraged to consider the ADB Group as a preferred creditor, not a family member who will forgive and forget. Perhaps the most effective measure would be to secure an agreement from the World Bank and the IMF that they would not approve new balance-of-payments loans, or at least begin disbursements, until arrears to the ADB were cleared. Assessment of the financial gap to be met should, after all, incorporate repayments to the ADB Group. Furthermore, the Bretton Woods institutions also have an interest in a healthy regional bank.

3.   The Bank will have to set its own example by holding the line on administrative expenses, one of the few areas under its direct control. Given the many operational functions requiring greater resources, as outlined above, significant savings will have to be achieved in other parts of the Bank. Furthermore, cost cutting has become such a universal phenomenon across the industrialized world, not to mention Africa, that the Bank can hardly justify otherwise. The recent 50 percent devaluation of the CFA franc, the local currency in Abidjan, makes it all the more reasonable to expect budget cuts, possibly including salaries and benefits. However, staff should not be targeted until significant savings are achieved at the level of the board.

4.   Among the various measures that would reassure the capital markets and rating agencies, none would go farther than an increase in the nonregional share of authorized capital and votes, as already recommended. This would send a clear message that the strongest economies remain firmly committed to the Bank and well positioned to ensure that internationally recognized financial norms are respected.

5.   The Bank has already been under considerable pressure from its nonregional members to limit its total nonconcessional lending to levels well below those of the early 1990s, but it has been a real tug-of-war. It makes good sense to endorse openly this cautious approach, for two reasons. First, such restraint would limit the need for borrowing, keeping its liabilities under control and giving it time

to improve its financial position. Second, the external indebtedness of most regional members is simply too high to justify larger amounts of commercial borrowing on their part. Third, more aggressive lending would likely push the Bank's exposure beyond prudent levels in the few remaining countries.

6.   In addition, the Bank must adopt a more explicit country-risk policy. While some progress has been made on this front, and it is politically contentious to push further, past experience offers little choice. Too many apparently reliable members have since fallen into arrears. Internationally acceptable criteria for creditworthiness must be adopted, which will inevitably exclude most if not all low-income, category A members from Bank lending. If the ADF VII replenishment negotiations were still stuck on this point in early 1995, it was with good reason. It is neither in the interest of the Bank nor the members concerned to pursue further nonconcessional lending for the time being. Furthermore, but quite secondarily, it is unrealistic to expect the nonregional supporters to accept lending criteria fundamentally different from those of the more robust World Bank in its African operations.

7.   The nonregional members, on the other hand, have been reluctant to fulfill their obligation to assist the Bank in grappling with external factors threatening its financial viability. In particular, a trust fund facility is necessary to clear up arrears that may otherwise be intractable. If donors agreed some time ago to provide similar assistance to the much stronger World Bank, there is no obvious rationale for depriving the ADB Group of such help. The ADF VII replenishment seems likely to include something along these lines. However, it will have been several years after the World Bank was assisted and will not represent additional resources. The reluctance of the nonregional members on this front does not encourage understanding on other matters by certain regional counterparts.

8.   Indeed, the prospective fall in the value of the Fund's replenishment is equally serious, not to mention the failure of one nonregional member to honor its commitment under ADF VI. (The situation has been further aggravated by the probable loss of two full years as a result of the protracted negotiations, though here the regionals must share the responsibility.) If Bank lending is to be cut back, and borrowers encouraged to accept this, more concessional lending will be needed to meet the foreign exchange and other development requirements of regional members. Furthermore, some Fund loans inevitably provide the foreign exchange that helps borrowers repay old Bank loans. Having authorized a fourth capital increase of 200 percent, the nonregional members now have some obligation to help the ADB Group cope with the consequences. Otherwise, if

repayments begin to exceed new disbursements, creating a net resource "reflow" from the borrower to the Bank, there will be less incentive for the borrower to remain current with repayments and the Bank's arrears will only worsen. Unfortunately, donor countries seemed set to ignore these considerations during the ADF VII negotiations.

The Blueprint: Bank Strategy

The Bank is, in 1995, under incredible pressure. The Knox Report has called for much more attention to the basic lending operations of the Bank and to the identification, design, appraisal, implementation, and evaluation of projects and programs. The persistent debt crisis, regional integration, private sector development, the environment, gender issues, and poverty alleviation all demand follow-up to the preliminary steps taken so far. The Committee of Ten's 1989 vision of the Bank as a center of excellence, leading the debate on Africa's development strategy, awaits action. Now the African Advisory Council has underlined the critical importance of governance to the work of the Bank. And while each proponent recognizes that more resources will be necessary to do a proper job, the total resources available are falling rather than rising.

The time has come for some tough decisions about where the Bank is going to make a difference. It was perhaps a noble idea to try to be all things to all people, but it came at a high price. To quote the Knox Report once again, "The Bank is pulled in all directions by conflicting goals and attitudes of its shareholders. This is perhaps the most important cause of the Bank's inability to deliver quality sustainable project support to Africa."[1] The shareholders and senior management are both responsible. Everyone has pushed their own ideas without really asking what the opportunity cost would be, what sacrifices would have to be made.

Now net income has evaporated under mounting arrears. Administrative costs and staff levels will be frozen if not cut. With the prospect of lower nonconcessional lending for the foreseeable future, income from loan repayments is likely to fall even if arrears are reduced. The regrettable, but apparently inevitable, decline in concessional funds means fewer resources to back new themes once they have been adopted. Lower targets will relieve some of the pressure on Bank staff, but they will also restrict the room for follow-up lending, which is usually necessary to breathe life into new ideas. Fewer resources will focus the minds of borrowing members, rendering them less amenable to new bank initiatives that divert funds from their own priorities. Cutbacks in bilateral aid will further exacerbate the situation.

In this harsh new context, the Bank must develop a clear vision of what its comparative advantage is, where it wants to concentrate. This cannot be done in isolation. One must look around at the host of other agencies active in Africa, starting with but going far beyond the World Bank. Where can the ADB make a special contribution by drawing on its established areas of expertise? What are others doing well enough without the ADB? The board made one small step in this direction during 1993, rejecting management's proposal for a cooperation agreement between the Bank and the UN Centre for Human Settlements. The degree of overlapping interests was just too small. More decisions of this type will have to be made.

The standard response is that the African character of the Bank represents the unique contribution it has to offer. But what does that mean? There can be no doubt that the major role of African shareholders, the process of electing the president, and the dominant share of African professionals on staff have made for a distinctly different culture from that of other lending and donor agencies, most notably the World Bank. These have resulted in a Bank that is generally more responsive to the demands of African borrowing members, more sympathetic to their problems, and more diplomatic in conducting its business.

It is less obvious what the net effect of this special culture has been. Such an approach can work in various ways, which may or may not promote the development effort. Some projects should be resolutely rejected and some conditions rigorously applied, in spite of borrower protestations. There have been times when the ADB Group has taken such tough decisions; but there have been many others when it did not. This African character should mean that borrowing members feel more comfortable in dealing with the institution, more ready to confide, less suspicious of advice. This too is true. However, often there has been no one to confide in or obtain advice from. The ADB Group should be able to exploit its unique position to act as a mediator between African governments and foreign funding sources, helping each side understand the other one better. The relationship between these two groups is often tense, frequently as a result of misunderstandings or differences in culture. The ADB Group has helped bridge this gap on occasion, but it could do so much more.

It is difficult to document how the African character of the Bank has made a real difference in the lives of Africans to date. We believe it has. It is more difficult to contend that this impact matches the resources so far committed to the enterprise. The management and staff cannot apply to good advantage their special understanding of

Africa, and their unique rapport with African counterparts, without a greater emphasis on portfolio and staff quality and the expertise that comes from concentration on a manageable set of problems. Neither borrowers nor other funding agencies will turn to an institution that lacks the expertise to back its good intentions. It is up to the shareholders, guided as always by management, to determine how the Bank will improve its focus in the coming years. Nevertheless, our task would not be complete if we did not offer a few ideas, albeit based on the limited information at our disposal.

1.   The Bank must get back to basics—its core lending operations and, especially, its projects. Project work is where the Bank has the bulk of its experience, yet this has been one of the most neglected areas. Other lenders and donors are still struggling with the challenge of effective project implementation and need the insights that an African institution should be able to bring to the task. The World Bank in particular seems to have lost some of its expertise at the project level through its focus on economic policy reform. As countries gradually rectify their policy environment, project lending will require higher priority once more. The Bank should position itself now to provide leadership in this area. In any event, a bank without a record of quality projects is ill placed to launch new initiatives.

2.   The Bank cannot neglect policy-based program lending. Project lending will not be successful without an improved policy environment, there is still a lot of work to be done, and balance-of-payments and budgetary support remain the highest priorities for many countries. However, the Bank will have to identify a few issues and countries where it wants to take the initiative. We have suggested above that the Bank concentrate on adjustment in sectors where it has already gained project experience and on broader macroeconomic reform in selected smaller countries. The Bank will then be able to compete on a more equal footing with the World Bank, in terms of its financial contribution and, more important, its knowledge. This will be important, not for the greater glory of the ADB Group, but for the recipient. The World Bank has not found all the answers, and in some small African countries the only alternative source of informed judgment may be the ADB Group.

3.   In the context of the above priorities, the Bank might do well to specialize in the social dimensions of adjustment, as well as the provision of institutional support. While its experience here is not extensive, neither is that of the World Bank. Both aspects should benefit from any superior qualitative understanding of the African condition that the Bank staff can provide. There is limited evidence from our Mali case study that the Bank has a better feel for capacity build-

ing. The Bank should be particularly well placed to help build the sense of local ownership that is now recognized as a major short-coming of many past adjustment programs. Pursuing institutional support toward better investment programming, project analysis and monitoring, and expenditure management is probably the best way to contribute to good governance in the short run. Highlighting the social dimensions would also provide a needed focus for the Bank's poverty alleviation strategy.

4.   Among the traditional sectors, agriculture deserves to retain the highest priority, in spite of the inherent difficulties involved. It will continue to be the economic backbone of most African countries for the foreseeable future, while themes like the environment, gender, and poverty alleviation also recommend such an emphasis. Though the ADB Group's record is very mixed, so is that of other donors. The Bank Group should build on the extensive experience gained by consistently allocating the largest share of its annual budget to agriculture. Furthermore, this sector has declined in importance among many other funding agencies, including the World Bank.[2]

5.   In general, themes like governance, poverty alleviation, the environment, and gender should influence the choice of priority sectors and then be addressed with a view to improving traditional lending operations. Apart from agriculture, they suggest a focus on education, small enterprise, and microenterprise. These would benefit women, address the growing employment problem, and contribute to governance by strengthening civil society. For the same reason, efforts to collaborate with NGOs should continue across all these sectors; but they should be brought into alliances with public agencies, not turned to as an alternative.

6.   Within these sectors, mechanisms must then be put in place to ensure that projects really do benefit the poor. Staff need to be assisted in identifying where environmental concerns or the role of women are critical to project success, and how to alter project design and implementation accordingly. The Bank should probably resist the temptation to launch many specialized environmental protection or "women's" projects for the time being, in the interests of focus. Many bilateral donors are already devoting considerable attention in this direction. Similarly, in policy-based lending, efforts to incorporate poverty concerns into program design deserve more attention than separate social funds. Such a choice by the Bank will not make life any simpler. It is often easier for environmental and WID staff to develop their own projects rather than work with others to integrate their concerns. It is also easier for management to convince shareholders that something is being done by pointing to such specialized projects.

7.   Because the private sector must inevitably play a central role in the future economic growth of Africa, the ADB Group must continue to expand its activities in some form. However, it is not clear that either its operations departments or the PSDU are properly equipped to deal with the private milieu. An independent structure along the lines of the IFC may be the answer, though the case for a separate African equivalent will have to be examined carefully. Any facility of this type should not be confined to large-scale firms but give special emphasis to small and medium-size enterprises, which have been particularly neglected in the past. Meanwhile, the Bank and the Fund proper should help establish an enabling environment for private investment. The Bank may have a special role to play in attracting foreign investment by providing the necessary advice and reassurances that both investors and national governments often require.

If the existing ADB Group is to extend itself well beyond its core project functions, it will have to do so selectively. It should look for issues where others are not demonstrating sufficient leadership and where there is a strong demand within the continent. And it should build on any strengths it may possess beyond its projects. By these criteria, the topics of external indebtedness and regional integration bear consideration, even though past initiatives in each case have been frustrating.

8.   Although the debt problem continues to be the overriding constraint to long-term growth in most of sub-Saharan Africa, it is not getting much attention. Indeed, with the turnaround in the fortunes of Latin America, there is a serious risk that the debt crisis will fall off the agenda of creditor nations. The ADB Group, as the only regional creditor, is the logical champion for continued efforts to resolve the problem. It is familiar with the financial issues at stake, and it sees the implications of the crisis in its daily work. There is also a strong self-interest, as its members' inability to service loans is threatening the Bank's own viability. Appropriate action could include lobbying in international forums, elaborating new debt-relief plans, and assisting member governments in debt management.

9.   As possibly the biggest success in regional cooperation, the ADB Group is also a logical proponent of regional integration. African leaders have committed themselves in principle but they need prodding in practice. Regional integration seems inevitable in the long run. Since it figures prominently among the original objectives of the ADB Group, it can hardly be neglected. The Bank could follow up on its southern Africa study in various ways, as well as finance similar ones in other regions. Now that AFREXIMBANK has

been successfully launched, the Bank will have to invest time and effort to see that it succeeds.

10.   There remains the vision of the Bank as a center of excellence in development thinking. Nothing is more powerful than ideas, and the influence of the World Bank is in good measure due to its prodigious research effort. But at least partly because of that impressive record, too many of the ideas "in power" in Africa originate outside. Africans need to take those ideas and blend them with their own if a successful African development strategy is to emerge.

We are tempted to apply the same reasoning here that we have argued holds true for the environment, gender, and most other themes—to focus on the core lending activity in the first instance. Despite repeated calls for the Bank to become an African source for new information and ideas, its research record has been disappointing. Output has been very limited as staff have been consistently sidetracked by more pressing institutional demands. What has been produced has seldom drawn on the Bank's own project experience.

Certainly, it is time to make a systematic attempt to draw lessons from its extensive history of lending. This would go beyond the standard postevaluation of projects to involve sectoral and thematic work. It could involve evaluation personnel; indeed they are starting to think along these lines. It should also incorporate some operations staff with a penchant for reflection. This research would not only benefit future lending, but it would also assist the broader community of donors and recipients. Through wider dissemination, including civil society, such work would also enhance the Bank's accountability.

To broach the larger issues of development strategy, however, the Bank must go much farther. It should strengthen its cooperation with the UN Economic Commission for Africa and its new management. It could and should reach out to the independent research community. There is much research expertise scattered around the continent that is seldom coordinated to focus on particular issues and generally lacks a high-profile venue to publicize its views. The Bank has already made some progress through the launching in 1989 of both a journal, *African Development Review,* and the annual *African Development Report.* In 1993, the latter drew on francophone, anglophone, and Arab scholars, including a few non-Africans, with a special focus on economic integration and structural adjustment.

The Bank opened the door to a major contribution in 1995. The *African Development Report* theme was to be "Structural Adjustment and Development in Africa: The Missing Links." To show how to go beyond structural adjustment and promote long-term development

is a big challenge, and one worth taking on. Perhaps not coinciden-
tally, the African Advisory Council chose a similar topic as its second
issue for deliberation. However, if the report is to have an impact, it
will need to be a tightly argued piece that focuses on a few key points
and at least implicitly challenges the so-called Washington consensus
in some respects.

To succeed in this and similar future endeavors, the Bank will
have to make a more serious commitment to research. We suggest
that a small but significant additional investment in a genuine
research capacity could make a big difference. Outside researchers
should be used more extensively, but an in-house capacity is really
needed to coordinate their contributions, absorb them, supplement
them, and provide the institutional endorsement that makes ideas so
much more effective. A concerted effort should also be made to
recruit senior non-Africans. The number of experienced and available African researchers is likely to be small, and the need for cross-
fertilization is especially important in the field of ideas. This in-house
capacity must be protected from the demands of senior management
for speeches and policy documents yet have their explicit support at
the highest level. It must build on project experience but go beyond
evaluation. Most of all, it must reinforce the few development priorities on which the Bank decides to focus.

Thus, we are compelled to reiterate the vision of the ADB Group
as a center of excellence, though the initial proposal by the
Committee of Ten was not favorably received by the Board of
Directors even in the halcyon days of 1990. Admittedly, our approach
would be rather more modest.[3] The beauty of research is that it is relatively inexpensive, compared to the typical development project,
and compared to the potential impact. A small investment can go a
long way. If the various forces at play mean that the ADB Group
must, regrettably, accept a smaller lending capacity for the medium
term, its contribution through new ideas could more than compensate. The trouble with research is that its payoff tends to be long-term
and difficult to demonstrate. In the current context of short-term crisis management and financial distress, there is likely to be considerable resistance to the idea of such an investment. But without such a
bold decision, the Bank is likely to find itself forever under the shadow of the World Bank, without its own place in the sun.

Certainly, the World Bank has cast a long shadow over the ADB
group. In every field or country the ADB Group has entered, the
World Bank has already been operating and typically continues to
operate with more staff, more funding, and more influence. The ADB
Group has tried to establish its own identity, primarily by maintaining its African character and by increasing its annual loan commit-

ments to the point where it would be a major player. Yet in almost every other respect, it has tended to replicate the World Bank, admittedly with considerable encouragement from the nonregional shareholders.

The African character of the "African Bank" has resulted in a different relationship with the region's members, one that might be described as "closer," figuratively though not physically. This has often produced results comparable to those of the World Bank. It has been difficult to find evidence of where this has translated into superior development impact. Surely it has, on occasion; but the Bank must now make some strategic decisions about where it will distinguish itself, to what ends it will devote its special status, and ultimately how it will justify its existence.

As a story of international cooperation in capacity building, the African Development Bank Group has been a success, of which Africans have been justly proud. It must now build on its unique character to develop specialized expertise in certain key areas through practice and research, communicating the lessons learned to the wider development community, and enriching the dialogue between recipient governments and foreign financiers. However, it will need to be selective in its choice of targets, then comprehensive in its approach to them, if its capacity is to make its mark.

Notes

1. ADB Group, "The Quest for Quality," p. 1.
2. Its share of World Bank lending in sub-Saharan Africa has been lower than at the ADB Group and fell to 11 percent in 1993 and a mere 5 percent in 1994. World Bank, *1994 Annual Report*, p. 80.
3. Where the Committee of Ten suggested 100 first-class professionals in Abidjan (plus another 150 supported around Africa), we would be inclined to think in terms of ten to fifteen for the time being.

APPENDIX

Table A1   Total ADB Group Loan and Grant Approvals by Country (in millions of dollars)

	1967–1972	1973–1975	1976–1978	1979–1981	1982–1984	1985–1987	1988–1990	1991–1993	Total
Central Africa	8	87	173	345	459	841	1,307	981	4,201
Angola	0	0	0	0	61	53	5	151	270
Burundi	0	13	9	67	39	52	22	84	287
Cameroon	3	5	13	36	70	119	202	202	649
Central African Republic	1	11	19	16	34	14	26	37	158
Chad	0	9	24	15	0	78	65	74	266
Congo	4	3	19	41	32	118	67	0	283
Equatorial Guinea	0	0	9	9	8	25	18	31	99
Gabon	0	10	19	31	20	44	152	331	606
Rwanda	0	5	21	49	42	46	50	44	256
São Tomé and Principe	0	16	9	1	2	48	65	18	158
Zaire	0	15	32	81	152	245	635	9	1,169
East Africa	14	39	135	317	500	512	864	929	3,310
Comoro Islands	0	0	11	31	23	0	0	13	78
Djibouti	0	0	0	3	15	22	31	37	108
Ethiopia	0	11	13	75	135	166	338	389	1,126
Kenya	7	7	31	55	103	48	171	169	592
Madagascar	0	0	19	32	131	41	89	64	376
Mauritius	0	7	11	27	11	52	8	40	156
Seychelles	0	0	8	9	18	10	60	24	129
Somalia	3	4	29	28	9	71	49	0	193
Uganda	4	10	13	57	56	101	118	193	552
North Africa	18	62	127	266	376	1,633	2,496	3,196	8,173
Algeria	6	3	19	0	0	249	517	574	1,368
Egypt	0	6	22	96	113	262	770	490	1,757
Libya	0	0	0	0	0	0	0	0	0
Mauritania	1	11	21	13	19	37	125	61	289
Morocco	3	13	29	55	53	740	506	1,188	2,588
Sudan	4	13	20	45	0	125	190	55	452
Tunisia	4	16	16	57	191	220	389	827	1,720
Southern Africa	11	57	149	395	517	626	916	1,336	4,007
Botswana	0	14	1	59	88	115	90	42	409
Lesotho	0	7	22	40	45	47	51	93	305
Malawi	5	7	35	35	79	49	107	187	505
Mozambique	0	0	19	90	75	4	147	270	604
Namibia	0	0	0	0	0	0	0	32	32
Swaziland	2	3	27	30	15	26	14	94	211
Tanzania	3	12	33	69	44	137	126	216	639
Zambia	1	14	13	72	115	134	170	96	615
Zimbabwe	0	0	0	0	57	114	212	305	688
West Africa	17	134	297	380	617	1,209	2,392	2,435	7,481
Benin	0	11	33	24	22	70	69	69	299
Burkina Faso	2	13	23	20	51	23	68	110	310
Cape Verde	0	0	9	28	32	18	47	38	172
Côte d'Ivoire	1	10	29	21	31	91	581	420	1,184
The Gambia	0	5	2	37	38	24	44	45	195
Ghana	0	17	28	32	84	98	257	108	624
Guinea	0	8	21	22	97	71	223	110	553
Guinea-Bissau	0	0	15	31	18	34	78	3	178
Liberia	2	10	21	23	107	0	3	0	166
Mali	1	17	33	27	35	100	76	114	403
Niger	1	4	22	23	59	10	37	41	197
Nigeria	5	6	0	0	0	525	767	1,020	2,323
Senegal	2	17	12	40	26	127	61	205	489
Sierra Leone	2	7	17	28	0	1	51	92	198
Togo	1	9	32	24	17	17	30	60	189
Multinational	10	2	48	26	78	114	163	80	520
Total	78	381	929	1,729	2,547	4,935	8,138	8,957	27,692

Source: ADB Group, Compendium of Statistics, various years.

Table A2   ADB Group Nonconcessional Lending by Country (in millions of BUA)

	1967–1972	1973–1975	1976–1978	1979–1981	1982–1984	1985–1987	1988–1990	1991–1993	Total
Central Africa									
Angola	0	0	0	0	45	28	45	87	205
Burundi	0	4	0	16	24	0	4	0	48
Cameroon	3	4	11	21	56	80	132	142	449
Central African Republic	1	0	0	10	4	0	0	0	15
Chad	0	0	2	0	0	0	0	0	2
Congo	4	6	15	24	29	92	48	0	218
Equatorial Guinea	0	0	7	0	0	0	0	0	7
Gabon	0	8	15	24	19	40	89	239	434
Rwanda	0	0	3	0	9	0	4	0	16
São Tomé and Principe	0	0	0	0	0	0	0	0	0
Zaire	0	12	20	39	87	119	347	0	624
East Africa									
Comoro Islands	0	0	0	10	0	0	0	0	10
Djibouti	0	0	0	0	0	0	0	0	0
Ethiopia	0	0	0	7	34	35	108	57	241
Kenya	7	6	17	37	67	0	55	12	201
Madagascar	0	0	0	5	62	0	0	0	67
Mauritius	0	6	9	18	7	37	5	26	108
Seychelles	0	0	4	0	14	6	5	17	46
Somalia	3	0	0	0	5	0	0	0	8
Uganda	4	8	10	38	38	7	20	15	140
North Africa									
Algeria	6	2	15	0	0	184	379	414	1,000
Egypt	0	10	10	48	91	207	531	289	1,186
Libya	0	0	0	0	0	0	0	0	0
Mauritania	1	1	5	5	15	0	47	0	74
Morocco	3	11	23	46	51	574	354	811	1,873
Sudan	4	7	5	7	0	17	36	28	104
Tunisia	4	13	12	46	188	171	287	593	1,314
Southern Africa									
Botswana	0	2	1	35	81	44	48	19	230
Lesotho	0	0	0	17	12	7	0	28	64
Malawi	5	6	15	0	44	0	0	15	85
Mozambique	0	0	5	36	45	0	13	0	99
Namibia	0	0	0	0	0	0	0	0	0
Swaziland	2	2	15	25	5	11	3	47	110
Tanzania	3	6	3	35	0	0	0	10	57
Zambia	1	12	10	28	66	94	61	10	282
Zimbabwe	0	0	0	0	28	84	136	200	448
West Africa									
Benin	0	6	8	3	0	7	0	0	24
Burkina Faso	2	2	0	4	23	0	0	0	31
Cape Verde	0	0	0	10	2	0	0	0	12
Côte d'Ivoire	1	8	20	16	29	77	404	273	828
The Gambia	0	2	0	9	10	0	0	0	21
Ghana	0	15	20	18	25	35	133	1	247
Guinea	0	7	7	5	38	24	99	44	224
Guinea-Bissau	0	0	1	10	0	0	0	0	11
Liberia	2	9	13	19	73	0	0	0	116
Mali	1	0	5	0	0	0	0	12	18
Niger	1	0	7	11	8	0	0	0	27
Nigeria	5	5	0	0	0	389	519	590	1,508
Senegal	2	6	8	30	0	28	0	115	189
Sierra Leone	2	6	4	3	0	0	0	0	15
Togo	1	3	11	4	0	0	0	0	19
Multinational	10	2	30	0	50	45	22	5	164
Total	74	195	366	718	1,384	2,438	3,980	4,109	13,264

Source: ADB Group, Compendium of Statistics, various years.

Table A3   ADB Group Loan and Grant Approvals by Sector (percent)

Sector	1967–1972	1973–1975	1976–1978	1979–1981	1982–1984	1985–1987	1988–1990	1991–1993	Total
Agriculture	19	27	24	35	28	38	20	22	25
Public utilities	24	31	31	21	25	18	25	20	22
Water	8	11	16	10	9	6	8	9	8
Power	11	10	10	8	11	9	15	8	11
Telecommunications	5	10	5	3	5	3	2	3	3
Transport	41	31	26	23	23	16	14	14	16
Industry	15	8	9	13	12	12	17	17	15
Social	0	3	10	8	12	9	9	12	10
Education	0	1	7	5	8	7	7	8	7
Health	0	2	3	3	4	2	2	4	3
Multisector	0	0	0	0	0	7	15	15	11
Total	100	100	100	100	100	100	100	100	100

Source: ADB Group, *Compendium of Statistics,* various years.
Note: Prior to 1982, lines of credit to development banks were not classified by sector. To obtain our sectoral totals for these earlier years, we assumed that one-half of such lines of credit went to agriculture and one-half to industry.

Table A4   ADB Group Loan and Grant Approvals by Lending Instrument (percent)

	1967–1984	1985–1987	1988–1990	1991–1993	Total
Projects	87	63	61	64	67
Lines of credit	10	13	9	12	11
Sectoral investment and emergency rehabilitation	2	7	6	3	4
Sectoral adjustment	0	8	9	7	7
Structural adjustment	0	6	11	10	8
Technical assistance	1	2	3	4	3
Total	100	100	100	100	100

Source: ADB Group, *Compendium of Statistics,* various years.

BIBLIOGRAPHY

For organizations, where a title is given in italics, it is a published document. Titles in quotation marks are internal documents.

ADB. *Rating Agency Review*. 1994.

ADB Group. *Africa and the African Development Bank: Current and Future Challenges*. Report of the Committee of Ten. 1989.

———. *Africa and the African Development Bank: 25th Anniversary 1964–89*. Report of the Committee of Nine. London: Euromoney Publications and ADB Group, 1989.

———. "The African Development Bank and the Environment." May 1994.

———. "The African Development Bank Group in the 1990s: Operational Programme for the Period 1992–96, and Beyond." 1992.

———. *African Development Report 1993*. 1993.

———. *Agreement Establishing the African Development Bank*. 1988.

———. *Annual Report*. Various years.

———. *Audited Financial Statement*. Various years.

———. *Compendium of Statistics*. Various years.

———. "Country Environment Profile: Zimbabwe." Environment and Social Policy Working Paper Series, No. 2. 1994.

———. "The Democratization Process in Africa, Governance, and the Role of the African Development Bank: Recommendations of the ADB African Advisory Council." Unpublished report, January 1994.

———. *Economic Integration in Southern Africa*. Oxford: ADB, 1993.

———. "Environment: Implementation of the Guidelines and Programmes for Enhanced ADF-VII." ADF-VII/CM.1/93/05. April 1993.

———. "Guidelines for the Implementation of the Action Program for Poverty Alleviation." May 1994.

———. "The Nature and Magnitude of Poverty in Sierra Leone," by C. L. Lufumpa. Environment and Social Policy Working Paper Series, No. 1. May 1994.

———. "Operational Programmes and Administrative and Capital Expenditure Budgets." Various years.

———. "Poverty Alleviation Policy and Experience: The Perspective of the African Development Bank." Unpublished paper by Miriam Pal, April 1995.

———. "Poverty Alleviation Strategy and Action Programme." ADB/BD/WP/92/104. September 1992.

———. "The Quest for Quality." Report of the Task Force on Project Quality. April 1994.

———. "Regional Development Finance Institutions and Economic Integration." Unpublished paper by Basil C. Muzorewa, November 1990.

———. "Role of the African Development Bank in the Treaty Establishing the Panafrican Economic Community." Report of the task force appointed by the president of the Bank, August 1992.

———. "Status Report on Implementation of the Private Sector Development Program." June 1993.

———. "Study of the Bank Group Experience in Policy-Based Lending." ADB/BD/IF/93/84. April 1993.

———. Study on Economic Integration in Southern Africa in a Post-Apartheid Period. 1993.

ADB Group Office of the Executive Director for Canada, Korea, Kuwait, Spain, and Yugoslavia. Annual Report. Various years.

ADB Group Operations Evaluation Office. "Annual Review of Evaluation Results, 1989." ADB/BD/WP/91/129. September 1991.

———. "Examen des Résultats de Performance des Projets Post-Evalués au Cours de 1988." ADB/BD/WP/89/32. April 1989.

———. "Review of the Results of Operations Evaluation 1992–93." ADB/BD/IF/95/67. March 1995.

———. "Revue des Résultats de l'Evaluation des Opérations 1990–91." ADB/BD/WP/93/21. March 1993.

———. "Synthesis of Project Performance Results, 1982–87." ADB/OPEV/88/10. November 1988.

"African Aid Bank Pressed to Tighten Lending Policies." Financial Times, May 13, 1994, p. 1.

"African Bank Meeting Runs into Sands." Financial Times, May 13, 1994, p. 4.

"African Development Bank: The Tough Task of Promoting a Continent's Progress." Euromoney supplement, October 1985.

"Africa's Lenders and Borrowers Fall Out." Financial Times, May 14, 1994.

Amegavie, Yewon Charles. La Banque Africaine de Développement. Paris: Pedone, 1977.

AsDB. Review of the Bank's Major Financial Policies. November 1992.

Australia International Development Assistance Bureau (AIDAB). "Review of the Effectiveness of Australia's Membership of the Multilateral Banks in Achieving Australia's Development Assistance Objective." Canberra: AIDAB, December 1991.

"'Chaotic' Bank Threatens Africa Soft Loans." Financial Times, May 10, 1994, p. 1.

Cornia, G. A., and G. K. Helleiner, eds. From Adjustment to Development in Africa. Oxford: Oxford University Press, 1994.

DANIDA. Effectiveness of Multilateral Agencies at Country Level: AfDB in Kenya and Sudan. Prepared for DANIDA by COWIconsult. Copenhagen: DANIDA, Danish Ministry of Foreign Affairs, 1991.

Diaku, I. "African Development Bank/African Development Fund: Problems and Prospects." In R. I. Onwuka and A. Sesay, eds., The Future of Regionalism in Africa. New York: St. Martin's Press, 1985.

Ebong, Ime Ekop. Development Financing Under Constraints: A Decade of the African Development Bank. Bonn. Neue Gesellschaft, 1974.

Fordwor, Kwame Donkoh. The African Development Bank: Problems of International Cooperation. New York: Pergamon Press, 1981.

Gardiner, Robert K. A., and James Pickett, eds. The African Development Bank 1964–1984: An Experiment in Economic Cooperation and Development. Abidjan: ADB Group, 1984.

Global Coalition for Africa (GCA). *Annual Report: African Social and Economic Trends*. Washington, D.C.: GCA, 1992 and 1993.

International Finance Corporation (IFC). *The African Project Development Facility: Report on Operations for 1993*. Washington, D.C.: IFC, 1993.

———. *Annual Report*. Washington, D.C.: IFC, various years.

Jerlstrom, Bo. *Banking on Africa: An Evaluation of the African Development Bank*. Stockholm: Swedish Ministry for Foreign Affairs, 1990.

Kappagoda, Nihal. *The Multilateral Development Banks: Volume 2, The Asian Development Bank*. Boulder, Colo.: Lynne Rienner, 1995.

Lele, Uma. *Managing Agricultural Development in Africa*. Washington, D.C.: World Bank, 1989.

Mingst, Karen A. *Politics and the African Development Bank*. Lexington: University Press of Kentucky, 1990.

"Mounting Arrears Weigh on African Bank." *Financial Times*, May 11, 1994.

"New Concerns on Development." *Financial Times*, May 13, 1994, p. 17.

North-South Institute (NSI). "Ahead from the Lost Decade: The African Development Bank Gathers Strength." Briefing paper No. 30. Ottawa: NSI, 1991.

———. "Crossroads or Cross-Purposes: Inter-American Development Bank at 31." Briefing paper No. 25. Ottawa: NSI, 1990.

———. "Giants and Microstates: Can the Asian Development Bank Cater for All?" Briefing paper No. 29. Ottawa: NSI, 1991.

Overseas Development Institute (ODI). "The African Development Bank: Facing New Challenges." Briefing paper. London: ODI, 1992.

Rwegasira, Delphin G., and Henock Kifle. "Regional Development Banks and the Objectives of the Bretton Woods Institutions." Paper presented at the conference "The International Monetary and Financial System: Developing Country Perspectives," Cartagena, Colombia, April 18–20, 1994.

Shaw, Christopher L. "Par Inter Paribus: The Nature of Power in Cooperation. Lessons (for the United States) from the African Development Bank." *African Affairs* 90 (1991): 537 558.

"Third World Hope: Development Bank in Africa Transcends the Region's Despair." *Wall Street Journal*, May 16, 1989, p. 1.

UN Economic Commission for Africa (UNECA). "African Alternative Framework to Structural Adjustment Programmes for Socio-Economic Recovery and Transformation." Addis Ababa: UNECA, 1989.

———. *An African Alternative to Structural Adjustment*. Addis Ababa: UNECA, 1989.

———. "The Khartoum Declaration" presented at the International Conference on the Human Dimension of Africa's Economic Recovery and Development. Addis Ababa: UNECA, 1988.

"An Unhappy Anniversary." *Southern African Economist* 7, no. 5 (June 1994): 3–6.

"Update on New Agenda for Africa." *Africa Recovery*, December 1993, p. 4.

"Very Good BAD." *Jeune Afrique Economie*, no. 130 (April 1990): 110–125.

Wodie, Francis. "The African Development Bank and the African Development Fund." In D. Mazzeo, ed. *African Regional Organizations*. Cambridge: Cambridge University Press, 1984.

World Bank. *African Development Indicators 1994–95*. 1995.

———. *Annual Report*. Various years.

———. "Effective Implementation: Key to Development Impact." Portfolio Management Task Force Report. September 1992.

———. *Reducing the Debt Burden of Poor Countries: A Framework for Action.* September 1994.

———. *Sub-Saharan Africa: From Crisis to Sustainable Growth: A Long-Term Perspective Study.* 1989.

———. *World Debt Tables 1994/95.*

———. *World Development Report.* Various years.

INDEX

About the Book
and Authors

The multilateral banks are powerful forces in the international community, providing loans of more than $250 billion to developing countries over the past half-century. The best-known of these, the World Bank, has been studied extensively, but the "regional development banks" are little understood, even within their own geographic regions.

This book looks specifically at the policies and projects of the African Development Bank, which, like the other multilateral banks, is being criticized increasingly by grassroots organizations, environmental groups, and others.

Drawing on case studies, the authors respond to some basic questions: Has the African Development Bank in fact been an effective agent of development? In its effort to assert its African character, has the Bank made a contribution distinct from the World Bank's inevitably larger involvement? They also assess the Bank's ability to address the urgent challenges of indebtedness and poverty, and to improve its own governance and management, including tackling the problems of mounting arrears and falling income.

E. Philip English is a Washington, D.C.–based economist, having worked at both the North-South Institute and the International Development Research Centre in Ottawa, Ontario. He worked at the African Development Bank from 1985 to 1988 and is the author of *The Great Escape? A Study of North-South Tourism, Canadian Assistance to Haiti,* and *Canadian Assistance to Senegal.*

Harris M. Mule was for fourteen years deputy permanent secretary and then permanent secretary in the Kenyan government's Ministry of Finance and Planning, and for a further five years in senior positions at the International Fund for Agricultural Development. He is on the boards of the International Food Policy Research Institute in Washington, D.C., and the African Capacity Building Foundation in Harare, Zimbabwe.